THE THREE A'S OF GRACE:

Awareness, Acknowledgement, Action

THE THREE A'S OF GRACE:

Awareness, Acknowledgement, Action

GRACE WAIRIMU

EST. 2019

BLKDOG

www.blkdogpublishing.com

This book is dedicated to my mum and dad, Rev. Monica Mburu and Bishop Josephat Mburu, who inspire me and continue to encourage me; my children Annalyne and Wilson, who fill my life with so much love and joy; and my family and friends.

I am truly blessed.

ACKNOWLEDGEMENTS

A heartfelt thank you to Annalyne and Wilson for their support and dedication throughout the writing of this book. You have played a fundamental role in its completion, without which it would not have been possible. Thank you for your love, encouragement, patience, and enthusiasm for its publication.

I could not have written this book without the love, wisdom and support of my dear parents. To my mother, thank you for being the unwavering source of strength and compassion in my life. Your endless patience, your belief in me, and the sacrifices you made to ensure I had the opportunities to grow and expand have shaped my life. Your words of wisdom have been a guiding light in my life, and your love continues to inspire everything I do.

To my father, your hard work, determination, love, and dedication to our family have taught me invaluable lessons. You have shown me the power of resilience and the importance of perseverance. Your quiet strength has always been a foundation upon which I have built my own courage. I am eternally grateful for your guidance and the wisdom you have passed down to me.

You have instilled in me a deep sense of purpose and a belief that anything is possible when we trust our inner strength. This book is as much yours as it is mine. Thank you for being my rock and greatest inspiration.

Grace Wairimu

INTRODUCTION

What is reality? How do you determine what is real and what is not? Your reality is what you are aware of. If you are not aware of something, it is not a reality to you, even if it exists. I have chosen to introduce this book with one word; 'Awareness'.

The dictionary describes awareness as the knowledge or perception of a situation or fact. Our awareness therefore is our reality. The life we are physically aware of today is full of insecurity and struggle. Every day, something is happening somewhere in the world that makes us feel powerless and helpless. Some of the events we are witnessing lately, from politics to security and wellbeing, make us feel as though there is no hope for the future.

But this book is here to tell you that you are not powerless or helpless. You have more power than you realise. The purpose of this book is to help you realise that there is power within you that you might not know exists.

It is based on the teachings of Jesus, and focuses on 'grace', the unmerited favour. It looks at some of Jesus' bold statements and declarations; some of which may seem implausible or farfetched—but which point to a completely different reality than we are aware of or experiencing.

Our reality is based on what we experience through our five senses. If we can't see it, touch it, smell it, hear it or taste it, it does not exist. We are limited by our senses; but there is a whole life out there that is beyond our five senses, which

Jesus was pointing us to when He said, 'If your eye is single, your whole body shall be full of light.'

He was referring to the inner eye of the spirit that is present in all of us. It is our guide, the still small voice of intuition. We hear this voice when we are still. The busyness of life and the noise around us makes it difficult to hear.

Think about this. When you're going through a challenge and you get to a place where you realise you can't handle it, you stop trying. Some people say they 'give-up', others 'surrender'. In that moment when you are resigned to the fact that the situation is beyond you and you allow your mind to rest, an idea comes to you; or you see something you hadn't noticed when your mind was racing, and you're inspired to do something. That is the voice of intuition guiding you.

If you follow the guidance and act on the inspiration, you will find yourself on the other side of the challenge. You won't even know how you arrived at the solution. This is why we are told to still our minds — 'Be still and know that I am God.' [Psalm 46:10] This voice is present in everyone; we are just not *aware* of it. Sometimes we confuse it with some of the many thoughts that flow through our minds every minute. We often ignore it.

Let us look at some of those *bold* statements:

'If you can believe, ALL things are possible to him that believes.' Mark 9:23

'He that believes in me, the works that I do shall he do also; and greater works than these shall he do...' John 14:12

'Take no thought for your life, what ye shall eat, or what ye shall drink...Behold the fowls [birds] of the air: for they sow not, neither do they reap, nor gather into barns; yet your heavenly Father feeds them. Are you not better than them?' Matthew 6:25-27

'Whatever things you desire, when you pray, believe that you receive them, and you shall have them.' Mark 11:24

'Can the children of the bridechamber [guests of the bridegroom] mourn, as long as the bridegroom is with them?' Matthew 9:15

'Before they call, I will answer, while they're yet speaking, I will hear.' Isaiah 65:24

This last one, unlike the others, is not Jesus' direct words but the words of God through Isaiah, the prophet who prophesied His birth. God was making a promise about a time that would come, when He would hear His people even before they called. A time when the laws of God would be written in the hearts of people and not in a tablet as it was then. [Hebrews 8:10]

Their reality at the time was different. They were estranged from God. He saw them as 'a people who provoked Him to anger continually to His face'. [Isaiah 65:2] You may say we are not any better, we do the same all the time. The difference is, there was no remedy for sin back then. They were under the law (Old Covenant) and the only way out for them was to spill blood through animal sacrifices. Today we are under the New Covenant of grace, which came through Jesus.

The prophesy was pointing to a time when all that (anger, condemnation, and material sacrifices) would be a thing of the past. That time is now, the time we are living in, made possible by the coming of the Christ — the saviour. [Romans 8:1] The *ultimate* sacrifice.

It is He who is now telling us that, if we believe, we can do the things that He did, and nothing shall be impossible for us. But we do believe, right? Why then are so many things not possible? Why are we ravaged by disease, poverty and insecurity? Let us look at two other statements that Jesus boldly made, which we may have taken for granted for lack of *awareness*—but which could well be the key to transcending these limitations.

These statements tell us *who we are* and what we are entitled to as children of the Most High. They include:

'The kingdom of God is within you.' Luke 17:21

and

'I have said, Ye are gods, and all of you are children of the Most High.' Psalm 82:6

Jesus repeated this last statement as a question to a group of people who wanted to kill Him for 'claiming' to be God — *'Is it not written in your law, I said, Ye are gods?'* [John 10:34] These statements have been reinforced by the Apostle Paul in different scriptures which we will explore and discuss at length later in the book.

The *awareness* of the kingdom of God, *'within us'*, helps us see Jesus' perspective when He said these things including, nothing shall be impossible for us, and we can do all things. It ties closely to the question, 'Can the children of the bridechamber mourn, as long as the bridegroom is with them?' The children of the bridechamber are the guests of the bridegroom. Jesus in this context is the bridegroom. He was answering a question about fasting, why the disciples of John fasted but His own disciples did not.

His answer implied that his disciples did not need to fast [mourn] as long as He was with them. The same bridegroom who walked with them physically, healing and performing other miracles, now lives within us. Why should we mourn? He is the 'Christ in us, the *Hope* of glory'. [Colossians 1:27] Why should we lose hope when the hope of glory is living within us?

We are not meant to suffer and struggle through life or mourn, 'begging' Him to move mountains for us when we know these facts, or when we are aware of His kingdom within us, every one of us; when we 'know' that the power that raised Jesus from the dead, the same power He used to heal the sick and the lame is in us.

Yes, challenges will come, but depending on how we meet them, they will help us evolve and be who we were created to be. It is often in our darkest moments that we have the greatest insights, because in these moments we are in touch with our inner selves; the part of us that is usually neglected due to the busyness of life and the noise around us.

These challenges, no matter how complex, are not meant to crash us but to be transcended. The power to transcend them is within us. We were created for great things. The kingdom of God is a kingdom of power and authority; with it comes the spirit of power, love and sound mind and not fear or helplessness. [2 Timothy 1:7] When we fully embrace these truths not just theoretically, but practically as well, we can surely move our own mountains. [Matthew 17:20, Mark 11:23] We have the power and authority to do that.

You are not under the law but under grace

Several years ago, I was facing a challenge that felt hopeless. I had prayed about it, but nothing was happening. It felt like God was a million miles away. After waiting for answers that didn't seem to come, I settled for what I felt was the only way forward. It wasn't the best solution, but it felt like the only solution.

I had all these questions and thoughts in my head that made it unbearable to think. 'Doesn't the Bible say God hates divorce? Didn't I vow before God and many witnesses that till death do us part?' One early morning, having not slept a wink in the night, I woke up, picked up my Bible and randomly opened it. The verse my eyes fell on said, 'You are not under the law but under grace.' [Romans 6:14]

Under normal circumstances, I would ponder its meaning and likely seek out other verses for support. But I knew exactly what it meant for me at that moment. It was a direct answer to the questions on my mind. I did not know much about law and grace. I knew grace was unmerited favour, the fulfilment of the Old Covenant, but beyond that, I knew very little. I had never thought about what it meant in relation to everything else in the Old Testament/Covenant, which represents the law.

From that moment I made it my mission to enlighten myself and, as the saying goes, when the student is ready the teacher appears. All the information I needed started to make itself available to me as though it was waiting for me to ask. It opened my mind to the true meaning of the words, 'It is finished'. These are the words Jesus uttered in His last moments in a human body. I also understood the meaning of the statement, 'The letter kills, but the spirit gives life,' [2 Cor 3:6] the letter being the law and spirit, the grace of God.

More recently, I had another similar encounter. I was going through an emotionally trying time after my mother suffered a stroke. Living abroad and not being there to physically offer my support made me feel helpless. She recovered from the stroke, thankfully, but later developed some complications. It was then that I began to question the word of God, such statements as 'nothing shall be impossible', 'we can do all things' and 'we can do the things that Jesus did and greater if we believe'. They felt unrealistic and unattainable. I wondered who they were written for.

I was working on my laptop when a thought about Jesus saying, 'I and the Father are one' crossed my mind. I searched the words and found the scripture. The story starts with Jesus talking to a multitude as He often did. He spoke in parables which many of them did not understand. Some said He was mad. That He had a demon. As I got to the part where they wanted to stone him, words appeared to jump out at me. I immediately assumed it was a problem with my laptop screen.

When it cleared and I focused back on the screen, the words that caught my eyes said, 'Is it not written in your law,

I said, Ye are gods?' [John 10:34] Rather than carry on reading, I began to wonder what law Jesus was referring to. I took a little detour to get clarity as it all seemed a mystery. I knew from the way the words bounced on my screen that there was something important that I needed to know. If it hadn't been for that, I would probably not have taken notice.

I found the words in Psalms 82:6; 'I have said, Ye are gods; and all of you are children of the most High.' I will come back to that in a moment. Going back to the scene where Jesus was about to be stoned for 'blasphemy', we see how it all played out, almost dramatically.

One moment, His accusers were condemning Him for 'claiming' to be God, and the next He was telling them that they too, 'are gods', the children of the most High. These are the same people who had rejected Him and sought to have Him killed. They were triggered by His claim that God was His father.

Now He is not only telling them that the same God is their father too, but also challenging their knowledge of the law, the same law they were using against him. He continued to reason with them,

"If he called them gods, unto whom the word of God came, and the scripture cannot be broken; Say ye of him, whom the Father has sanctified, and sent into the world, Thou blasphemest; because I said, I am the Son of God?"
John 10:35-36 (KJV)

Going back to the law to which He was referring, notice His words, "Is it not written in your *law*?" He was reminding them that they were bound by the law, and that law said they were gods and the children of God, the same things they were condemning Him for claiming to be. Until the law was fulfilled through His death and resurrection, they were subject to it. How could they then use it to condemn Him if it said the same about them?

According to their law, the punishment for blasphemy

was death by stoning. But if that law said they were all gods and children of God, then His claims were well founded and not blasphemous. The same book of Psalms says His word is forever settled in heaven, meaning it cannot be challenged. [Psalm 119:89] It cannot lie or contradict itself. If it says ALL, it means all, excluding no one, Jew or Gentile, free or bond, male or female. In today's language, it means every race, creed and gender. We are all gods, the sons of the Most High.

In another incident, when Jesus was being questioned, this time by a group of Pharisees who wanted to know when the kingdom of God would come, He answered,

> *'The kingdom of God comes not with observation...*
> *The kingdom of God is within you.'* Luke 17:20-21

This is a very powerful statement. If you know what a kingdom stands for, then you know you are powerful. This is the kingdom of the king of kings, not just some earthly kingdom. In this kingdom dwells all the fulness of the Godhead. [Colossians 2:9] Armed with this knowledge, we begin to see ourselves as God sees us. Much as it may be hard for us to wrap our minds around it, He sees us as gods. He sees us not as mere men but spiritual beings with His full power and authority within them.

In this life, we are always in the process of becoming. Grace declares us righteous while we are still sinners. [2 Cor. 5:21] Life is an ongoing process of growth and expansion. It continues to evolve, and as we grow in our belief/faith and trust, so does our capacity to receive greater awareness and become more —there is no limit to what we can become. You are always becoming more of who you are meant to be. The best of who you can be is not something you reach at a specific point in time, but a constant state of becoming.

We are meant to be more like God/Christ as that is who we are at the core—our innermost being. His word says, 'As he is, so are we in this world.' [1 John 4:17] He created us in

10

His image and endowed us with the power to create our world using our minds and words, just as He created the world. [Prov. 4:23, 18:21] Image also means likeness.

This book is here to tell you that no matter what your life may look like right now, you are not a victim of your circumstances but the creator of your reality. Your ideal reality is not distant; it is flowing towards you as you evolve to align yourself with it. Through unwavering faith and trust in the process, you can transcend any limitations and live the life you desire, in perfect health and abundance. This is the life you were created to live, a full life.

It is the life Jesus had in mind when He declared His reason for coming, 'I am come that you may have life and have it in full' or more abundantly. [John 10:10] You can rise above doubt, replace fear with faith, and begin to see every experience, no matter how challenging, as a step toward your highest good. You can begin to enjoy the future promised in Jeremiah 29:11.

The scripture that Jesus quoted saying, we are gods, the children of the Most High did not end where He ended His quote. It went further to say, 'But ye shall die like mortals ...' [Psalm 82:7] Why didn't He include this part? The Psalm he quoted from says, 'I have said, Ye are gods; and all of you are children of the most High. But ye shall die like mere mortals and fall like one of the princes.' Some translations say you shall die like men and others like mortals.

This was a statement of how it was then. We were created immortal but lived and died as mortals. But Jesus was on a mission to change all that. His job description was to fulfil the law and provide a way out of condemnation, reconciling God's children back to Him, [2 Cor 5:18] restoring our original nature – restoring our position in the Godhead, our union and oneness with God.

In the Old Covenant, we were condemned to live and die like mere mortals, but upon Jesus' death and resurrection, all that would be reversed. We *'would'* have the power to transcend all limitations. May be even death. We would no longer live and die like mere mortals. I use the word 'would' because, He was yet to die and resurrect when He said these things. He had not fulfilled the law yet, meaning grace had not come.

Grace, which represents the New Covenant came by Jesus while the law was given by Moses. [John 1:17] His mission was to supply the demands of the law, and the law demanded blood. That's why upon His death, His blood became the atonement for all our sins, shortcomings and everything that kept us in bondage.

Today, we can enjoy the freedom that people back then did not when we know who we are. To know who we are, we have to understand not only what Jesus did but what He accomplished for us. He undid what Adam did, freeing us from all curses, including the curse of the law and that of Adam. [Galatians 3:13] The curse of Adam says we must toil and sweat for everything.

Jesus fulfilled that one too, (Yes, He did!) that's why He says, 'Take no thought for your life, what you shall eat or drink,' adding that the birds of the air toil not, yet they are fed and looked after. So are the lilies of the field, He says. [Matt. 6:28] All those statements that seem a little farfetched and overpromising are not metaphors or empty claims. They are statements of *eternal truth* and not even some future events because the word of God is already settled in heaven. Nothing we do or do not do will change it.

What we do or not do only changes the conditions of our life, the physical life. The answers to our prayers exist *now* in this moment. They are not waiting to happen but to be realised. If I hadn't opened my Bible that morning as mentioned earlier, for example, I would have been convinced that my prayers were not answered or God did not hear me, yet His word says He hears us before we call. My answer was already there waiting for me to align myself with it.

The word of God is true, when it says our prayers are

answered before we ask, believe it. It may be that we look in the wrong places for the answers. Within is where all our solutions are. It is 'in stillness and in confidence' of who we are that we find the 'salvation' that is already provided. [Isaiah 30:15] That salvation is the solution to our problems, all of them. All the answers to our prayers already exist, waiting to be realised, hence reminded to 'stand still and see the salvation of the Lord'. [Exodus 14:13]

When we are still, we hear the inner voice and when we act on it, it leads us to the answer that is already available. When Jesus said, 'It is finished', He meant He had accomplished what He came to do. He fulfilled the law, every one of the commandments. This is what He says about it,

> 'Do not think that I came to destroy the Law or the Prophets. I did not come to destroy but to fulfil.'
> Matthew 5:17

By fulfilling the law, He did away with the fear of condemnation and judgement, replacing it with righteousness and unconditional love. His desire is for us to know who we are and awaken to the power within us, the same power that He operated in, to realise that we are one with Him and because He is one with God, we also are one with God. To awaken to the truth that the power that raised Him from the dead resides in us. [Romans 8:11]

In all these statements and more (not mentioned here), He was communicating one message, unravelling what to this day remains a mystery; that *we are one with God, and what God can do, we too can do because it's His power that works in and through us.* [Ephesians 3:20] If you are one with God, your neighbour is one with God, and I am one with God, doesn't that make us all one? Why then do we fight against each other? We are only fighting against ourselves. Paul put it this way:

> 'There is neither Jew nor Greek, there is neither

bond nor free, there is neither male nor female: for you are all one in Christ Jesus. And if you be Christ's, then are you Abraham's seed, and heirs according to the promise.' Gal. 3:28-29

'But he that is joined unto the Lord is one spirit'
1 Cor. 6:17

'Beloved, if God so loved us, we ought also to love one another. No man hath seen God at any time. If we love one another, God dwells in us, and his love is perfected in us.
Hereby know we that we dwell in him, and he in us, because he has given us of his Spirit.'
1 John 4:11-13

When Jesus said we too can do the things He did and greater, He was looking at it from this perspective; that we are one with Him — one with God the Father. We should also look at it from the same perspective and allow it to change our self-concept; to start seeing ourselves as powerful and capable of anything we can conceive in our minds/imagination.

When you see yourself as one with God, it will not be too hard to see yourself transcending limitations as Jesus did. Paul understood these concepts better than anyone. This is what he says:

'For who hath known the mind of the Lord, that he may instruct him? but we have the mind of Christ.'
1 Cor. 2:16

He is talking about spiritual discernment, saying that the natural man cannot receive or perceive the things of God as they are foolishness to him. We are not natural men if we acknowledge this gift and accept it. We have the mind of Christ; a natural man or *mere mortal* does not have the mind of Christ. The preceding verses say that we have received not the spirit of the world, but of God 'that we might know the things that are freely given to us of God'.

If Jesus says we are gods, let us embrace it. It is one of the things He has freely given to us — One of the greatest gifts we could ever receive from God. It is not easy to change some of the beliefs we have held for years, this is why we need spiritual discernment. Paul addresses this, urging us to be 'transformed by the renewing of our minds'. [Romans 12:2]

Renewal is not something that happens once, it is constant. Just as God's mercies are new every day, renewing of mind should be a continuous process of evaluating our beliefs and doing away with what no longer serves us. If you are struggling or living in lack (scarcity or poverty), you must learn how to use your gift. You must learn how to wield the power God has freely given you.

The first step is to be *Aware* of it. It is your identity and your power to transcend these limitations. If you have been identifying with things outside of yourself, you will learn that everything is within you, the whole Godhead or nature of God. This is what it means to be created in the image or likeness of God. It does not necessarily mean physical image as God is spirit.

If you didn't already know, you now know that you are made in the likeness of God, you have the mind of God, and the kingdom of God is within you in all its fullness and glory. That is your identity! It is very empowering when you internalise it. The second step is to *Acknowledge* the power therein, and the third is to walk in it; *Action*.

We are called to live a life of freedom and power, and to *rest* in knowing who we are. It is our heritage and birthright. Once you become aware of who you are and acknowledge it, you are led from within, in other words, you are inspired to act. It is important not to ignore this inner guidance as the inspired action you take is the answer to your prayer. It is your power to transcend that problem you thought was insurmountable.

This is what the Three 'A's of Grace is about. The A's

stand for Awareness of who you are, Acknowledgment of it, and, most importantly, Action. Just as faith without action is dead, becoming aware of these truths and acknowledging them without acting on them is pointless. It won't make a difference in your life.

It is easy to become aware of the presence of God within us and even acknowledge it but, unless we act on the inspirations or guidance that come from it, we will forever be looking for answers in the wrong places and claiming that God does not hear or answer our prayers.

This book will not only tell you but also *show* you how to step into the grace that has always been available to you, enabling you to use that power to overcome challenges and limitations, and live life as God intended.

The *awareness* of the presence of God in you changes your *reality*. When you are conscious of His working in, and through you, you begin to see life differently. You become a co-creator of your own life with Him, 'For it is God who works in you both to will and to do of His good pleasure'. [Phil. 2:13] He says:

> *"I am come that YOU might have life, and that YOU might have it more abundantly."* John 10:10

Today become AWARE of who YOU are and walk in that power; — It is the power that overcomes the world.

CHAPTER ONE

One with God

In him we live, move and have our being.

During hard times, we often feel a disconnect that sometimes leads to withdrawal from daily activities, friends, family and life in general. Some describe this feeling as emptiness or a sense of being lost. It feels as though our entire system is out of sync, or the rhythm of life is suddenly offbeat. If this feeling is left unchecked, it can easily lead to clinical depression. The discomfort is, however, not always negative. It awakens strength and resilience within us we may not have realised we had.

How often have you heard someone say, 'I don't know how I survived that?' I have lost count of the times I've heard people say, 'I don't know what I'd do if this or that happened?' and then – it happens. Yet, they make it through. We all have an incredible ability to rise above life's trials, no matter how overwhelming they seem. This is because there is a power within us waiting to be discovered, a power far greater than anything we could ever conceive outside ourselves. When we tap into it, we can heal, overcome weaknesses, and transcend limitations. In short, we can do all things!

This is not an easy concept to wrap our minds around

especially when we are in the middle of a challenge. I struggled with it. I questioned my faith, not because I didn't believe in God, but because life constantly reminded me of my failures. I pursued dreams that crumbled. I built relationships that fell apart. I initiated projects that didn't see the light of day, yet the words '*I can do all things'* were constantly echoing in my mind.

What was I doing wrong? I would wonder. I know I am not alone in this — his is life, its highs and lows, its unexpected twists and turns. I have seen others struggle too, to a point where my problems seemed like nothing in comparison. You probably have felt that way too, one moment you think your world is over just because you're dealing with a challenge, then you see someone going through a much bigger challenge. Would you swap positions?

Some years ago, a family friend, young and full of life, suffered a sudden heart attack. We were all just beginning our journey as parents; our firstborns were babies. We all had so much to look forward to. One Sunday afternoon, returning home from shopping with his wife, he collapsed on the kitchen floor. The doctors fought hard to save his life. He was placed in the Intensive Care Unit, his life hanging by a thread.

When his wife called from the hospital, we could not believe how one minute they were at the supermarket and the next in the ICU. I believed with every fibre of my being that God would heal him. When we went to see him, his family was there. I assured them that he would make it, even though he was on life support. The family did not believe in God; they called Him 'the man upstairs'. I encouraged them to believe in His healing power, and together, we laid hands on him and prayed.

We woke up the next morning to the news that he had passed away in the early hours of the morning. His family had made the painful decision to have his life support switched off. It must have been a difficult decision to make. I could not believe what was happening, it was unreal. It was like watching a movie with a terrible ending. I believed in the power of prayer, and I did not have any reason to believe otherwise. Was it God's will? Was his time up? Would he have survived if the life support had not been switched off? May be he'd have survived but brain damaged. I had all these questions and possible outcomes.

This was the very first time I started to ask myself some hard questions about faith, God's will, and how our actions influence our outcomes. I may not have had clear answers, but I did learn something, that no matter what you're dealing with, it could be worse. It could also be better. Whatever plate you're served, it's not the worst no matter how bad it is, nor is it the best, no matter how good it is.

Today I understand that how we respond to challenges determine the outcome. God is not always responsible for each and every thing that happens in our lives. Do we respond from fear or from faith? This is the determining factor. Sometimes we don't even respond, react to things. At the time, I was angry at myself for giving the family false hope and part of me was angry at them for being so quick to make that decision.

There was also a part of me that was angry at God. I felt let down. In my reasoning, He had the perfect opportunity to prove Himself to the family and may be help them know Him. Looking back, I realise that I did not truly know Him either. I believed in Him, but I did not understand Him. Though I didn't call him the man upstairs, I was not any different from them.

The reason they called Him the man upstairs is because the general understanding of God is a deity who lives in heaven, looking down on us and calling all the shots. Deciding who needs to be rewarded and who needs to be punished. I, too, saw Him as distant — separate from me, living in Heaven, issuing commands and deciding fates from afar. I knew He is omnipresent, but the reality of Him living in or within me was not something I was consciously aware of.

The Apostle Paul, in Colossians 1:26-28 calls it a 'mystery' which has been hid from ages and from generations, 'Christ *in* me the hope of glory'. It's not surprising then, that a lot of people do not know that Christ is in them. It may have been hidden but not anymore. The same scripture says it is now 'made manifest' to His saints. His saints are those who acknowledge Him, they see His power working in them from the inside out.

The truth is, God is not far from us, nor is He calling all the shots. As a matter of fact, He is closer than our own breath because He is in us. He is Emmanuel, God with us. He animates our being, *"In him we live, move and have our being."* Acts 17:28 — We exist within Him, and it's not just us who exist within Him, 'He is before all things and by Him all things consist'. [Col.1:17]

He has given us free will. We create our lives from the freedom He has given us and the abundance He has made free for us to access and enjoy. Free will is the highest expression of unconditional love, in that we are free to make choices right or wrong. It is in making wrong choices and decisions that we learn. God does not penalise us for making mistakes, He helps us correct them if we're willing to learn.

Having said that, even though the mystery has been revealed, we still cannot know everything from beginning to end. This we are told in the Book of Ecclesiastes: 'He has made everything beautiful in its time. He has also set eternity in the human heart; yet no one can fathom what God has done from beginning to end.' [Eccl. 3:11]

Sometimes, *awareness* makes all the difference. It shifts our perspective and helps us see things in a new light. The awareness of God in us and not a distant figure looking down from Heaven, eliminates fear and the sense of helplessness we feel when things go wrong, and though we may not know everything, we know that the end (outcome) is good because His plan for us is good.

It eliminates the feeling that we are victims of some power out there that we have no control over. That fear robs us of our strength because, instead of standing firm and knowing we can handle anything that comes our way, we start blaming ourselves, God or others. We feel small and incapable of standing up to the challenge. We anticipate punishment when we fall short, and should any misfortune befall us, we attribute it to the fact that we fell short; we see it as a punishment.

When we realise we are one with God, we are freed from feeling trapped, judged, or condemned. This awareness also helps us detach from the outcome when we commit something to God. We no longer carry guilt or blame when things don't go our way or don't materialise as expected. We live with the awareness of Christ in us, the hope of glory. This awareness helps us focus more on God's love than on our failures. We become more attuned to His love, forgiveness and compassion than our shortcomings.

With this awareness, we learn to love ourselves. We accept our flaws and gladly learn from the mistakes we make without judgement or fear of it. We obey, not out of fear of punishment but conviction. We no longer seek validation, approval, or acceptance from others, because they already emanate from our being. Instead of looking for these things in the external world, we become one with them.

We become one with love, joy, peace, compassion, healing and all the attributes of God, which are already within us. We lose the need to be right in the eyes of the world. We also learn to hear God's voice within us, the still, small voice that is never wrong.

Knowing that our prayers are heard before we even pray enables us to be grateful for the things we need as though we already have them as our needs are supplied at the point of need; never early or late. With this awareness, we enjoy the freedom that comes with knowing we have power over any circumstances, and that we are not victims, beggars or prisoners of our external conditions.

I recently came across an allegory that captures this concept so beautifully. It's about a man who was arrested and locked in a dungeon. A fierce jailer, carrying a heavy, rusty key, took him to the back of the dungeon and threw him into a cell, slamming the door shut with a loud bang that echoed through the walls. He was left in the dark, his mind shattered by the noise and the fear that accompanied it.

For twenty years, he endured this. Now and then, the door would open with a loud noise and creaking, and the jailer would walk in and leave some food and water for him without saying a word. He would then pull the door shut with the same ear-splitting bang. Over time, the man's despair deepened, and he began to lose the will to live. One day, in despondency, he decided to end it all.

His only plan was to attack the jailer the next time he came. He believed this would be his end, perhaps it would bring an end to his torment. He had nothing to lose. He carefully mapped out his attack—examining the room, noting the jailer's routine and calculating his every move. As he got close to the door, he noticed there was no lock—just a simple knob. Surprised and confused, he reached out to turn it. To his astonishment, the door swung open.

He had never gotten this close to the door before. Could it have been unlocked all this time? Had he been a prisoner of his own imagination all these years? For twenty years, he had believed he was locked up in a cell, unable to escape. But the truth is, the door had never been locked. He could have walked out at any time. As he stepped through the rusty, unguarded gate into his newfound freedom, only one thought echoed in his mind: 'Why didn't I do this sooner?"

He did not know he was free. He lacked the knowledge that would have set him free. His lack of *awareness* had kept him trapped in a false belief for years. Some of us are prisoners of false beliefs. We stay stuck in situations, feeling helpless and powerless when all we need is a shift in perspective to walk out of them. Often, our jailer is fear, past experiences, limiting beliefs and poor self-concept.

Our beliefs about ourselves can keep us trapped for

years. We feel small when faced with challenges, not realising that the one who's in us is greater than anyone or anything in the world. [1 John 4:4] We fail to recognise the immense power within us. This power lies dormant until we become aware of it.

Just like the man in the cell was intimidated by the appearance of his surroundings, so are we often intimidated by our circumstances. But just as those physical appearances were illusions, so are the external pressures and challenges we face. They train and help us to evolve beyond the limitations of our five senses.

Our physical senses can only perceive the world in its current form, but these challenges invite us to use our inner senses; our intuition, our spiritual perception, and our connection to something greater than ourselves.

The prisoner's locked door, which appeared so ominous, was a symbol of the mental cage he had built for himself. Once he grew tired of his confinement and decided to seek a way out, he found that the door had always been open. Freedom only comes when we change the programming of our mind. When we change the way we're looking at something, a situation or a challenge.

This happens when we come to the end of ourselves and decide we have had enough. The prisoner's decision to act and take the first step came from being fed up with waking up to the same reality every day for years. It ultimately led him to the truth: he was never really trapped. He simply needed to shift his thinking and become *aware* of the *truth* that was always present. The truth did not suddenly appear, it was always there. He became aware of it.

This is something only we can do for ourselves. It starts with the decision to get unstuck. Are you tired of struggling, are you tired of being ill, weak or living in poverty, are you tired of the way things are? Do you wish things were different? You're the only one who can make that decision, and once you do, the battle is half won.

The next step is to focus on the solution, which is being

unstuck or free. You may not know how, but that's not important. What's important is the solution. Don't focus on the problem or the how. Always focus on the end result even when you don't have a plan. What you focus on grows; if you focus on a problem, it gets bigger. If you focus on the solution, you eventually find it.

Challenges are not roadblocks; they are opportunities to listen more closely, to reflect, and to realise that there is always another way. There are solutions beyond what we can see with our physical eyes or sense with our natural senses. When we start asking ourselves questions like, 'Is this all there is? Is this the only way to live?' Something begins to shift within us and, as we start to act on the guidance that comes from within, doors open.

These quiet, intuitive nudges may sometimes be mistaken for random thoughts, but they are often the voice of our inner guide, our true self or true identity guiding us toward freedom. We don't hear this voice when our minds are overwhelmed with worry and anxiety. But when we slow down, quiet the noise and tune in to our inner wisdom, we begin to hear it. And when we *choose* to act on it, to step through that door, we realise that the path to freedom is never wrong, it just requires courage.

That decision sets the ball in motion. It's like embarking on a journey not knowing where it might take you; you have to have faith. Imagine you had no eyes; how could you see? Consider these statement I mentioned earlier: *'If your eye is single, the body is full of light.'* What did Jesus mean by that? Would one eye provide better vision than two? This is his full statement:

> *'The light of the body is the eye: if therefore your eye is single, your whole body shall be full of light. But if your eye be evil, your whole body shall be full of darkness. If therefore, the light that is in you be darkness, how great is that darkness! No man can serve two masters: for either he will hate the one and*

love the other, or else he will hold to the one, and despise the other. You cannot serve God and mammon.' Matthew 6:22-24

Understanding this concept can change everything about how we live, how we deal with fear and anxiety, and handle life's challenges. Fear is often the root cause of our troubles, but the key lies in where we choose to focus our attention, do we focus it on our fear or faith? We can't focus on both because they cancel each other. Faith drives out fear and fear drives out faith. It's just like light and darkness. They can't exist together.

The 'single eye' is the eye of the spirit, our inner eye that sees beyond the physical world. This eye is never wrong because it perceives things that the physical eyes cannot see. When we realise that we are one with God and acknowledge his residence in us, we align ourselves with our inner guide, which is His spirit. By allowing Him to be our guide, we begin to perceive things that are not immediately visible, tangible or audible to our physical senses.

The single eye, the spirit of God within us is single-minded; it knows only one power—God's power. Many people believe in both the power of God and that of the devil, but the single eye sees only one power: the power of good. Evil power is the misuse of God's power. When one uses the only power there is negatively, it produces negative outcomes.

Consider this; 'If your eye is evil, your whole body will be full of darkness'. You cannot have both light and darkness coexist. The moment light enters a dark room, darkness flees. In the same way, you cannot believe in the power of God and, at the same time, believe in the power of the devil. There is only one power; what we call evil power, or the power of the devil is the power of God used negatively.

The devil has no power. When you believe that he does, you live in bondage, always looking over your shoulder. You live in fear, and fear is the opposite of faith. Once you give in to fear, you leave the door open for every misfortune because where fear is, there is doubt and worry. The three are cousins, you let one in, they all move in and steal every good thing that God has lined up for you.

When you focus your attention on one power, you rule out any other, just like when you turn on the light, darkness disappears. Training your mind to focus on one power is like learning to drive; if you focus on avoiding the kerb, you end up hitting it. If you focus on the road, you avoid the kerb all together. Whether or not the kerb exists, it does not bother you. The key here is to focus on what you want rather than what you do not want.

When you purpose to see good in any situation, something good always comes out of even the worst of situations. It is our choice to decide where we want to put our focus, on fear or faith. Fear, we're told has torment. [1 John 4:18] Faith neutralises fear. Faith is the antidote for fear. If we could focus on the good and have a single eye, we would erase fear from our consciousness.

If we could just focus on the conviction that we are aligned with the *highest and only* power, we would no longer be afraid of making mistakes or failing. Fear would be unknown to us. We would just be. When you focus on not failing, you fail, but when you focus on success, you do not fail. The difference between faith and fear is that faith sees the invisible and affirms it, while fear sees the invisible and dreads it. Both look toward what has not yet happened, but one looks with hope and trust and the other with dread, expecting catastrophe.

Did you know we are commanded not to fear? 'Have I not commanded you? Be strong and of good courage; do not fear or be dismayed: for the Lord your God is with you wherever you go.' [Joshua 1:9] Our creator knows what fear does to us, just like a car's manufacturer knows what happens when you fill your car's tank with the wrong fuel. The manufacturer doesn't plead with you to use the right fuel, he states it in the manual and expects you to follow it.

We are meant to simply be — to rest in who we are. When we rest in God, we express Him because He works through us and in us for His glory. We weren't created to strive or wear ourselves out trying to make things happen. With God's guidance, we can live a stress-free life and be grateful rather than strive/struggle.

> *'For it is God which works in you, both to will and to do of his good pleasure'* Philippians 2:13

Having a single eye, in this case, means you are only focused on the good. You are not looking over your shoulder or watching out for the 'devil'. It also means that you waste no time focusing on negative things or things that steal your joy. Paul, teaching on this subject instructs us to think on the good – the positive.

This is what he says,

> *'Finally, brethren, whatever things are true, whatever things are noble, whatever things are just, whatever things are pure, whatever things are lovely, whatever things are of good report, if there is any virtue and if there is anything praiseworthy, think on these things.'* Philippians 4:8

What he's simply saying is to stop giving attention to negative energy, which we call evil or the devil. We must not strive to prove ourselves or work to earn God's love, we are already resting in that love. A love that knows no fear.

> *'There remains therefore a rest to the people of God. For he that is entered into His rest, he also hath ceased from his own works, as God did from His. Let us labour therefore to enter that rest, lest any man fall after the same example of unbelief.'* Hebrews 4:9-11

Unbelief is the only thing the Bible refers to as 'unforgivable'. It is so serious, it is referred to as blasphemy against the Holy Spirit; a sin that by law was punishable by death.

When I was seven, I remember hearing a sermon about blasphemy against the Holy Spirit. The sermon was in my dialect (Kikuyu) and blasphemy against the Holy Spirit in Kikuyu is *'Kurama Roho Mutheru'*, direct translation being, 'insulting' the Holy Spirit.

I had stayed behind after Sunday school just so I could play with babies and hopefully get to hold them. Sometimes their parents allowed us to take them home when they became restless as our house was only a stone's throw from the church, allowing them to enjoy the service without distraction. My younger brother and I would feed them and make up songs to entertain them as they ate. We would then lay them down to sleep until the end of the service when their parents would pick them up.

The sermon caught my interest, and I found myself wondering about this unforgivable sin. That day I stayed and listened to the whole sermon. I wondered what it would mean to be unforgiven forever. It would obviously mean going to hell. That terrified me. No one would want to go there, so why would anyone insult the Holy Spirit, I wondered.

The more I thought about it, the more I felt a strange urge to do it. It was almost magnetic. It's like looking at a saying, 'Wet paint, do not touch,' or telling a child not to touch something. There is something that pulls you to it, making you want to touch even though you know you shouldn't. The more you think about it, the more inclined you are to give in to it.

I couldn't resist the urge. What was I going to call him though? In my understanding at the time, an insult is when you call someone a dog, a cow, a monkey or anything they're not. None of those animals felt right or befitting the Holly spirit. Inasmuch as I 'needed' to do this, the insult did not have to be terrible. It had to be something nice; not so big or rough. I ruled out the cow, the dog and definitely not a monkey.

These are all animals we had at home except for the monkey. We also had a very friendly and cuddly little cat. It felt more appropriate for the mission. Having that sorted, the next worry was where to do it. No one had to know what I was up to. Up to this time, I had not talked to anyone about it.

Behind my grandmother's house was a gently sloping lawn where my little brother and I spent hours sliding down the soft green grass, relishing the simple joy of those carefree moments. This time I was there on my own, and not for fun. A part of me was sad that I was going to be unforgiven forever, and the other part was excited about doing something that no one would dare to do. I had taken the whole thing literally.

Today I know that it is impossible to blaspheme against the Holy Spirit once you have entered His rest. Many scriptures point to *unbelief* as the blasphemy against the Holy Spirit because it comes between us and God's fullness. Unbelief is the inability to believe, the absence of faith or lack of it. It blocks the good that is meant to flow into our lives, thus negating His power.

It is therefore unforgivable in the sense that the person who lacks faith has no means to acquire what is rightfully theirs. He therefore shuts himself out, because the gifts of God are received by faith. They are not physically perceived or received. This is the scripture that the sermon was on.

> *'Any sin and blasphemy will be forgiven man, but blasphemy against the Holy Spirit will not be forgiven.'* Matthew 12:31-32

When Jesus said, 'It is finished,' He meant that God had

provided everything we need and will ever need. All there is for us to do is to receive, and we receive by faith through believing. In other words, faith is the key to the Kingdom, and if unbelief is the absence of faith, there is no way to access anything within the kingdom.

It's simply having a treasure box and no key to open it, so you have a box full of all the things you desire but you cannot open it, what good is it? In the kingdom is where everything is, unconditional love, forgiveness, provision, healing or wholeness of body, mind and spirit, eternal life, happiness, joy and abundance of every form, be it spiritual, physical or material wealth.

He has provided it all. Our job is to receive. If the key is faith, how can anyone receive it? This is how unbelief negates God's power. We're told to seek the kingdom first because, once we find the kingdom we have found everything we need in this life. [Matt. 6:33] In this kingdom lies the power to transcend all limitations, without which we cannot have a full life, which, as we saw earlier, [John 10:10] is the reason Jesus came.

It is our unbelief that keeps us stuck. It blocks the flow of the spirit because God does not impose. Unbelief, lack of sufficient knowledge, wrong beliefs, long-established customs and traditions that do not align with the will of God, and our self-concept among other things hinder the supernatural working of God in our lives.

This was evident in Jesus' own hometown, according to the Gospels of Mark and Matthew. He performed many miracles everywhere He went but could not do much in His own hometown. This is not because He did not want to or that He had no power there, but because of the people's unbelief.

> *'And he could there do no mighty work, save that he laid his hands upon a few sick folks, and healed them. And he marvelled because of their unbelief.'*
> Mark 6:5-6, Matthew 13:58

People in Jesus' hometown did not believe He was the son of God. They knew Him as a carpenter, the son of Mary and Joseph. They knew all his brothers and had seen Him grow and probably play with their children as a boy, we are not told that much; we are told very little about His life growing up. 'Is this not the carpenter, the son of Mary, the brother of James, and Joses, and Juda, and Simon?' they asked. [Mark 6:3] They did not recognise Him as God, and for that reason, His power did not work for them.

He was willing, but they were not ready to receive. When we acknowledge His sovereignty, His power works in and through us, and we begin to see the fruits. It is our faith that activates His supernatural power in our lives; the reason the word says, 'Without faith, it is impossible to please God.' [Hebrews 11:6] We lock ourselves out of the things we need to live a full or abundant life that He came so we could have.

A full life is a successful and victorious life, free from limitations such as disease, poverty etc. It does not please Him to see His children struggle with these things when He has done everything to enable us to live free of them.

Grace Wairimu

CHAPTER TWO

Metanoia

Be transformed by the renewing of your mind.

etanoia is a Greek word for change of mind or renewal of mind. Scientifically, the mind encompasses many functions and processes, including thought, memory, perception, cognition, imagination, emotion, consciousness and many more. It plays a big role in how we perceive things and ultimately deal with them. Having a wholesome concept of ourselves can make a difference in what we allow in our minds and how our mind functions.

A Harvard University lecturer, William James said, 'Man, by changing the inner attitudes of his mind, can change the outer aspects of his life.' If we want to change our lives, we must start by changing our thinking because everything happens in the mind before it becomes a reality. Even the creation started as a thought in the mind of God, then a word; 'Let there be...' and it was, except for man who is different from all creations. He is a creator himself. He creates His world by His thoughts and words; *'As he thinks in his heart so is he.'* [Proverbs 23:7]

Heart and mind are sometimes used interchangeably, especially in the Bible. It is where man shapes his life and creates his world. The heart is the core of your being, your thoughts, will, conscience, and values. It is in the heart and mind that thoughts and feelings reside, and that is what creates your life. We are cautioned to guard them as they determine the course of our lives.

> *'Keep your heart with all diligence; for out of it are the issues of life.'* Proverbs 4:23

Good News Translation says, 'Be careful how you think; your life is shaped by your thoughts.' This is reinforced by Paul's words in Romans 12:2, urging us to be transformed by the renewing of our minds. Transformation happens when we renew our minds, changing the course of our lives. Sometimes wrong thoughts and beliefs can lead to a life that does not align with our desire.

To change that, all we need is to renew our mind; evaluate our thoughts, believes, customs, traditions etc. and change whatever does not support our purpose or where we want our life to go. If you have a mind, and we all do, you can change your life. That means we can all change our lives by changing or renewing our minds.

Sometimes, what keeps us from embracing change is fear of the unknown. This keeps us in a loop, doing the same thing repeatedly and getting the same results because we are too afraid to step out of the familiar zone and explore possibilities. If we could silence fear and be open to the unknown, we would realise that beyond our fear is a whole new life of endless possibilities.

Metanoia also means repentance. When you realise that what you held as true is not real or true, and decide to move away from it, you are going through repentance. You are rejecting the lie you believed in and embracing the truth you now know to be right. This is what Paul was talking about, addressing the Romans, to repent from their old ways and embrace the new consciousness of truth.

They had many traditions that did not necessarily

benefit them but kept them in bondage. He was urging them to free their minds, then they would know God's perfect will for them. [Romans 12:2] You may have been born subject to conditions that made you feel powerless; you don't have to stay in that position of powerlessness. All you need is to change or renew your mind. Change the way you think about yourself and the situation you are in.

We are powerful beyond our imagination because the omnipotent creator of the universe lives within us. Repentance happens when you allow this power to take over your life and change you from the inside out. Paul, speaking to the Roman church, said, 'I delight in the law of God after the inward man.' [Romans 7:22] The outward man is a natural man. But the inward man is spiritual man. The inward man influences the outward man, transforming his outward/physical life.

The inward man is our true self. It is the spirit of God in us. Repentance, therefore, is the radical change of mind towards life. It is when you allow the inward man to influence the outward man, not the other way around. It is when you allow the God within you to take the driver's seat. You begin to see life differently, and more importantly, your self-concept changes. You cease to see yourself as a victim of life but a victor or a conqueror. This process is called 'surrender'.

Surrender is the willingness to trust in the intelligence of life, that everything is happening for your highest good and to participate fully in that; to use every experience for growth and evolution whether you perceive it to be good or bad, even when you don't understand. It is to trust and know that life will show you.

When the COVID-19 pandemic hit, my youngest child had just gone to university, and that gave me the freedom and flexibility to move to a town of choice not determined by conditions such as the schools the children went to or the ability to be physically available for them. I could live and work anywhere I wanted. It was exciting; freedom is always exciting.

So, the pandemic found me in a new town, many miles away from everyone I knew and everything familiar to me. Long story short, when everything was shut down, I registered with a local agency to work at a COVID-testing centre. It was scary, but others were doing it; nurses were still working in hospitals, paramedics were still responding to emergency calls and attending to COVID-19 patients, and even taxi drivers were still in operation. What was there to fear?

Besides, it was only for a short period, I thought. That was not to be. The longer the situation lasted, the more impatient and frustrated I became. I had heard a preacher on TV talk about perseverance and how some situations we find ourselves in are 'tests' that we must pass. According to the preacher, the more you resist, the longer the situation lasts; the tests keep repeating themselves until you pass.

The message was that you must pass the test. It took me a very long time to pass this one, and through it, I learned so much about myself, about the ego, and, more importantly, about surrender.

Surrender is simply accepting what is and allowing. You accept where you're at and allow life to lead you to the next step. It's only when you accept that you realise you are right where you should be at that moment even if it doesn't feel or look that way. I had to change my mind about the whole situation. Instead of complaining, I became grateful that I was not a victim of the virus and that I was able to help.

By this time, things had advanced, and we had moved from the testing centre to actual wards where we looked after COVID-19 patients and those who were recovering from it. I began to see things from a different perspective and was glad that I was not there as a patient. I could have been. There was nothing special I had done to keep myself from the contracting the virus. Seeing people die helped me appreciate my position and the fact that I was useful in some way.

One of my favourite authors, Dr Wayne Dyer, made a

profound statement in one of his books, *Wishes Fulfilled*: 'If you change the way you look at things, the things you look at change'. This is the meaning of metanoia, transformation through change in our way of thinking. It's simply not allowing external conditions to influence our internal condition. Two people could be looking at the same thing and have different interpretations of it depending on their states of mind. Our state of mind informs our worldview.

Fear, for example, is a concept that paralyses. I call it a concept because it is conceived in the mind and not necessarily real. When confronted by something we deem life-threatening, we are filled with fear. Sometimes, our mind tricks us into thinking we are in danger. Most of the time, the things we fear do not exist in the present moment; we anticipate them, much like a false prophecy.

Fears like the fear of failure, disease, loss, or simply fear of the future are all insecurities that cloud our minds and shift our focus away from harmony. They are mostly psychological. Though they do not exist in the moment we start having the feeling that something bad is going to happen, they in many cases materialise. This is because we attract what we focus on. Evaluating these fears and consciously changing the way we think about them is the first step towards freeing ourselves from them.

The secret is to use our minds to stay in harmony. Once we realise that our thoughts are causing us uneasiness, we must change them by focusing on harmony. To focus on harmony is to focus on the solution because solutions come when we are still and not when we are anxious. It's like a drowning person: the harder they fight trying to save themselves, the deeper they sink.

Among the many things that Apostle Paul talks about is the state of our minds, encouraging us to control our thoughts, bringing them to the obedience of Christ.

'Pulling down strongholds, casting down

*imaginations and every high thing that exalts itself
against the knowledge of God, and bringing into
captivity every thought to the obedience of Christ.'*
2 Cor. 10:4-5

What Paul is telling us is to dismantle entrenched patterns of thoughts, false beliefs or mental 'fortresses' that resist truth. In other words, to break free from our mental prisons, to reject any distorted mental images and assumptions (imaginations) and replace them with truth. Things like ideologies, egos and pride exalt themselves against the knowledge of God. He's telling us to challenge them and bring them under God's wisdom.

King Solomon, who was known for his wisdom and still is, says in Proverbs, 'A man who rules his spirit is better than one who takes a city.' [Prov. 16:32] They are both talking about self-control or being able to control our minds and emotions. He adds that a man without self-control is like a city without walls. [Prov. 25:28] A city without walls is weak and vulnerable, it is without defence.

Human imagination is one of the most powerful functions of the mind or tools that God has given to man. It is where we create things that are not seen. We can build a whole city in our imagination or fly to a faraway land that nobody knows about and build cities there. That's the power of imagination. It is important to train ourselves to use our imagination to create, not just anything but what we really want in our lives and those of others.

We must learn how to use it and use it well — positively. Using it negatively is what Paul refers to as 'imaginations that exalt themselves against the knowledge of God'. Our imaginations must align with the knowledge of God, not against. When you imagine something, you concentrate your thoughts on it. The reason we must learn how to use our imagination is that what we concentrate on manifests in our lives.

It does not matter whether it's positive or negative, if you focus on it long enough, you capture it. In other words, it manifests in your life. A good example is how a camera works. We use cameras all the time these days. To capture an object on the camera, you only need to focus the lens on the subject steadily and persistently for as long as you need to, then press the button or squeeze if it's analogue. If the object shifts or someone suddenly walks in front of it as you press the button, you capture what is in focus.

It's the same with our minds. We must train our minds to focus on what we want to capture or attain. If we want good health but focus our mind on disease, we capture what we focus on, the disease even if it's out of concern for someone who has it. If we constantly think about it or worry about it, we risk getting it. It is not superstition; it is the creative power of the mind.

We must not entertain any thoughts that create fear. Fear is our worst enemy. The things we fear most have a way of showing up in our lives. Job discovered that and said,

> *'For the thing which I greatly feared has come upon me, and that which I was afraid of has come unto me.'* Job 3:25

When you fear something, you tend to obsess about it. You may catch yourself thinking about it subconsciously, yes, subconsciously because it's no longer a conscious thing. You have entertained the thought so much that it has been picked up by your subconscious mind. We will discuss that later in the book.

Focus on what you want in your life. When your focus is on abundance, for example, there must be no thought of scarcity. Our thoughts must be positive, constructive, and harmonious. They must be consistently and effortlessly directed to the desired outcome. Remember Paul's teachings from the previous chapter. 'Whatever things are good, whatever things are pure and of good report, think on those things.'

Sickness and lack or scarcity are not good, pure, or of good report. Instead of occupying our minds with them, the sick should see themselves as well and whole, and the poor as rich, lacking nothing. That is how they align themselves with the solution. If someone you know or in the family is sick, see them the way you would like them to be, well and healthy. That way, you are focusing on the desired outcome — the solution.

The secret here is to change our thoughts from the old condition we want to get rid of, to the new one we wish to produce, and remain in that state. To keep talking or thinking about the old condition is to affirm its existence. Instead, think about the new desired condition single mindedly. We must always be single eyed.

When God promised to restore the fortunes of Judah and Jerusalem, He instructed the people to prepare for war. They were not an army but a group of regular people; they were scared because they felt weak and unprepared. He instructed them to say, 'I am strong,' especially when they felt weak. [Joel 3:10] He wasn't asking them to lie or pretend, He was encouraging them to change their self-image. This is the same concept; we must always think and proclaim the desired outcome.

In another story documented in Judges 6, the Israelites were under the oppression of the Midianites, who had a big army and were much stronger. The Israelites had no army and were scared. A man named Gideon was working secretly, hiding away from the enemies. An angel appeared to him, addressing him as 'mighty man of valour'. [Judges 6:11-12] The angel knew he was hiding out of fear, which did not make him brave or mighty. According to the dictionary, valour means great bravery, especially in battle.

He was not mocking him or being sarcastic, he was showing him who he was on the inside. Gideon accepted this new identity and led his people to victory with only three hundred men against their enemy's army of over a hundred thousand men. To him, it was a new identity but to the angel, that is who he was. He just didn't know it. He only needed someone to remind him who he was. Once he aligned himself with the truth, he found the courage to face his enemies.

The point to note here is that the truth was already set. The angel knew it, God knew it, but Gideon didn't. That's why he addressed him as 'mighty man of valour', a great warrior. We too may not know who we are, we have accepted the idea of being broke, weak, sick etc for so long we think that's who we are. We're only seeing the physical, the outer man, but God looks on the inside. [1 Sam. 16:7]

Even for us, the truth is the same, that things in the spiritual realm, the invisible, are perfect and in order. We just have to align with that truth through our thoughts, words and action, and above all, through faith. When you have a negative thought, declare the opposite. Declare you are strong when you feel weak, you are well when you're sick, not just with empty words, but with conviction, believing every word you say.

That doesn't mean you should not seek intervention when you're sick. Your inner physician should be your first respondent as He is the closest to you. He's in you. You don't have to go looking for Him or to make calls as He's already aware, even as you make those calls. If you stay awake at night worrying for your child's future or feeling frustrated with their behaviour, stop worrying and start seeing them as God sees them.

See them as the angel saw Gideon; see what you want to see in them and speak to them from that perspective. Rather than criticise them or tell them how useless or stupid they are, call out the greatness in them. The genius is in all of us waiting to be discovered. When you do this, you are changing your mentality to the equivalent of the desired outcome, which will, in time, prove itself in your experience. You are changing your world and the world around you.

Our world is a manifestation of mental activity which develops within us, the imagination. Thinking and speaking negatively of a situation reinforces it. Through our imagination, we escape from the limitations of the senses and the bondage of reason. Our natural senses are limiting as they tell us what is possible and what is not. In the unseen world, all things are possible.

Paul, talking about the natural and the spiritual nature of man, says that the natural man does not perceive the things of the spirit because they are foolishness to him. Some things cannot be discerned with natural senses and reason, no matter how educated one might be. There comes a time in life when we must 'crucify' logic and the intellect and allow the flow of life to show us what our physical eyes cannot see. Gideon's father, Joash did not see the bravery in his son, but the angel did.

This flow of life for someone who has discovered the kingdom of God within him is God, the creator of the universe. He sees us in our true identity, not as we are physically but as we are in Him. It does not matter what your understanding of God is, whether you call Him Life, Love, Truth, the Way, the Universe, Infinite Intelligence, Source, etc. What's important is that you know we are talking about the Creator of Heaven and earth, Emmanuel — God with us. We will talk about His name later.

When He looks at us, He sees His son, He sees Himself. How so, you may ask. He, Jesus died for us all while we were yet sinners and clothed us in righteousness, which is grace, or the person of Jesus (God). That is what He sees, it's like looking in the mirror and seeing your reflection. He sees what we are on the inside and not what we are in the physical, just like He saw a brave man in Gideon.

It is not easy to change a habit, especially if you're trying to do it overnight. It takes time, discipline, and persistence. Once the new habit becomes established, it becomes more automatic and natural. That is how 'mental equivalent' is built. Gideon did not try to convince the angel that he wasn't the man He thought he was, he changed his mentality and rose to the occasion. He changed his self-image and began to see himself as the angel did.

To align yourself with who you are on the inside, you simply change your mentality and maintain the new one; for example, if you currently see yourself as poor, start seeing yourself as rich. You change your mentality to what you want to achieve, be it health, success, wealth etc. All these things are within you, you just need to align yourself with them. Rather than focus your mind on beating a bad habit, see yourself as God sees you and the habit will fall away without so much self-effort.

Just as light drives out darkness, so does grace drive out what is unlike itself or what does not align with it. Like Gideon, you just need to remember who you are. The most important point to remember here, is not to talk about problems as if they exist. Don't own something you do not want by calling it yours, i.e. my disease, my cancer, my diabetes etc.'

Bear in mind that just because it afflicted you does not mean it is or was yours in the first place. It never was. Begin to think, act, and talk as if the problem is already solved, whether physically gone or not. Before a condition disappears physically, it must disappear from your mind. This is what faith is about. It starts from within and then appears on the outside because the outside is the projection of the inside.

Your words must be in alignment with your mind — your thoughts and emotions. Saying you're healed while thinking the opposite will not bring the desired outcome because it lacks faith.

Why are words so powerful?

According to Jesu's teaching, what goes into the mouth does not defile a man because it does not enter his heart but the belly, and then gets dispelled. But what comes out of the mouth is what defiles a man. He goes on to explain that what comes out of the mouth comes from the heart, and what comes from the heart is what defiles.

While the Bible uses the heart and mind interchangeably, the heart is associated with emotions or feelings, and the mind thoughts. When we don't guard our hearts, negative emotions come out of our mouths as negative words that cause chaos in our lives and those of others. Words reveal what is on the inside, and according to Jeremiah 17:9, the heart is deceitful and desperately wicked.

If negative emotions can cause chaos in our lives, positive emotions must have the opposite effect. Did you know that the Bible says laughter is medicine? This is what it says, 'A merry heart doeth good like a medicine: but a broken spirit dries the bones.' [Prov. 17:22] A two-minute conversation, whether face to face or on the phone can tell you what's in someone's heart by the choice of words, tone and attitude.

It is believed that an average person has approximately sixty thousand thoughts in a day. Most of these thoughts come and go unnoticed. The human mind is like a river flowing with thoughts throughout the day. It takes discipline to know what thoughts to ignore and which ones to entertain. It is not those you ignore that impact your life but the ones you allow to get to the heart or to influence you.

While you may not control every thought that comes to mind, you can control which ones you give life to by words. Thoughts come in; words go out. What comes out of your mouth can heal or kill. They can also make you sick; they can build or break. Words can bless or curse. [James 3:10] Life and death are in the power of your tongue. [Proverbs 18:21] Unspoken thoughts become real once impressed upon the subconscious mind, but spoken words are live and active. That's why we must choose our words wisely.

If your thoughts are right, your words will be right. If these two are consistent, then they will manifest on the outside. There is no renewal of the mind without faith. Faith builds what doubt and fear have destroyed. It opens doors to all the desirable things in life. [James 1:17] It is the link that connects us with our creator. It puts us into contact with our infinite power, the power within us, opening the way to unlimited possibilities and unlimited resources.

We can only rise as high as our faith; no one can do anything greater than what he believes he can do. It takes faith to see beyond obstacles, to see the way beyond difficulties and to refuse to allow anything to divert our focus. To build a mental equivalent of freedom, vibrant physical health, abundance, or a growing understanding and conviction of God, we must have faith and not entertain any doubt.

Paul describes faith as the substance of things hoped for, the evidence of things not seen. [Hebrews 11:1] If you can see something, you are not *hoping* to see it. You already know it is there, so no faith is required to see it. But for that which you cannot see, you have no evidence of it. The evidence of its existence is your faith. If you have no faith it exists, then, to you, it does not exist. It is impossible to build a mental equivalent of something you have no faith in. You cannot visualise it. You cannot 'see' it.

Without faith, there is very little you can achieve out of the unseen, the supernatural realm. When we look at the world around us with our physical eyes, we see disharmony, fear, chaos, and all kinds of difficulties. There are wars, severe weather conditions, crimes and diseases. It's easy to get discouraged, disillusioned and fearful. But the best way to conquer this fear and disillusionment is to have faith in the unseen and to use your words to declare what you want to see, to imagine it constantly and to be grateful for it.

It is important also to count the good in your life amidst all the chaos. This helps you see that there is still good in the world despite all the chaos and disorder. Allowing your mind to rest while doing what you can is the best way to effect change, no matter how insignificant you might think that change is. It shows appreciation of God's presence within and around us, His guidance and wisdom.

We are told to pray without ceasing. [1 Thes. 5:17] We must be in constant communion with God, not necessarily on our knees but in our minds, even as we go about our normal duties. Praying without ceasing is to remain consciously aware of the working of the Spirit throughout the day, it is not impossible. Some people say that 'the mind is the workshop of the devil'. That is because it is always active and, if untamed tends to lean on the fearful side, manufacturing thoughts of fear and disillusionment.

When tamed, it is the workshop of the Creator. It neutralises fear, replacing it with ideas and motivation to act positively, leading to a solution. It opens the mind to possibilities previously unknown, making man a co-creator with His creator. Once we discover the kingdom within, our minds become the workshop of God.

One of the people whose lives demonstrate this attitude is David, the father of Solomon. He lived in awe and acknowledgment of the goodness of God. In other words, 'He prayed without ceasing'. He lived each moment in the attitude of worship and thanksgiving. He meditated on the goodness of God and deliberately chose to see good in everything. In one of his Psalms, he says,

> *'I praise you because I am fearfully and wonderfully made; your works are wonderful; I know that full well.'* Psalm 139:14

He had no doubts whatsoever that his mind was the workshop of God. It brought forth beautiful poems and music. He was talented and creative. There is this one Psalm he wrote that I find to be both a prayer and affirmation, instead of asking for what he needed, he gave thanks for it. It effectively demonstrates the concept of believing you have received what you pray for, even before you see it. It says:

> *'Bless the Lord, O my soul, and forget not all His benefits:*
> *Who forgives all my sins and heals all my diseases.*
> *Who redeems my life from destruction and crowns me with lovingkindness and tender mercies.*

Who satisfies my mouth with good things so that my youth is renewed like the eagle's.' Psalms 103:1-5

In just a few lines of poetry, he covers almost all areas of life, from forgiveness of sins to health, security, provision and renewal of youth. Instead of asking God to take care of these concerns, he thanks Him as though they are already taken care of because he knows they are. It is done, and so be it.

David must have known how our body and mind work to say that we are fearfully and wonderfully made. When Paul, in the New Covenant, wrote about transformation through the renewal of the mind, he must also have known something about the power of the mind. Let us look at how our mind works.

The part that thinks and analyses things all the time is the conscious mind. It only rests when we go to sleep. The subconscious mind then takes over. There is yet another part of the mind, the superconscious mind. This is the mind of God. It operates in us when we let it. This mind respects free will; it will never overstep.

The Conscious, the Subconscious and the Superconscious mind

The mind has two main parts, not counting the unconscious state: the conscious and the subconscious. The conscious mind is also called the objective mind or waking mind. It learns through observation, experiences, and education. It deals with external things as it has contact with the environment through the five senses: sight, smell, touch, hearing and taste.

It is our daily guide in our objective life and physical environment, also known as the three-dimensional world. Our reasoning faculty is the noblest attribute of our conscious mind, but it is essentially finite and primarily for the three-dimensional world.

The subconscious mind, on the other hand, is

unrestricted by our objective senses, physical form or earthly conditions, nor impeded by the processes of finite reasoning. It is the subjective mind, also called the sleeping mind. Unlike the conscious mind, which uses the senses, the subconscious mind is controlled by suggestions from the conscious mind.

It is the seat of our emotions, the intelligence that makes itself manifest when the conscious mind is sleeping or dormant. It sees without the use of eyes and can leave the body and travel around like in a dream or a vision. It is one with infinite intelligence and boundless wisdom.

The third part is unlike the other two. It is the *superconscious mind.* This is the mind of God within every man, the divine plan of the creator. When you follow your intuition leading you to safety, avoiding danger you did not know about; it is the infinite spirit guiding you from within. It is the divine plan, the infallible guide within you. This infinite spirit opens the way to great abundance. It is a magnet for all that belongs to it by divine right.

To access it, man must take the first step and ask or seek. Few people have access to superconscious mind. It is where ideas of great works and discoveries are found. Deep spiritual experiences and miracles such as healing are also found there. In the Bible, we learn about several people who accessed this part of the mind while asleep. A good example is Jacob, who wrestled with 'an angel' until daybreak.

This was not a physical event. He was sleeping. It happened in a vision of the night when his conscious mind was asleep. When he woke up, he named the place 'Peniel', 'For I have seen God face to face, and my life is preserved.' He said. [Genesis 32:30] Scientifically, our sleep and wake cycle is regulated in the brain, where a gland called the 'pineal gland' plays a key role by producing melatonin in darkness (night), helping us to fall asleep and maintain deep sleep, and suppressing it in daylight.

This cycle is called the Circadian rhythm. It tells the body when to sleep and when to wake up. It also affects other body processes like hormones, digestion, body temperature etc. When the body's clock fails to function normally, it can lead to dysfunction in the body or ailments, including depression and mental imbalance. Research shows that when this gland is activated, people witness supernatural healing and other supernatural experiences. It activates the genius within.

Jacob must have had his pineal gland activated, which makes me wonder about the relationship between the two names, Penial, the name he gave the spot where he saw God, and Pineal the gland. On another occasion, he was away from his home, on his way to a place where his father had sent him to find a wife. He was tired, and it was getting dark. He decided to rest and carry on with his journey in the morning. He took a stone for his pillow and lay down to sleep. [Gen 28:11]

In his sleep, he saw a ladder resting on earth, reaching up into heaven and angels of God going up and down the ladder. He then saw God standing above the ladder. He introduced Himself as 'the God of Abraham, your grandfather...' and promised to protect him wherever he went. [Gen. 28:12] When Jacob woke up, he said, 'Surely the Lord is in this place, but I did not know it.' He took the stone he had slept on and set it up to commemorate the event. He called the place Bethel. 'It is surely the house of God and the gate of Heaven.' He said.

Another person who had this kind of experience is Solomon, the son of David. He is known as the wisest and wealthiest man who ever lived. He received his wisdom and wealth in a dream. His father had died, and he had become the king. In a dream, God told him to ask for anything, and he would grant it. He asked for understanding to rule the people as his father had, with wisdom and truth. God granted his request and added riches and honour, which he had not asked for. He also promised to lengthen his days.

'And Solomon awoke; and behold, it was a dream.'

1 Kings 3:15

Wouldn't we all want to have that kind of a dream! He celebrated with his servants and gave thanks to God. All that God promised in the dream came to be.

How Thoughts and Emotions Affect Your Physical Experiences

Thoughts impressed on the subconscious mind by the conscious mind through beliefs, imaginations, or convictions are brought into our lives as a condition, an experience, or an event. The subconscious mind is like soil, which accepts any seed you deposit in it, whether good or bad. It accepts any idea, good or bad. Like the soil, no one knows what you planted until it shoots up from the ground and is physically visible as a seedling, a plant, and then fruits if it bears fruits.

You cannot plant a mango seed and harvest oranges, you reap what you sow, literally. Likewise, anything you accept and believe to be true is accepted by your subconscious mind and manifested in the physical world. Ideas are conveyed to your subconscious mind through feeling. If you feel something deeply like joy or sadness, it will make an impression on the subconscious mind, and you might find yourself thinking about it subconsciously or even dreaming about it.

Anything you believe or hold as true, whether it is factual or not, is impressed on the subconscious so that if you are presented with a similar situation, the subconscious mind produces the results it produced previously. Sometimes, if you do something enough times, you can do it without engaging your conscious mind. Your subconscious mind knows how you react to certain things so well that when faced with those conditions, you react impulsively, like always. You don't even need to think about it.

A good example is our beliefs and superstitions. We know them, and they work like clockwork. It's not some magic or evil power; it's the power of belief. Let's say you believe if you have a hot drink before going to bed, you wake up at a certain time in the night, may be midnight or 2am on the dot. If that belief is strong enough to be picked up by the subconscious mind, it will wake you up at exactly that time whenever you have a hot drink before bed. The subconscious mind obeys what the conscious mind tells it.

If you fear something bad will happen, avoid dwelling on the thought or verbalising it. You cannot fool your subconscious mind because it takes cues directly from your conscious mind. It is not what you say that is impressed on the subconscious mind, but what you believe or feel strongly. The best way to deal with such thoughts of fear is to use the one thing that neutralises fear, faith.

Always decree harmony, health, peace, and abundance, not just with words but with conviction. Consistently feed your conscious mind with positive and empowering thoughts, and your subconscious will respond accordingly. Developing an attitude of gratitude helps shift our mindset towards contentment and abundance as it reminds us of the blessings already present in our lives.

Gratitude is a transformative practice that can profoundly influence your life. It shifts your focus from disharmony to harmony and from lack to abundance. It rewires your brain and enhances your emotional well-being and, ultimately, your physical health. As mentioned earlier, gratitude is the quickest way of breaking free from negative thought patterns. It helps you align more with your desires, leading to a happier and more fulfilling life.

Giving thanks shows you have faith in the good present in your life whether seen or unseen. Being healthy and prosperous is the normal way to be. It was God's vision for man since creation. Mental coercion or too much effort to achieve these states indicates anxiety and fear and can work against your best intentions. When your mind is relaxed, it is open to ideas and when you accept an idea, your subconscious mind goes to work to execute it. The feeling of health produces health, and the feeling of wealth produces wealth.

Imagination plays a big role in this; it is our most powerful faculty. You must have heard the saying 'If you can imagine it, you can achieve it'. It's a quote by William Arthur Ward, an American motivational writer and poet, and it's accurate. The best part is, imagination is free. You can imagine anything, however obnoxious; there is no limit to what you can imagine and there are no restrictions in the world of imagination.

Imagine yourself healthy, living in harmony and abundance. Imagine the fulfilment of your desire. Before you go to bed, remind yourself that you're healthy and prosperous and be thankful for it even if you don't physically see it or feel it at present. Tell yourself that everything you need has been provided and fall asleep in that state of mind. Every man has the power to bless and multiply, heal and prosper. Seeing yourself in this states in your imagination is blessing yourself.

You do not have to strive or slave hard; abundance is a mental conviction. Build into your mentality and subconscious mind the idea of abundance, health and peace. You get into a perfect mental discipline by thinking, speaking, feeling and doing all that is required for change with effective and productive action. It is not enough to know that your desires are granted. You must act accordingly. You cannot keep asking for something you have already received; instead of asking consistently, give thanks with joy. Maintain the conviction that you have received without wavering. I will return to this point in later chapters.

Some people see life as a battle, others as a game. It all depends on the state of your mind because the actual battle is in the mind. Once you win the battle in your mind by changing the internal state, your external world changes. You will then begin to see life as something to be enjoyed rather than dreaded, even what we has not unfolded yet. Your physical experiences will begin to reflect you internal life.

We are what we are by virtue of the consciousness from

which we think. If we think from the consciousness of sonship, we draw strength from these words; 'Son, you are always with me, and everything I have is yours.' [Luke 15:31] God has everything, there's nothing you could ever need or ask for that He hasn't. As His son's all that He has is ours. Being sons of God makes us gods and heirs of His kingdom.

I will say it again that the real battle is in the mind because that is where everything happens. This is where we shape our lives by the choices we make. There is a verse in the Bible that is often misquoted; it says our enemies [foes] are those of our household. [Matt. 10:36] It refers to our mind and not our family members.

Your mind is the source of all your fears, anxiety and doubts, which are your worst enemies. It tells you things that are often not real or true in the form of negative thoughts, which when believed or acted on could cause a lot of tension and negative outcomes. It is your mind that tells you are going to fail even before you launch that great idea God put in your heart to pursue.

The mind has a hard time accepting new things, ideas and concepts, but once it does, doors begin to open. It just requires discernment to know what to accept and what to disregard. Some people say, follow your heart — but we have seen that the heart is deceitful and wicked. We can all learn something from the wisest man known to have lived:

> 'Be careful how you think; your life is shaped by your thoughts. Never say anything that isn't true. Have nothing to do with lies and misleading words. Look straight ahead with honest confidence; don't hang your head in shame. Plan carefully what you do, and whatever you do will turn out right.'
> Proverbs 4:23-27

This is a short summary of what makes up a healthy self-concept. We tell lies when we are hiding something, when we don't feel good about ourselves, often out of guilt or shame. It tells us 'Not to hang our heads in shame' regardless of the situation. It calls us to express ourselves authentically [with honest confidence].

This is only possible when we can control our mind. It is far better to control your mind than a nation; a man who can control his mind is more powerful than one who controls a city. [Proverbs 16:32] One who can control their emotions is more powerful than one who has great wealth and influence.

CHAPTER THREE

The Secret Place

He that dwells in the secret place of the Most High...

He that dwells in the secret place of the Most High shall abide under the shadow of the Almighty. These are the opening words of the popular ninety-first Psalm. They are powerful, reassuring and a promise of safety, but what is this secret place?

The author, King David, lived in reverence of God. He constantly meditated on His word and generally lived a life of gratitude. He was not perfect; he had flaws like any of us, but what is most notable in his writing is his adoration of God and affirmation of His love (God's love), protection and blessings over his life. He talks about the Almighty as his refuge and fortress. He was aware of God's presence around him and consciously chose to 'dwell' in that presence. From this we learn that the presence of the Almighty is the secret place, a place where God's love for him overshadowed his own love for Him.

David passionately spoke about God's love for him as opposed to his own love for God. Despite his shortcomings, he never doubted that God loved him. He instinctively understood grace, even though he lived long before it was revealed; he lived many years before the birth of Jesus and grace came through Jesus. He seemed profoundly aware that his relationship with God was rooted *not* primarily in his own devotion, but in God's unwavering love and grace. This was a different way of thinking as the commandments demanded that they 'love God with all their hearts, minds and soul'. This was the greatest commandment in the law. [Matt. 22:36-37, Deut. 6:4]

Rather than strive to love God with all his mind and strength, He rested in His love for him. That is what grace asks us to do. In Psalm 23:6 he says, 'Surely goodness and mercy shall follow me all the days of my life.' In Psalm 36:7 he says, 'How excellent is thy lovingkindness!' Some translations say, 'How priceless is your unfailing love, Oh God!'. He speaks this way of God throughout the book of Psalms, affirming the words of Jeremiah; God appeared to Jeremiah saying, 'I have loved you with an everlasting love; therefore, with lovingkindness have I drawn you.' [Jer. 31:3]

These revelations were making way for grace, the greatest miracle that could ever happen to the human race. How could anyone love God with all their heart, mind, and strength? The Israelites never figured it out even after seeing all the things he did including raining down manna for them and drying up the sea. They also saw Him turn rivers into blood. [Psalm 78:36-45]. But He turned things around and said, okay, you can't do it. I will show you how it's done. I will love you instead. That's how grace was conceived.

Looking at it from this angle, we realise that we do not so much rely on our love for God, but His for us. He loved us first and like David, our confidence, praise and repentance are all responses to this amazing love. When we're conscious of this, we trust that His love is dependable even when we fail. God's love for us does not depend on what we can do for Him, give Him or on our good or bad conduct. It is steadfast; unconditional. David, as previously noted, was not perfect by his own merit. He failed like we all do.

He committed a crime most people would not even come close to in a lifetime; he arranged for an innocent man to be killed in battle and took his wife for himself, then covered up the murder. I will not go into the details of his repentance and forgiveness at this point but what I want to point out is his ability to pick himself up and return to the 'secret place,' resisting the inner voices telling him he did not deserve God's love and forgiveness. Grace is the roadmap to the secret place.

While most of us think we must earn God's approval, love, forgiveness etc. by being good, never failing, or by doing or not doing, David knew about being 'still' in God's presence. Grace is simply undeserved or unmerited favour. It leads us to repentance, resulting in good deeds and not the other way around. We often think that we have to be a certain way or do certain things to earn God's love and blessings. Acts 17:25 says He does not need anything that we can supply by working for him since He is the one who gives. David knew this.

Jesus, questioned by the Pharisees, who saw His disciples pluck and eat corn on a Sabbath day, answered them, 'Have you not read what David did?' David, according to Matthew 12:1-5 entered into a house of God and ate bread that was not lawful for him to eat because he and his men were hungry. Jesus was not saying 'look, this man was so rebellious' with pride as if being rebellious is a virtue. He used him as an example not only to tell them that there was nothing wrong with plucking corn on a Sabbath, but also to pass a message they could not understand at the time. The message of *grace*. Did David already know about grace?

Jesus knew what He had come to do, and though He had not physically achieved it, He had the end result in mind. He had come to free the people from bondage of every kind, not just sin. 'It is for freedom that Christ has set us free.' [Gal. 5:1] In His consciousness, it was already done. The Pharisees could not do any work on the Sabbath because it was prohibited according to the law. Though Jesus had not fulfilled that law yet, He did not need to observe it, nor did His disciples. They were in a different consciousness, the consciousness of grace. They lived in a different reality.

This is when you set an intention and begin to live as though it is already done. It's from this consciousness that Jesus said, 'When you pray, believe you have received whatever things you desire, and you shall have them.' [Mark 11:24] Similarly, Christ sees us as righteous even though we sin, in reality no one is without sin and there is no small sin and big sin when it comes to grace. The Law demanded different penalties for different sins, but under grace, all sin is equal, and none is unforgivable except unbelief—which is a personal choice, not a result of God's punishment or condemnation. We sin with or without knowing, by thought, words, action or inaction.

What Jesus was practising and teaching is simply the art of living in or from the end or wish fulfilled. It is knowing that our prayer or intention is already fulfilled before we see the evidence, and that we're forgiven even before we fall into sin. It is this knowledge that allowed David to say, 'Bless the Lord Oh my soul, *who forgives all your sins and redeems your life from destruction.'* [Psalms 103] He saw himself as forgiven, not just for the past or present mistakes or sins, but for all his sins, even the ones he had not committed yet. This can be triggering for a lot of people because there is a part of us that does not want to accept that we continually sin or fall short even though deep down we know it's true. I will discuss this further in the coming chapters.

On another occasion, Jesus was asked why His disciples never fasted. This is what He said, 'Can the children of the bridechamber [bridal party/groom's guests] mourn, as long as the bridegroom is with them?' [Mark 9:15] He is the groom. For as long as He was with the disciples, they did not need to fast. He interpreted fasting as mourning. The presence of a bridegroom means celebration. People feast and celebrate at weddings. In the same manner when we have Christ living in us, every moment should be celebration time not mourning.

People in the Old Covenant mourned when they

wanted God to hear them. They fasted and tore their clothes; some even smeared their faces with ash. Today we don't need to do all that. He hears us before we call. If the disciples did not need to mourn because He was physically with them, how about us? He lives within us. We are the brides of Christ, He is the bridegroom and every moment of our union with Him is a wedding, calling for celebration.

Jesus gave the example of David because David somehow knew the secret. His secret was to dwell in the secret place of the Almighty, the presence of God. He also referred to this secret place as his hiding place — 'You are my hiding place; you will protect me from trouble and surround me with songs of deliverance.' [Psalm 32:7]

Where is this Secret Place?

David gives us the secret to enjoying God's protection and provision, which is to dwell in the secret place, but we still don't know how to get there. Though it sounds like a place you physically go to that no one else knows about, it is, on the contrary, a place everyone carries around with them. This is why he says that no matter where he goes, even if he makes his bed in hell, this presence of the Almighty is there. It is his *awareness* of the presence — his *consciousness* of God in his life.

In his day, the statutes of God were written in a physical slab or scroll. But David knew God and was conscious of His presence around him all the time. With or without the law, he had a personal relationship with Him that did not require any rules. In one of the scriptures, he is described as 'man after God's own heart'. Today, with the coming of Christ, the statutes of God are written in our hearts, fulfilling the promise, 'I will put my law in their inward parts and write it in their hearts.' [Jeremiah 31:33] Today, we find spiritual truths within our consciousness. If you truly want to know something, before asking your pastor or church elder, sit in stillness and quiet confidence and listen. The Holy Spirit is a counsellor.

The secret place of the Most High is our own consciousness. David lived in the consciousness of this presence. Through the awareness of it, he took it everywhere he went. There was nowhere he went that this presence was not, simply because he was conscious of it. It's the same with us in this present day; if we are not aware of this presence, it lies dormant in us. We must become aware of it and allow it to inspire us to act as it inspired David. He did great things, some of which would not have been possible without God's input.

He praised God even in his darkest moments, and especially then; he picked himself up and returned to the secret place within his consciousness. He knew he couldn't hide from God. "If I say, 'Surely the darkness will hide me and the light become night around me,' even the darkness will not be dark to you; the night will shine like the day, for darkness is as light to you." He said.

> 'Where shall I go from your spirit? or where shall I flee from your presence?
> If I ascend up into heaven, you are there: if I make my bed in hell, behold, you are there.
> If I take the wings of the morning, and dwell in the uttermost parts of the sea,
> Even there shall your hand lead me, and thy right hand shall hold me.
> If I say, Surely the darkness shall cover me; even the night shall be light about me.
> Yea, the darkness hides not from thee; but the night shineth as the day: the darkness and the light are both alike to you.' Psalms 139:7-12

It is easy to assume that the secret place of the Most High is a house of worship like a church, mosque, temple or a synagogue, but these are houses we go to and cannot physically be there all the time. We don't have to be in these houses to commune with God because He does not live there. We have so far established that He lives within us.

'The God who made the world and everything in it is the Lord of Heaven and earth and does not live in temples made by human hands, as if he needed anything. Rather, he himself gives everyone life and breath and everything else.
Acts 17:24

It is good to go to these houses, but how often do we go there? One or two days a week, what about the rest of the days? You can remain in communion with God both in these houses and outside—because communion with God is not a one-day-a-week event, or even two or three. Nor is it restricted to a place, time, or posture. It is a moment-by-moment awareness of His presence.

There are several things we can learn from David: that we cannot hide from God, we can maintain the awareness of His presence through meditation, thanksgiving and praise anywhere at any time, and that we do not rely on our love for God but His love for us which is unfailing and unconditional. This is how he dwelt in the secret place of the Most High. The dictionary describes the word dwell as to 'live in'. It is not to visit or to hop in and out once in a while. It is a constant state of being.

David raised his vibrations through praise and thanksgiving, not that he always had things to keep him happy 24/7, but he chose to stay in this elevated state through the awareness of the presence of God around him. Through the awareness that God is good, and he wants the best for us, he was able to thank Him and praise Him even before he physically received what he was trusting Him for. This is a principle called 'the assumption of wish fulfilled'. In other words, praying from the conviction that your prayer is already answered.

Instead of saying, 'God heal me' for example, you thank Him for healing you. Instead of saying, 'God help me' you thank Him for getting you out of that sticky situation while you're still in it. It shows complete trust in the goodness and faithfulness of God. Jesus once again talks about prayer In Matthew 6, saying that we should not practice our righteousness in front of others to be seen by them. But when we pray, we should 'enter into our closet, shut the door and pray to our father, who is in secret' and He will reward us openly.

He also cautions us against using many pointless words, as our Father already knows what we need before we ask. [Matt. 6:6-8] Did He mean we must literally go into a physical room and close a physical door? How about praying on public transport, in open spaces, or while walking? Can we not pray in places that have no doors or privacy?

He was talking about the 'upper room', a metaphor for our consciousness—the secret place. This place, only you know and only you can access. Whatever goes on in there, no one else knows. This is why it is a secret place. What you say in this place is only between you and God, who dwells in you. Whether we are at home, at work, on public transport or in open spaces, we can commune with Him in our minds through prayer or meditation.

This is what Paul was talking about when he said to Pray without ceasing. [1 Thess. 5:17-18] He meant to always be in communion with God. To retire in thought within our own consciousness, withdrawing our attention from the outer world and come boldly to the throne of grace — to have confidence in His love and the fact that we are complete just as we are.

Once we enter this secret place, we find mercy and grace. We no longer have anything to declare or prove. We just rest in the stillness and awareness of His presence where we are whole, lacking nothing.

'And ye are complete in him, which is the head of all principality and power' Colossians 2:9-10

With this assurance, it does not matter what is

happening around us, we no longer identify with appearances but choose instead to trust in God. 'I will say of the Lord, He is my refuge and my fortress; My God, in Him will I trust.' David continues to say, 'Surely, He shall deliver thee from the snares of the fowler and the noisome pestilence.' [Psalm 91:3]

If you are familiar with this Psalm, you probably understand that the protection the author talks about is not just physical but also psychological. A fowler, from the dictionary, is someone who catches birds, and pestilence is a fatal disease or plague. The Bible is, however, not to be interpreted literally. Noisome pestilence is any kind of danger, physical, mental, material or spiritual. It can be anything that threatens your welfare.

'Thou shall not be afraid of the terror by night, nor the arrow that flies by day, nor the pestilence that walks in darkness, nor the destruction that wastes at noonday.' [Psalm 91:5] All these are representations of all our problems, whether physical, emotional, spiritual, financial or relational. The arrow that flies by day and destruction that wastes at noonday are those that we are aware of like financial or relational problems. They are not hidden. Pestilence that walks in darkness are those that we are unaware of. Some ailments, for example, take months or years to present symptoms. We're unaware of them because they are hidden from us until they present symptoms.

Our problems can be classified as belonging to either the conscious or the subconscious mind. The arrow that flies by day and the destruction that wastes at noonday belong to the conscious mind, while terrors of the night and pestilence that walks in darkness are those of the subconscious mind. Modern psychology has shown that most of our difficulties have their roots in the depths of the subconscious mind. Examples include fear, anxiety, depression, paranoia and other complexes of the mind. We cannot see them, they are hidden and only come to the surface when triggered.

Some of these complexes can be destructive; a danger

to us or others. Paranoia, for example, may not be seen as a big problem but a paranoid person who thinks everyone is out to get them may act in a way that endangers them or others. People suffering from mental illnesses such as depression can harm themselves, and those suffering from paranoid schizophrenia, for example, can be a danger to others. These are examples of pestilences that we are protected from when we dwell in the secret place of the Almighty.

'For He shall give his angels charge over you to keep you in all your ways.' Psalm 91:11

This beautiful love letter to whoever receives it also says that He, the Almighty or the Most High, will set him on high because *he has known His name.* He, the Almighty, will be with him in times of trouble. Note that it does not promise that there will be no troubles but that He will deliver him and answer him when he calls. Not only will He honour him, but also satisfy him with a long life. This Psalm is packed with nuggets of information to which we must pay attention.

One, it is important to know God's name. Here, we see the author use such names as the Most High, the Almighty and God. While we know he is referring to the Creator of the universe, we cannot be so ignorant as to think that everyone recognises Him as the one true God. Nor can we ignore the fact that these are not names, but titles—just as 'Father' is. There is power in a name, and it is important to know the name of your God, the god who has residency within you.

It is also an honour to have a long life. Living long is something to aspire to and not to be dreaded. Modern living has created some kind of anxiety around long life. It is not unusual to hear young people say they do not want or wish to get old. People fear growing old because of the challenges associated with old age such as dementia and general decline in cognitive functions and mobility.

You cannot have a long life and not grow old, but you can grow old gracefully and enjoy a long life. What we are learning here is that it is not God's will for us to die young or to suffer from illnesses or plagues. His will for us is to live long and have a full human experience.

'With long life will I satisfy him and show him my salvation.' Psalm 91:16

A Bible promise is a statement of consequences that naturally follow from certain thought patterns and states of consciousness. Negative thought patterns will tell you it is not good to live long, which is rooted in fear and if you hold that thought in your consciousness, it becomes true for you. You either die young or have complications in old age simply because what you hold as true in your consciousness becomes your reality. It is done to you according to your faith/belief.

The Bible is a book for everyone no matter what their beliefs are, and so are the promises in it. God is not a respecter of persons; when He sends down the rain, it rains for everyone, rich or poor, good or bad, young or old, whether they believe in Him or not. It is up to us to accept or reject what He has freely offered. We have free will. Furthermore, principles are impartial; they apply to everyone without exception much like the laws of nature. This brings to mind a joke my dad used to tell us about stubbornness when we were kids, that if someone was truly stubborn, they would never drown in a river.

Rivers too adhere to their own natural laws and principles; they will never flow upward. If you're in its way as it flows downward, it does not matter who you are, it takes you with it. The river and I had a complicated relationship when I was growing up, I fell in a lot, so I know what it's like to be on the other side of nature—stubborn or not stubborn.

The Psalm ends with a promise of protection, that the Almighty will show us His salvation. This is a promise that all our complexities are dissolved by the truth, the realisation of God within us.

CHAPTER FOUR

The Name of God

I will set him on high, because he has known my name.

When God appeared to Moses in the wilderness, He introduced himself as the God of his father and the God of Abraham, Isaac, and Jacob. Moses knew without a doubt it was God's voice he was hearing. But what would he tell the people when he returned from the mountain? Who was he going to tell them he had been speaking to?

'What am I going to tell them your name is?' he asked. 'I Am Who I Am, tell them "I AM" has sent you.' God replied. When Isaiah prophesied the birth of Jesus, he said he would be called Emmanuel – God with us. [Matt. 1:23, Isa. 7:14] In another scripture, he said, 'For unto us a child is born... His name shall be called Wonderful, Counsellor, The Mighty God, The Everlasting Father, The Prince of Peace.' [Isaiah 9:6] None of these is a name, they are all titles except Emmanuel.

It is believed that Isaiah lived about 700 years before the birth of Jesus. He was not around when Jesus was born but had prophesied about Him on several occasions. When He was conceived, an angel appeared to Mary and gave her the news of the child she was going to carry and what His name was going to be. Joseph, her husband, was also given the same message by an angel in a dream. They were both told His name would be called Jesus. [Matthew 1:21, Luke 1:31]

Jesus in Hebrew is Jeshua, Joshua or Jehoshua, meaning Jehovah is salvation or Yahweh saves. They are all the names of God. He could have given Moses any of these names, but He chose 'I AM'. When we say, 'I am', referring to ourselves, we are talking about ourselves together with God, who is in us – Emmanuel. We are evoking the name of God. Now, you may be wondering: if Isaiah prophesied that His name would be called Emmanuel, why did the angel say He would be called Jesus? Isn't that a contradiction? I wondered that too.

In the first chapter of Matthew, we are told about the angel appearing to Joseph in a dream about the conception and birth of Mary's baby boy. The angel told him that he, 'would save his people from their sins'. Jesus means saviour, the Lord saves.

> *'And she shall bring forth a son, and thou shalt call his name Jesus: for he shall save his people from their sins.'* Matthew 1:21

> *'Now all this was done, that it might be fulfilled which was spoken of the Lord by the prophet, saying, Behold, a virgin shall be with child, and shall bring forth a son, and they shall call his name Emmanuel, which being interpreted is, God with us.'* Matthew 1:22-23

The angel told Joseph that the birth of Jesus was fulfilling Isaiah's prophesy, that a virgin would bear a child whose name would be Emmanuel, meaning God with us. Since His resurrection, He is not only with us, but *in us.* So, Christ in us, is our salvation — 'Christ in us the hope of glory'. [Col.1:27] There is no contradiction.

Paul calls it a '*mystery*' which hath been hid from ages and from generations, but now is made manifest:

> '*To whom God would make known what the riches of the glory of this mystery is among the Gentiles, which is Christ in you, the hope of glory*'
> Colossians 1:27

He says this about Him:

> '*Wherefore God also hath highly exalted him and given him a name which is above every name: That at the name of Jesus every knee should bow, of things in heaven, and things in earth, and things under the earth; And that every tongue should confess that Jesus Christ is Lord, to the glory of God the Father.*'
> Philippians 2:9-11

This takes us back to the introduction, where we discussed being one with God, seeking the kingdom and acknowledging the sovereignty of the king. When we say, 'I AM', we are talking about our inner identity, the person that God created us to be. We must, therefore, see ourselves the way God sees us; complete as we saw in the previous chapter, 'And ye are complete in him, which is the head of all principality and power'.

He sees us as capable of anything because it is He who works in us. We set our desires and intention; He brings them to life because we have our being in him. '*In Him, we live, move and have our being*' Acts 17:28

The Power of I AM
Moses was astounded when God told him what He wanted him to do. It sounded impossible to him. He did not have an army to fight Pharaoh; he was on the run after killing one of Pharaoh's soldiers. How could he go back there? God

wanted him to go back to Egypt and lead the Israelites out of slavery.

He started to run all the cycles of thoughts we run through our minds when overwhelmed by tasks we deem to be beyond us. 'This is too big for me, how am I going to do this?' He belittled himself like we often do. 'Who am I that I should go to Pharaoh and bring the Israelites out of Egypt?' he asked.

'I will be with you,' God reassured him. Though we may not have this kind of a dialogue with God or encounter, this is exactly what happens in our lives daily. An idea comes to mind and what do we do? We talk ourselves out of it; 'I am not strong or smart enough, I do not have the resources, I cannot do it'. 'Can't' is the devil! If you're looking for a devil to blame for your failures, 'can't' is your culprit. Your fears and doubts are your devil. God is always saying, 'I put the idea in your mind, I will be with you. Just follow your desire and obey the still small voice (intuition]. I will do the rest.

Moses, like any of us, was looking at his own being, the ego-self and not the 'I AM' or the inner being. He was thinking about his own strength, which was nothing in front of Pharoah. There was no way he could confront Pharoah in his own strength. He needed a paradigm shift, like we all do. He needed to see himself as God was seeing him. He needed to change his mind and have a different concept of himself. The new paradigm allows the weak to say, 'I AM strong' and the sick to say, 'I AM well'. This is because we are declaring the power of God in us, and not our own.

By ourselves, we can do nothing. [John 15:5] Instead of thinking of our own inability, we become aware of Him working in and through us. Anything that comes after 'I Am' must reflect that awareness, that it is not by our might but by His power that works in us. Attaching the name of God to disempowering words or statements is taking the name of God in vain. See Exodus 20:7; there are repercussions for taking the name of God in vain. There is power in your tongue, and you evoke this power whenever you say I am. Whatever you declare to be, you become.

Our 'I AM' must be cantered on God. *Whatever we attach our 'I AM' to becomes our reality.* If you say I am not capable of this, whatever it is, you will find that you cannot do it, because it is done unto you according to your faith. Moses finally embraced his 'I AM' and led the Israelites out of Egypt with God by his side. He walked with them, physically leading them through the wilderness as a pillar of cloud by day and a pillar of fire by night. He also spoke to them even though most of them were too fearful to hear His voice. He reminded them who He was and what he expected from them:

> *'I am the Lord your God, who has brought you out of the land of Egypt, out of the house of bondage. You shalt have no other gods before me. You shalt not make unto thee any graven image, or any likeness of anything that is in heaven above, or that is in the earth beneath, or that is in the water under the earth.'* Exodus 20:1-4

Knowing God's name and who you are go hand in hand. When you know who you truly are, you know who God is. When you know who God is and who you truly are, you know what you can and cannot do. His word says we can do all things. *God can do for you only what you allow Him to do through you.* Moses wanted to see his people free from bondage in Egypt, but he had to allow God to do the work through him.

Daunting as it was, he knew it was the only way to free his people and himself. He was already on the run after attacking a soldier, trying to protect one of his people from the soldier. He was a prince at the time after being found in the river as a baby and running away to hide in the wilderness meant giving up the privileged life he had become accustomed to since he was a baby. Faced with the task of liberating his people, he had to trust God and not himself. God works through us to do the impossible, but we must allow Him to; otherwise, we will never know we could do those things.

The Israelites' journey was physical, ours is spiritual. God speaks to us through the voice of intuition as opposed to thunder and lightning. We do not have to wait to see a burning bush to hear His voice. Sometimes He speaks to us through dreams and visions, sometimes through other people and many other different ways.

Throughout the journey from Egypt to the promised land, the people made sacrifices to God, and God provided them with food from Heaven; manna fell from Heaven, ensuring they had enough for each day. They sacrificed animals as burnt offerings to him. That was only for that time when everything was physical. There was going to be a new covenant in future, which Jeremiah prophesied. In this new covenant, they would no longer have to make these kinds of sacrifices. God's law would no longer be written on a tablet but in the hearts of people.

This new covenant would be made possible by the coming of Jesus the Messiah, about whom Isaiah and Micah prophesied. He would be the last to shed blood as an atonement for sins. He would be the ultimate sacrifice, and no blood of any animal would be required or accepted after that as a sacrifice for sins. Today, no one needs to make any blood sacrifice or any form of sacrifice to be forgiven or to receive any form of blessing from God. We receive everything by grace, unmerited favour. All we must do is be aware of this grace and receive it freely.

We do not need to 'sow a seed' in form of material things to receive anything from God inasmuch as giving is good and acceptable. We should give because we want to, and not to be blessed, healed or otherwise. You cannot do deals with God or bribe him. He's already given of himself freely to anyone who's open to receive. This is the new covenant that came with the resurrection of Christ, not to do away with the law of Moses but to fulfil it as we saw earlier. *'The letter kills [law], but the spirit [grace] gives life.'* [2 Cor. 3:6] So many of them died because they were disobedient, which was consistent with the law.

Grace is about freedom; *we have freedom when we know the truth.* You must have heard the popular saying, the origin of which is the Bible, 'You shall know the truth and the truth shall make you free'. [John 8:32] It is also popularly said that knowledge is power, but knowledge is not power unless you apply it.

There is a big difference between someone who knows something and applies it in his life and one who knows and does nothing with the knowledge. Knowing something and not acting on it does nothing for you. It does not empower you in any way. The real power that makes a difference is in the action. We must apply what we have learnt to qualify it to be power. We must reclaim our birthright of freedom by learning to appropriate the name of God, the I AM.

I AM means the Limitless One, the Holy One who inhabits eternity, whose name is Perfect. The scripture says,

> *'And this is life eternal, that they might know Thee, the only true God.'* John 17:3

He is everywhere and in everything. His presence within you is always seeking to express itself at higher levels through you. Remember God is spirit, He can only perform physical activities through people like you and me who have physical hands and bodies. He wants to do great things through you; He wants to heal and give hope to others, He wants to visit the vulnerable and the needy and even raise the dead. He raised the dead and said we can do greater things than He did.

Unless we open ourselves to him, unless we fully surrender our will to His, we will never know what we're capable of. We are the channel of the divine. We must listen to the still small voice inside for instructions. As I write this,

I am reminded of the words of Isaiah, 'Whether you turn to the right or to the left, you will hear a voice saying, *'this is the way, walk in it.'* [Isaiah 30:21] There is always that little voice whispering in our conscience, trying to catch our attention and give us instructions.

We ignore it often because we don't recognise it or are unsure whether we should listen to it. We lack discernment. Sometimes we are too busy. We must be attentive and trusting. Just imagine if Moses saw a burning bush and thought, 'Oh, that's weird, it must be witchcraft. This must be the devil. I need to get out of here fast!'

This is a possible reaction in today's world because we attribute a lot of things to the devil or evil powers. We are more aware of the 'other' power than the only power. When you are aware that there is only one power and one presence, you will not be so quick to see the devil in everything. Instead, you will see God, and instead of judging and dismissing everything you don't understand, you will take a minute to ask, *'what am I learning from this?'* You will then listen to the inner voice for answers.

Our answers are always within us because the all-knowing and all-seeing God is within us. I heard someone say that the all-seeing eye is the eye of the devil; the devil is not all-seeing or all-knowing. He used to be an angel before the fall, the reason he is referred to as a fallen angel. Angels are neither omniscient nor omnificent.

Moses stilled his mind, and so should we when faced with situations we don't understand. We should not be too quick to judge. We should instead call upon this infinite wisdom within, the I am, and let it reveal to us the things that we need to know. These situations should remind us to 'be still and see the salvation of the Lord'. When we call out to this infinite wisdom, it reveals to us things that we do not know. [Jer. 33:3] It reveals to us things that we need to know.

Salvation doesn't always mean to be saved from sin but also to be rescued from our current problems, difficulties or challenges. If you are hungry, food saves you. If you are thirsty, water quenches your thirst; if you are dying of thirst, it saves your life. The God in you leads you to a place where you find what you need, be it food, water or other supplies. The intelligence in you tells you to turn right or left, to call this person or that person; it may even tell you what places or routes to take and which ones to avoid.

Always have a deep conviction that all is well or will turn out well despite the outward appearance or reasons why a problem might not be resolved. Remain steadfast in the consciousness of victory and never of defeat. Be single-minded. Think about the desired outcome and not the problem. God is a limitless and infinite being, and man is the individualisation of God-consciousness. We may refer to God as He, not necessarily because He is male.

To say that He is one thing, male, female or otherwise, is to imply a limitation on His part. He created us, unique and individual, to express Him in different and unique ways. Male or female, the physical aspect of our being is irrelevant spiritually because spirit does not have gender, and we are all spiritual beings having a human experience.

No one can be you, and you cannot be anyone else. You may admire someone because of the way they carry themselves and even find yourself wanting to be like them; but they have a part to play and so do you. If you try to be them, or be like them, you're neglecting your part. They are expressing God in their own individualistic and unique way and so should you. You can only do that by being you, being authentic. God did not create copies. He created perfect individuals with unique differences, all serving different purposes that are equally useful in the collective whole.

A body does not have all hands, even though hands might appear to do the most work. Doing the most is not synonymous with being the most important or the best. We are all equally important in the eyes of God, though we express Him differently according to our individuality. We also do not always see things in the same way. One person may use the power of I AM positively, and another may use it negatively, either knowingly or unknowingly. The outcomes will not be the same in these cases, even though God intended for everyone's reality to reflect His goodness and grace. This is where free will comes in. We must respect people's choices inasmuch as we want them to have positive experiences.

We are often tempted to see other people as 'others' – because they don't look like us, they don't believe like us, think like us, or act like us; for these reasons, we want nothing to do with them. We think we are right, and they are wrong. This, most of the time, is our ego talking or thinking. Our ego tells us we are better than others or higher in our perceived hierarchy when, in fact, there are no others and there are no hierarchies in the kingdom of God.

We are all trying to find our way back to Source, and one way or another, we get there. And when we do, we realise we are one. We have always been and always will be. The word tells us that, 'Every knee shall bow' – everyone will come to that place of realisation at some point. It does not matter how long it takes, what matters is that it happens. As Paul said:

> *'If anyone is confident that he belongs to Christ, let him also consider that just as he is Christ's, even so are we Christ's'* 2 Corinthians 10:7

We may not all have come to that place yet, but somehow, we are all searching. We may not all know what we are searching for, but when we find it, we know.

> *'People have for years looked for God everywhere, when all this time He is the word in their mouths a thousand times a day—it is called the I AM.'*
> Dr Joseph Murphy

In one of his books, Dr Murphy describes I AM as 'pure being', the reality of you and the living spirit within you.

'It was never born, it will never die, water drowns it not, fire burns it not, wind blows it not away ...' We have confidence in Him because this is true of Him. Murphy goes on to say, 'He is the ageless one, the eternal God working in and through us.'

The next time you say I am this or that, remember who you are talking about. Know that the person whose name you're evoking is not weak, never sick, poor, frustrated, desperate or powerless. Honour Him with the words of your mouth. It pleases Him. The book of Revelations says we overcome by the blood of the Lamb and the word of our testimony. The two go hand in hand, your faith and your confession. Your belief, confession and actions must align. That is what constitutes faith.

CHAPTER FIVE

Christ Consciousness

Herein is love made perfect, ...as he is, so are we in this world.

Christ consciousness and God consciousness are one and the same thing as the two are one. Christ is God the father manifested in human form, to walk among us, die for our freedom and live within us as a guide, counsellor and comforter. When He walked among the people before crucifixion, a man called Philip asked Him to show them His father. He did not expect the response he got. Jesus, amazed that even after being with him for so long he did not truly know who He was asked him, 'Don't you know me, Philip, even after I have been among you such a long time?'

'Anyone who has seen me has seen the father.' He answered before asking yet another question, 'Don't you believe that I am in the Father, and that the Father is in me?' We now know this for a fact, thanks to Philip. Jesus went farther to explain this, knowing it was not an easy concept to grasp even to this day. He ensured that there was no more doubt or confusion about it. 'The words I say to you I do not speak on my own authority. Rather, *it is the father, living in me, who is doing his work.* Believe me when I say that I am in the father and the father is in me.' [John 14:8-11]

It is evident that Jesus was conscious of the Father working in Him and that the things He did, including the miracles, such as turning water into wine or raising the dead were done by the Father through Him. He was conscious of the power of God moving in and through Him as we are today. Further down the chapter, He told Philip that whoever believed in Him would also do the works he did, even greater.

Being God/Christ conscious is simply being conscious of the working of God in our lives just as Jesus was conscious of the Father working in Him. It is the awareness of the presence and power of God in us. Christ consciousness, therefore, is the conviction that Christ lives and works in us and through us, and that in this world, we're just like Him. If we were bold like Him, we could also say, 'Anyone who has seen me has seen God' because 'as He is, so are we in this world'. [1 Cor. 2:16]

Every moment of our lives, we're evolving to be more like God because that is who we are on the inside, and at some point, our outside must reflect what is on the inside. In this consciousness, we can also claim to have a consciousness of grace because grace is the person of Jesus, the manifestation of Christ. *'For the grace of God has appeared that offers salvation to all people.'* Titus 2:11

In this consciousness, we realise that our life is fully supported and provided for by the grace of God. That, by ourselves, we cannot sustain our lives. Only by grace and the unconditional love of God do we live and are who we are. It's in Him we live, move and have our being. [Acts 17:28] This is now beginning to sink in, it's not repeated by accident. This realisation helps us retire within ourselves with a sense of inner peace, knowing that we do not have to carry all the burdens of life by ourselves. We realise there is a greater power than ourselves, working behind the scenes to support our effort.

We subsequently stop striving to be, to acquire more and more of this or that, we even stop resisting evil and rest in that grace. [Matt. 5:39] We put down the sword and rest in the stillness; we find strength in quietness and in trust. [Isa.30:15] Grace is not a power; it is a presence, and in this presence, there is no need for power, only joy and gratitude. 'In thy presence is fulness of joy.' [Psalm 16:11] There cannot be fullness of joy where there is pain, disease, lack, etc. These things are dissolved in the same way that darkness dissolves in the light.

In Christ/grace consciousness, we fully understand what it means to 'take no thought or not to be anxious about anything' because we are at rest. Grace functions as wisdom, inspiration, harmony, peace, health, wholeness, and completeness, as well as the source of all knowledge flowing through you, in you, and as you.

We live not by might nor by power but by the spirit of God. This spirit is our guide, our provision and defender. It's not even by good work or conduct/behaviour, but by his grace alone. [Titus 3:5-7] It is also by grace that we are justified, and through grace, we claim to be righteous. Through grace, we transcend the need to be right, to judge, to lead or be led, to be praised or applauded, we just rest in being who we are. The need to prove ourselves or convince others fades. We let the divine Consciousness flow through us, animate our being, and live through us. Here, not even sin has power over you.

> '*Sin shall have no dominion over you, for you are not under the law, but under grace.*' Romans 6:14

This grace transcends all laws, including the law of karma or cause and effect. What does the scripture say about law and grace? We saw earlier that the law kills, but grace gives life. The law was given through Moses as a schoolmaster to guide the people. [Gal. 3:24] Those who failed to observe it made sacrifices through offerings of bulls and other animals, depending on the magnitude of the sin committed. The blood of those animals was the sacrifice that made the atonement for their sins. If you had no animals to sacrifice, there was no salvation for you; you had to die; it was the law, but since grace came, we no longer need a schoolmaster.

Jesus did it all before declaring, 'It is finished!' In Christ-consciousness, you no longer need to be conscious of the law because Christ is the 'end of the law for righteousness to everyone who believes'. [Romans 10:4] You also do not need to be conscious of sin. Remember you cannot serve two masters. You cannot be conscious of grace and at the same time be conscious of sin. Sin has no power in the presence of grace. That does not mean you no longer sin, it means sin has no claim over you, the debt has already been paid.

Because God's law under the New Covenant is written in the heart, you find yourself doing what you ought to do without much effort or struggle. Being 'good' becomes your natural state. But even good people sin, we all fall short, so what does good mean in the face of grace? Jesus asked the people, 'Why do you call me good?' He did not see himself as doing anything special; He was just being himself. Besides, 'No one is good but God', He said. [Mark 10:18] We all bask in the glory of Him who is good. None of us, without God can claim to be good.

Likewise, when you're resting in the consciousness of grace, the power of God works in you, 'both to will and to do of his good pleasure'. [Phil.2:13] It's not about your effort or willpower. You find that the harder you try to break a habit through willpower, the worse it gets. We see too many people being 'tricked' to 'sow a seed' in order to have breakthroughs in life, mostly financial or health related, to beat a bad habit or be blessed. This seed is usually in the form of money or gifts; if you are giving money or gifts to get God's blessings, be it forgiveness, healing or material, how different are you from the people who sacrificed animals under the law? You cannot mix grace and law.

Move away from the law and into the grace that requires nothing but faith. Let faith be your seed. It is through faith that you access these things that are already available to you. If you want to sow a seed or give whatever gift you choose, do it out of love, not to receive a blessing or anything; you're not trading with God. When you are under grace, you are just being yourself, but you are in your higher mind, one with the mind of God. [1 Cor. 2:16] In this mind or consciousness, you find it is not a struggle to let go of grudges or resentment, to forgive or love even your enemies. The law kind of fulfils itself in your life, reinforcing the fact that grace fulfils the law.

In grace or Christ consciousness, your life expresses the attributes of God without much effort. You become the embodiment of love without trying or forcing yourself to love. Love is the emotion of goodwill—wishing for all men what you want for yourself. You wish even those who hurt or dislike you peace, joy, harmony and all the blessings of life without feeling like it's taking anything away from you. To you, it is giving, and the more you give the more you receive. If, however you give grudgingly, it does not count and therefore does not come back.

The healing power of God does not flow through consciousness that is anything less; if there is hatred, resentment or unforgiveness, His light must drive it out for it to flow through you. You must allow this to happen. The creation is not greater than the Creator; as much as you are one with God, He is still the Creator, and you are the creation.

You must pledge allegiance, devotion and loyalty to the I AM within you, the only presence and power—the only true God. He does not withhold anything from us. [Psalm 84:11] Everything we could ever want is already established in the consciousness of the individual. God's grace is our sufficiency in all things.

You are gods

When I read the scripture mentioned at the beginning of the book, 'You are gods', I could not think of anything else for days. It stayed on my mind, weeks and months. Then I decided to do something about it. Going back to the moment I read it, it was like an epiphany, like a light bulb moment. I was both excited and confused.

I felt like I had had a revelation, but what if I was wrong? What if I got it all wrong? In the days that followed, it was all I thought about. At the time it happened, when letters and texts appeared to jump out of the screen as I read them, I was sitting next to my daughter, both of us busy on our laptops. I turned to her and said, 'Guess what, we are gods.'

The look she gave me made me realise it was a bad idea to blurt it out like that. 'Mum' she paused, looking at me like something was wrong with me, 'are you okay?' she asked, still looking at me like I had lost my marbles., 'That's blasphemy, Mum.' She remarked.

I called my son who was also working, but in his room wanting to hear his opinion. 'You can't say that out loud.' He said. 'It doesn't sound right.' He added. I wondered if anyone else had at least read those words and what they made of them. The beauty of the days we are in is that any information you can think of is available online. You just need discernment to know what to take and what to disregard. I immediately embarked on a research, this time specifically on this topic. My search words were, 'You're gods'.

My research led me down some rabbit holes; I was all for it! One thing led me to another. I started to notice synchronicities that led me to what I needed without much effort. Before I come to that, let me take a little detour and show you how far I was willing to go to unravel the mystery. I am a curious person, and while my curiosity has not always landed me on a soft cushion, it hasn't landed me on a hard enough surface to stop me from exploring possibilities. During my research, I stumbled on a piece of information claiming that a plant called 'teacher' has answers to any question.

I thought it was funny and obnoxious at the same time. I did not give it a second thought. Then I found myself wondering how that was possible. How would you ask a plant a question in the first place? I decided to find out.

As the name suggests, this is a plant that teaches you what you 'need' to know. It answers your questions, but more importantly it teaches you things that you need know. It knows the difference between want and need. When you know what you need to know, you get the answers to what you want to know. There's a difference. I learnt that through interacting with it.

I wanted to learn more about this plant, also called the vine of the soul before committing to having a dialogue with it. I needed clarity and if a plant could talk, I was more than willing to listen. So, I started to gather as much information as I possibly could on it. I learned that it grows in the Amazon rainforest, and it takes four years to grow. Contrary to my assumption, you do not stand in front of it and ask questions, you drink from it like you drink orange juice form an orange. The 'juice' is brewed from the inner bark of the vine.

Do I have to go to the Amazon rainforest to have an audience with this teacher? I wondered. My research did not disappoint, I did not have to travel to the Amazon rainforest. Long story short, I was soon booking a flight, and everything was set for this experience of a lifetime, not in the Amazon rainforest but closer to home. I was excited and looking forward to it.

It was a month away. As days passed, the excitement slowly began to shift, leaning more towards anxiety and fear, what am I getting myself into? I questioned my sanity. '*What if this, what if that?*' You know the drill. A few days before my flight, I considered cancelling it all together. Then I had a strange dream. In the dream, I saw myself travelling to this place. The flight had landed, and I was pulling my suitcase on a dirt road. I could see where the event was taking place, and there was someone a few meters ahead of me and one behind me. We all had little suitcases, so I knew we were on the same mission.

We got to our rooms and started to unpack; then someone informed us that we were late and offered to take us to the conference hall where the rest of the people were. We could unpack later, he said. In the hall, I was met by an old friend, my best friend in primary school. I haven't seen this girl in years in real life. She looked exactly as she did back then. She told me that the first lecture had just ended, but not to worry as, 'Walter Russel' had left some notes for me. Before I could even ask who that was, She lifted her dress slightly to show me the notes written in the hem of her dress. I was baffled.

'He wrote this?' I asked. 'There he is.' She said, pointing at an older man in a twilight blue, vintage-looking suit. He stood out because everyone else was casually dressed. He also looked much older than everyone else. I could not understand how or why would write my notes in my friend's dress. It gave me an image of a young, spontaneous and humorous person, but looking at him I saw a serious and mature person – such a contradiction. Everything was mind boggling, even the way she talked about him, as if I knew who he was. I had never seen him or heard that name before, and I did not understand why he would leave notes for me.

When I woke up from the dream, I grabbed my phone and looked up the name before I forgot it. To my surprise, he was a real person who was now departed. He looked exactly as I saw him in the dream, even the suit he wore in one of his pictures looked exactly as I had seen it in the dream. He was born a whole century before me, which explained the vintage-looking suit. It was all so bizarre, but it gave me an opportunity to get to know him and try to figure out why he had been introduced to me in a dream especially because he was departed.

I learned that he had written many books before his passing; I immediately ordered two of them, titled, *The Universal One* and *The Secret of Light*. In another book that appeared in my search, but written by a different author, he was described as 'The man who tapped the secrets of the universe'. That was a lot to take in. It however gave me the confidence I needed to go ahead with the trip.

Fast forward to the event, I am sitting on a mat in a group of twenty people, most of us from different parts of the world. We have little glasses in our hands containing the juice made from the Teacher Plant. The host started off by giving us the History of the drink, why it's called teacher and what we can expect from it. He respectfully informed us that we did not have to drink it, it was okay to change our minds if we weren't sure. I felt like he was seeing right through my mind. I made my decision right there that nothing was going to stop me.

I had not learned to quiet my mind at the time, so thoughts came flooding in, telling me I might not get out alive. I started feeling a little stupid for being there and also for having those thoughts. Did I really think a tree could teach me something I didn't already know or explain things that I needed answers to? 'Maybe if I Walter Russel's books I'd find the answers I was looking for,' I thought.

Though I had ordered the books, they had not arrived by the time I travelled to the event as the dream was only a couple of days to the event. Thoughts kept coming in and out of my mind. I sat there trying to quiet my mind, telling myself to be still and be open to the full experience since I was already there. There was no turning back.

I took the drink in one gulp and sat quietly, waiting, constantly reminding myself why I was there. The background music was so calming and beautiful. It was about the sovereignty of God and how nature is an expression of His love and wisdom. An hour passed, then another. We had been made aware what to expect and how the drink would make us feel. It was already about three hours, and I wasn't feeling anything. Should I ask for more, I thought. I was expecting answers to questions that were on my mind, quietly praying that the questions were answered but forgetting to ask them.

The room was quiet, except for the background music and suddenly, I started to hear noises. People were already having their moment with this teacher. Why wasn't anything happening to me. Though I couldn't hear what the people talking were saying, it crossed my mind that I could speak to the invisible teacher and see what happened. I was subconsciously expecting 'the teacher' to appear so I could ask the question, but as it was not happening, I had to do something, *'C'mon teacher, give me something, show me heaven.'* I quietly said.

I didn't even get to ask the question I had in mind. Immediately, I saw the sun emerge from my right-hand side moving across to the centre. It was getting brighter and brighter as it moved. It stopped directly in front of me, now facing me directly and shining even brighter. I thought it couldn't get any brighter, but it kept shining brighter and brighter. I was, however, still able to look directly at what looked like a human face.

I was in awe. I wondered if it was the face of God. Even before I verbalised the thought, the sun started to smile, the smile kept getting wider and brighter, and the light even brighter. What puzzled me was how it kept getting brighter and yet I could see the face so clearly without burning my eyes. I smiled back at it and it smiled even more. At this point, I was burst out laughing. The orange-yellow rays of light became lighter, softer and warmer, until they were almost white. There seemed to be more colours blending harmoniously to create this beautiful sight I cannot quite describe.

The smile appeared to confirm my unspoken question. Then came a feeling of warmth and love emanating from the sun, reaching me as rays of pure white light. Without an ounce of doubt, I was aware I was looking at the face of God.

I felt it. I knew it. I don't know how long I might have been there, basking in that beauty and love that kept getting stronger and brighter as if there was no end to how strong and bright it could get. During this time, my mind was downloading information about God's unconditional love without any spoken words.

I perceived this information, which was being communicated telepathically. It's hard to explain the communication that was going on between me and what I perceived to be God. I am not saying that the sun is God, but He appeared to me in the form of the sun. I had seen that kind of light before in a dream where I had seen God/Jesus, but unlike this experience, I could not see His face due to the brightness of the light. In the dream He stood right next to me and gave me a little golden sword. Once the sword was in my hand, I saw myself in a beautiful garden full of colourful flowers. It was as if the sword had teleported me to this serene garden where colours looked more vibrant than in real life. That was over two decades back.

Here in this experience, I was not dreaming. My attention was then diverted from the centre where the sun was to my left-hand side. I saw trees and mountains emerge from that corner just as the sun had emerged from the right. They were dancing as they moved to the centre. It was even funnier seeing them dance than it was to see the sun smile. I laughed out loud, completely oblivious of my physical environment.

'What are you trying to tell me?' I wondered. Immediately, I telepathically got the message that He, God, was animating them as He animates everything He created. For the first time since the experience began, I heard the background music I had been listening to before it started. I also, for a split second, became aware of the other people around me. I was aware of the noise in the room. Some people were screaming and others crying.

I did not know if they were crying for joy or screaming in excitement, but I felt a little guilty for laughing. My attention quickly returned to the music as the trees and mountains continued dancing and moving closer to the sun. The song that was playing seemed to explain the view in front of me. I noticed that they were dancing to the rhythm of the music, which made me wonder if we were all seeing the same thing.

I could hear the words so clearly, as though someone was singing in my ear, 'You are the mountain, you are the river, you are the sky, you are the sea. You are the bright LIGHT in me. To see you in ALL is to see you in me, because I'm in you and you're in me'. The song went on to say, 'Petals of the lotus are many, but the flower is just one. Philosophies and religions are many, but the truth is just one.'

The words 'You're in me, and I am in you' continued to sound in my ears as my attention slowly drifted away from the music. As the music faded, the sound in my ears remained. It was as if someone was singing in my ear. The mountains and trees were still dancing. I wondered if it was God singing. It was the weirdest thing ever, the best experience I can remember. He communicated to me, without words, that He is in everything, He animates everything, and both humans, the nature and all created things are intertwined in unconditional love. The experience did not end there; the next day, the emphasis was on the light.

Very early in the morning, as soon as I had woken up, I noticed it was unusually dark and very quiet. It was pitch black I could barely see anything even the soft rays of light normally seen in the morning, piercing through the window. I didn't know what time it was, and no one seemed to be up yet. I was trying to reach for my phone so I could check the time without disturbing other people in the room. Then a message came to me saying, *When the light wants to come in, it cannot be stopped.*

In all these communications, apart from the background music and the words from the song whispered in my ears the night before, I did not hear an audible voice. I was hearing, but not with my ears. I perceived them. It was funny because when I had a dream about the event before it happened, the person who had left notes for me wrote a book about the Light, as I mentioned earlier. The book titled *The Secret of Light* was originally published in 1947. I could not wait to go home and read it.

I always knew that God is light. I also knew He spoke to people in mysterious ways, but nothing could have prepared me for that experience. Later that morning, we sat together to talk about our experiences the previous night. One of the hosts explained to me that my experience was talking about the light in me, which is God. He explained that we all have that light in us, but most of us do not allow it to shine due to ignorance or being unaware of it. In his words, 'It's like a candle put under a pot, except it does not completely go out. It leaves a spark, which when fanned lights up again.'

He explained to us that the work of the teacher is to reveal that light, and what we do with it is up to us. It was then that I was able to put all the pieces of my experience together, including God appearing to me as the sun. The sun produces the most or the brightest light—enough to light up the whole world. My whole experience was about the *Light*. I got one of the answers I was looking for, the confirmation that, we are gods because God lives within us.

We are gods when we know that we are, and when we allow Him to shine through. Before that, we are just like a candle put under a pot, meaning we are not expressing Him; in other words, we are not what we're meant to be. He is the light, and that light is in all of us. Our one job is to express it/Him, just like a candle's job is to produce light and illuminate its surroundings. Through this experience, I learnt a lot of things, some not directly related to the questions I had but also very important. Things that I needed to know.

I learned about fear, doubt, about good and bad, right and wrong, judgment, preconceived beliefs, self-preservation, the ego, all of which can hinder us from expressing this light and living the life we were created to live. In other words, they hinder us from realising our desires and dreams. I desired to have this experience, but thoughts of whether it was right or safe, and many other things that seemed to crowd my mind caused fear, which almost stopped me from going through with it.

Some of the things that hold us back are tendencies to 'self-preserve'. They kick off subconsciously, just like our legs start running when we sense danger. Sometimes there is no danger. This we cannot see unless we allow the light in us to illuminate our perception and judgement, allowing us to see through the shadows. The Bible tells us there is nothing bad, it's the mind that makes it so.

> *'To the pure all things are pure: but unto them that are defiled, and unbelieving is nothing pure, but even their mind and conscience is defiled.'* Titus 1:15

When you have a pure conscience, nothing is bad. When you see things and people the way God sees them in your consciousness, everything will be good because it's the mind that makes things good or bad. Once we consciously change the way we think about them, they change. It all depends on our state of consciousness, our state of mind. In Christ-consciousness, everything is pure. There is no need to fear. There is also freedom.

When we are guided from within, we cannot go wrong. The spirit of God is our guide when we are one with Him. He is the light in us, which lies dormant until we're aware of it and allow it to express itself through us. Inasmuch as we are all gods, His power does not work in us by default. We must give it permission to. If we want that power that helps us transcend the limitations of this physical life, we must be open to it and be conscious and intentional about it.

In his book, *The Secret of Light*, Walter Russell states that consciousness in man is his mortality. It never sleeps, and it never changes. *'It is the light which man is unknowingly seeking but assumes that the sensation of his brain is his thinking.'* He describes consciousness as man's storehouse of all knowledge, all power, and all presence. 'Consciousness is man's true self, his eternal self through which his omniscience, omnipresence, and omnipotence are expressed as he slowly becomes aware of their presence within him.'

His claims, both as a spiritual teacher and a scientist, are consistent with the fact that we are created in the likeness of God, every one of us. We are all looking for something, and that something is the *light within us*, the light that joins us together as one. We are all one regardless of religion, faith, background, race, colour, political differences and all. Just like the petals of a flower; the lotus or the lily that Jesus spoke about are many and the flower is one, we may have our different beliefs, faiths and traditions, but the truth is one – God is one.

There are no two Gods, two powers or other Gods. There may be other gods (small g), but God, the creator is only one. Similarly, there are no others; we are all one. The word says,

'And this is life eternal, that they might know thee, the only true God.' John 17:3

Your background would not make a difference, whether pagan, Christian, Muslim, Buddhist, name it. God knows it all. It would not matter what teachings you followed if the motive behind it was to seek the realisation of the truth. Ultimately, you would arrive at it. Different people have been led to that destination from many different directions, just like so many of us were led to the event from different countries, it did not matter where we were coming from or what route or mode of transport we took as long as we arrived at the designated destination.

The greatest miracle that has taken place in me since the experience is that I stopped judging people or myself. Self-judgement is as destructive as the judgement of others. Instead, I started seeing God in everyone as I see Him in me.

That does not mean I do no wrong or they do no wrong. It means I have more compassion for myself and for others. The designated destination for us all is back to Source, back to our creator. We must all return where we came from.

Everyone is doing their best; it does not help to beat yourself up or others. At some point, even those who have not yet discovered the light in them will come to discover it. In another one of his books, *The Divine Iliad*, Russell says,

> *'I am the Light; I alone AM. What I am, thou art. Thou art the Light. Thou art one with me. Man may know me by desiring to know me. To know Me is to be Me.*
> *Through My Light alone can Man know Me. Man is Light when he knows that He is Light. Man is Me when he knows that he is Me. All men will come to Me in due time, but theirs is the agony of waiting.'*

He is not referring to himself in this poetic writing but to the great I AM, the Light, the Truth and the Way. He echoes the scriptures in the twelfth chapter of John: *'And if I be lifted up, I will draw all men unto Me.'* When we discover the light in us and acknowledge it by allowing it to shine through, we lift Him up allowing Him to draw others to Himself. We do not have to convince anyone, we just need to let the light shine.

CHAPTER SIX

The Ego

I have now seen the one who sees me.

Who doesn't like to be seen? I can't think of anyone I know. People hate to be ignored. In the story of Ishmael, the first son of Abraham, a drama unfolds, much like something you would see in today's courts or reality TV shows like the famous Jerry Springer show.

We see a good and well-meaning couple; let's forget for a minute that this is 'the father of many nations', Father Abraham. He and his wife Sarah realise they are getting too old and have no child. Sarah advises her husband to have a child with their servant Hagar, to which he agrees. The moment Hagar becomes pregnant, she starts to despise and disrespect Sarah.

Sarah complains to her husband, who allows her to do as she wishes with Hagar. She begins to mistreat her, and as a result Hagar runs away from home. She's found by an angel near a spring in the desert. The angel advises her to go back to her mistress and submit to her. Fast forward, the baby is born and years later, Sarah has a child of her own, Isaac. Ishmael, Hagar's son, is a young teenager by this time.

There is a big feast to mark the birth of the new baby, Ishmael's half-brother Isaac. Sarah sees Ishmael mocking her, and she is enraged. She asks her husband to send him and his mother away, this time for good. Abraham knows it's not the right thing to do, but he does it to please his wife.

This is only a background story of someone whose life is captivating, yet not much is said about him. His name came to me in a dream, but I couldn't remember anything about the dream when I woke up. All I could remember was the name Ishmael. I looked it up and was led to the story of Hagar. My search (on the internet) did not find any other Ismael. I thought there must be something in his story that I needed to know. The only reference given was the scripture, the book of Genesis.

As I read his story, it was his mother's words that captured my imagination. Alone in the desert, having run away from the place she called home while pregnant, she must have been scared for both her life and that of her unborn child. In that moment of uncertainty, an angel appeared to her, and she automatically knew who he was. 'You are the God who sees me,' she said to the angel. 'I have now seen the one who sees me.' She added.

She must have felt alone and unseen to say that. I don't know how long she had been in the desert before the angel appeared, but she must have had a lot of thoughts in her mind. She must have been running the scenes of events that led up to her present situation like a movie. It reminded me of something I talked about earlier in the book, identity. It is usually when we are faced with challenging situations that we begin to have honest conversations with ourselves. It is when masks begin to fall off and we see things clearly.

In Hagar's situation, she probably started off feeling victimised and being angry at Sarah for being so 'inconsiderate', she must then have felt sorry for herself and even angry for feeling vulnerable. These are the cycles we go through in our daily living. They help us examine ourselves retrospectively. When you feel most overwhelmed, isolated and unsure, that is when angels show up. There are angels watching over us all the time. We may not see them or feel like they intervene when we need them to, but they do when there is need for intervention.

Sometimes we use the word desert or wilderness metaphorically to mean unpleasant or difficult situations. Most of the times, it is our ego that lands us in those situations like Hagar. Her ego must have convinced her that she was better off in the desert. She might have thought about what people might say seeing her so vulnerable, the assumptions and judgement from the neighbours or even family members. How could she face them? Our ego can protect us in some situations and destroy our lives in others. It has its place and purpose.

There might have been safer places to run to than the desert, but Hagar's ego would not let her. It blinded her as it so often blinds us. Being in the dessert can also mean withdrawing from normal activities and taking a break when things get overwhelming. We do this at certain points in our lives. We find ourselves in the desert, shut off from the people who care about us, sometimes even turning our backs on God. God however never turns His back on us. He sent an angel to let Hagar know she was still 'seen', meaning He still cared about her despite her attitude towards Sarah and the pain she had caused herself and her son Ishmael as a result.

We are told that God knew us before we were formed in our mother's womb, meaning we existed long before we were conceived. We did not have a care in the world the whole nine months we were in the womb. We did not have an ego either. Our mothers could do nothing much for us except ensure they ate well, rested and had regular checks. Who took care of us? Who made sure our bodies absorbed the nutrients they needed to develop? Who takes care of babies in the womb?

Babies come into the world pure and without an ego. All they know is the spirit that cared for them in the womb. Ishmael was in this position, a place of rest where everything flowed as it ought to without his input. While his mother stayed awake at night worried about their safety and their future, Ishmael had no care whatsoever. He did not care that they had no safe place to sleep at night or food to eat let alone other conveniences. He had no ego.

The ego starts to develop when we become aware of ourselves. By this time, we have learned and picked up a lot from our caregivers, society, and our surroundings. Children are like sponges; they soak up everything they see and hear. They learn by simply observing. With time they begin to learn who they are, identifying with things around them. As they grow older, who they were before birth, and as babies take a back seat until something happens much later in life that, like Hagar, makes them feel unseen.

Most of us can relate to this. When we are comfortable, we become ignorant of many important things. We tend to be complacent. It is only when our lives are disrupted that we start to have deep thoughts and serious conversations with ourselves. In these moments, we feel like we are in some kind of desert. These are the moments we are most likely to hear the still, small voice from within.

In Hagar's case, an angel found her in her desert and offered a solution that would help her return to safety, harmony and peace. He was her still small voice of reason. He instructed her to submit to Sarah, her mistress. She had to silence her ego or at least tame it. For as long as she harboured the feelings of self-importance which led her to disrespect and despise Sarah in the first place, she was going to find herself back in the desert. She needed to swallow her pride to return to harmony.

When the angel found her, he said, "Hagar, slave of Sarai, where have you come from, and where are you going?" She said she was running away from her mistress. Notice that the angel calls her 'slave of Sarai'. Hagar had long ceased to see herself as a slave, otherwise she would not have had confidence to disrespect her mistress. She was carrying the master's child. In her eyes, her status had been elevated from 'the slave of Sarai' to Sarai's co-wife. Her ego was too big for harmony.

The thing with ego is that we do not see it in ourselves. We see it in others but not ourselves. Hagar did not see anything wrong with her attitude towards Sarah. She most likely, genuinely thought it was Sarah who had a problem. 'Go back to your mistress and submit to her,' the angel responded, adding that he would increase her descendants so much that they would be too numerous to count.

That was her promise from God; she did not have to worry about her son Ishmael as God would bless him regardless of what happened in the future. Ishmael was already taken care of, his future was in God's hands and so was hers. The ego can be a blessing or a curse. While we may not annihilate it, we can tame it just like our minds. The ego is the identity we pick up as we grow older. It is the part of our human existence that has forgotten who we are and who carried us throughout our life before showing up in the world.

The ego identifies with people and things. It identifies with the physical world; things that are physically visible and has a hard time seeing what is not physically seen or perceived. Hagar was identifying with the wrong thing. She was identifying with her new status as the mother of Abraham's child. We are not innocent. We identify with our professions, marital or social status, material possessions, the fortune we have accumulated, and even things we have inherited from our families. We think that this is who we are.

When these things are no longer available, we have a breakdown; we do not know who we are any more since we have been stripped of our identity. We do not even know what to do with ourselves, it is as if life for us has stopped. But life goes on, with or without these things. The angel appearing to Hagar indicated that she was still 'seen', a reminder that she wasn't who she was because of what she was carrying. With or without the baby, she still belonged.

Like all of us, she had a soul that belonged to God, the Creator and Author of life and everything that pertains to it.

That is our real identity. It is not affected by what we have or what we lose. It is constant and eternal. God still cared about Hagar and the baby she was carrying. She was still valuable to her maker, and He promised to care for her. Being a slave did not make her any less valuable to God. On the outside, these are labels. God is not so much concerned with the outside even though it matters because it enables us to experience the world. The inner person is the one that remains when the physical experience ends. This is what God sees when he looks at us.

It is what the angel saw in Hagar. It did not matter that she was a slave or from a different region or even tribe. I believe she returned to Sarah with a different mindset. It is important to know that if all the things we hold so dearly were taken away from us, we would still be whole and no lesser beings because our true identity never changes, even with the changing outer conditions, social status and even economy. It is our ego or the outer identity that tells us 'we are finished'. That's a term I have heard people use when things go terribly wrong, like losing a job or when a business goes bust.

Ishmael means God listens. Everything that happened in the Bible so many years ago was meant for generations to learn from, and that is why the Bible never goes out of date. Just as we interpret Jesus' parables as metaphors and allegories meant to counsel, instruct and guide us, we should interpret everything in the same manner, otherwise, they would not mean anything to us. They will just be stories of people who lived in a different era, irrelevant to our modern life.

When the angel appeared to Hagar, he told her that God had heard her cry, and he would bless both her and her son. He would give her many descendants, and her son would become a strong man. 'He will be a wild donkey of a man,' the angel said. He also said that he would be against everyone, and everyone would be against him. [Gen. 16:12]

Though Hagar went back to Sarah's house and Ishmael was born in a safe environment, it did not last very long. From the tender age of thirteen, he was back in the desert where he grew up. This time, it was not Hagar's fault but his own. He mocked Sarah on the day she was celebrating Isaac's birthday, both were sent away for good.

God protected and provided for them as He had promised. Isaac, on the other hand grew up in the safety of their home, surrounded by love, warmth and security, a stark contrast to Ishmael who lacked most of these comforts in the desert. One day, having no food or water, Hagar left him under a shade and walked away, not wanting to see him die of thirst. She had forgotten that God had promised to provide for them. This was many years after the first encounter with the angel who promised to take care of them.

Hagar had forgotten about the promise because of all the challenges she encountered in the desert. The springs had run dry, and they had no water to drink. This is exactly what happens to us, once we are faced with lack or difficulties of different kinds, we forget the promise God gave us to never leave us nor forsake us. [Hebrews 13:5]

The angel appeared to her again in that moment of desperation and showed her where to get water from. It was not too late as Ishmael was still breathing. Though Haggar may have forgotten the promise, God had not.

The contrast between Ishmael and Isaac's lives is that Ishmael grew up to be a strong man, (warrior) with no knowledge of security or boundaries, while Isaac was disciplined but not as strong physically. Unlike Ishmael, He did not need survival skills that his half-brother needed to survive in the desert. Ishmael had to learn to hunt, something his father never had the opportunity to teach him, I imagine. We are told that Ishmael became an archer. [Gen. 21:20]

In their later lives as adults, Ishmael became a warrior/fighter, while Isaac was restricted and disciplined. The two brothers represent two different archetypes, not necessarily superior to each other but conflicting. They ended up in different regions (nations), and there were conflicts between them. The angel had told Hagar before Ishmael was born that her son would be against everyone, and everyone would be against him.

We see these conflicts today between nations, religions, and even families. They emanate from the ego. The ego is the cause of most of the things we attribute to the devil. We make the devil seem so powerful, almost as powerful as God, which is an insult to God. Ego causes competition, disagreements, jealousy, envy, hatred and many other negative outcomes, that many times lead to fights and wars, and all sorts of evil, including murder, neglect and lack of compassion.

Egocentric versus God-centric life

Abraham granted Sarah's wish to send Ishmael and Hagar away because God advised him to, for his own peace of mind, 'Do not be so distressed about the boy and your slave woman. Listen to whatever Sarah tells you, because it is through Isaac that your offspring will be reckoned. I will make the son of the slave into a nation also, because he is your offspring' Genesis 21:12.

It distressed Abraham to send his son away, but he obeyed. He loved the two boys. To him, they were both his sons. In dealing with the conflict between them much later in their lives, He tried to bring God back into the equation.

Isaac grew up knowing God, but Ishmael had married an Egyptian wife and lived a different kind of life from the one Isaac was raised in. Egypt was not a God-fearing Nation, it was where the Israelites would later be held captives and rescued by Moses. While Abraham and his household worshipped one God, the Creator of Heaven and Earth, Egyptians worshipped many gods. Abraham's life was God-centred, he put God before everything else in his life. His willingness to sacrifice Isaac is just one of the many instances where we see his dedication and faithfulness to God.

He introduced the idea that life is not meant to be 'egocentric' but 'God-centric', meaning we are not here just to serve ourselves but to serve God and others. We are here to serve a higher cause and to experience a higher state of consciousness that enables us to connect to a higher reality. The pagan world focused more on control and power, materialism and success, but Abraham knew another way of life. He lived that life.

The world is still the same today; the secular world focuses on these things to this day. There is nothing wrong with acquiring wealth; prosperity is a big part of God's plan for man. He says so in Jeremiah 29:11, 'For I know the plans I have for you, plans to prosper you and not to harm you, plans to give you a future and a hope.'

John, the apostle writing to a man named Gaius, said:

> *'Beloved, I wish above all things that you may prosper and be in health, even as your soul prospers.'* 3 John 2

He wished him prosperity in all areas of his life and not just the spiritual. There really is no debate about prosperity and material wealth, physical health and spiritual health. It is all in God's plan and will. It is our inheritance. The problem comes when we put material wealth before all else, even the giver, the one who makes it possible for us to acquire it. Wealth and prosperity is God's design and plan, He is the one who gives us the power to get wealth. [Deut.8:18]

Abraham never allowed his ego to keep him from honouring God no matter how wealthy he got. He became the patriarch that religions follow as a key figure to understanding the world. He introduced the concepts of justice, virtue, kindness and compassion. He sent his two sons to different parts of the world with a certain set of beliefs and philosophies. Ishmael was sent to the East, which is the land of the Arabs today. Having learned archery and acquired other survival skills in the desert, he took a more aggressive approach compared to Isaac.

Inasmuch as we have our own personal conflicts and self-interests, we must always be virtuous and kind. When it comes to the battle between living a spiritual life in a material world, we must have boundaries and self-control. We must also have discipline. Love without discipline is flawed and not strong enough to maintain peace and harmony. It is that kind of love for God that causes people to hurt each other in the name of God. It pushes us to fight those who do not agree with us.

It is not God's desire for us to fight for Him; He can do that for Himself, and He is doing it all the time. He is revealing Himself to people of all backgrounds and faith.

I recently read a book about near-death experiences where hundreds of people gave accounts of their experiences as they came close to the end of their lives. Some had been in a coma, others had been brought back through resuscitation, and some had even died and pronounced dead. Those who did not believe in God before the experience had a different story when they came back.

We do not have to get to the point of death to know that there are no differences on the other side, that there are no powers to fight for. There is only one power: the power of the one true God. The God that Abraham worshipped. The truth is, we have more in common than we are different. We all have a soul, and all souls originate from one source. In other words, we are all brothers and sisters, and at the end of our physical experience here, we all return to that source, our Creator.

We all have an indispensable life mission despite the paths we have taken in life. With our different skills, talents, opportunities, experiences, gifts and resources, each one of us has something to offer to the world, and that becomes our mission, we may call it a purpose. We can take those resources, harness them and direct them toward making our little corner of the world a little brighter and more harmonious. We can be bearers or ambassadors of *light* wherever we are and help others discover their own light (Light in them), and share in the blessing of Abraham:

> *'Blessed shall be thy basket and thy store. Blessed shall you be when you come in and blessed shall you be when you go out.'* Deut. 28:5-8

This is the blessing of Abraham, the father of many nations. According to the Bible, all of us 'wo are of faith' are children of Abraham, the father of faith, [Gal. 3:6-9] whose relationship with God accorded him many titles. Among them was a friend of God. He not only listened to God and obeyed, but he trusted him with everything he had including his son Isaac's life. His closeness to God was not rooted in performance, but in trust, honesty, and companionship. He shows us that faith is more than believing. It is walking with God, even when the path is rough and unclear.

He was a giver. We often feel like we have nothing to give because we have no money or material possession, but the truth is that these are not the only things we can give. Life is all about giving, just as nature gives to us every single day without fail. We wake up every morning, and the sun is out; the air is fresh, and the birds are singing. Even the scriptures tell us that His mercies are new every day. Our gifts, talents, experiences, good or bad and our time are all resources we can give.

We can encourage others not just with our good experiences but the bad ones also. People need to know that others have experienced the difficult things they are currently experiencing and survived. That gives them hope and assurance that they too can survive and move past them. Everybody needs hope.

CHAPTER SEVEN

Prisoners of the Past

To everything, there is a season, and a time to every purpose.

In his book, *The Power of Now*, Eckhart Tolle talks about the essence of freedom that comes from letting go of 'self-identification with one's personal history and life situation'. I was reminded of this, not too long ago when an innocent text message of less than five words sent me back to the past, over a decade ago. For a good few minutes, I was sobbing like a lost puppy. For those few minutes, I lived in the past, feeling every emotion I felt back then, as though it was happening all over again in that moment.

It's a trick the mind plays on us, making us forget that we're not in that situation. I caught myself and quickly snapped out of it. Seconds later, I was laughing about it. A thought, a word, or a memory can trigger emotions associated with that thought or memory, and if we dwell on these thoughts we easily find ourselves feeling every emotion we felt back then. Unless we are fully present in the moment, we can easily fall into the trap of being imprisoned by our past.

Everyone has a past, and not all of it pleasant. Some of our pasts can make us feel vulnerable, weak and powerless, but we are not in that past anymore. We may have worked hard to move away from it, but unless we are operating in the

Christ-consciousness, dwelling in the secret place, we will always find ourselves being pulled back because the subconscious mind seeks to return to its original programming. It always tries to go back to the dominant states especially those associated with the memory or thought currently on your mind.

When we think about something that makes us sad, we say it broke our heart; what's the relationship between the heart and mind? The mind produces thoughts and the heart emotions. To live in the present, we must not allow thoughts or memories of things that hurt us linger for more than necessary. If you hear news that upset you or bring bad memories, it is unwise to keep talking about them unless it's necessary. That way, you're guarding your heart, not out of fear but wisdom.

Many people have been hurt in the past, abused, neglected or betrayed, either as children or adults. While we cannot change what happened in the past, we can change how we deal with it in the present life. Each time we entertain thoughts of something negative that happened in the past, we are allowing it to influence our feelings, emotions, moods and even actions. We are giving it power over our present life, the life we have worked so hard to create.

We are creators; we choose what we want to create and remaining in the past emotionally and mentally is choosing not to create something different or new. When we fail to consciously create something different, we find that we attract similar situations even when we're physically trying hard to move away from the past. The past does not define anyone, nor does it have to determine the future. It does not mean that because you had a difficult past your whole life has to be difficult. You can consciously choose to create a different path by choosing your thoughts, emotions and words.

Just as you have cut physical ties with the past, you must cut mental and emotional ties as well. While I am not saying it's easy to forget these things, we can train our minds to transcend them and not allow them to steal our 'now'.

Whether it happened ten or twenty years ago or yesterday, today is a new day with new possibilities. Holding on to the past denies us the opportunity to see the new possibilities because we are blind to them. The truth about the past is that it is gone. It does not disqualify you; it prepares you for the future.

It humbles you so that you never forget who gets the glory when the breakthrough comes. What the master potter forms with the shattered pieces is more beautiful than what was never broken. You do not have to keep playing old movies that bring nothing but sadness and defeat. Everything in life is a frequency. If you don't like the movie or music your mind is playing, change the frequency. Change the channel.

Sometimes, you will find that even those people who hurt you have something good you remember them for. Change the frequency and tune in to that or something else that makes you feel more empowered. You also must be able to separate between someone who did something to hurt you and what actually hurt you. That can help you see things in a fresh perspective because not all offenders offend maliciously. Good intentions can backfire, and because we have no way of seeing someone else's intentions, all we see is the outcome. Regardless of what was done, forgiveness is key, it makes way for healing.

Without forgiveness, it will be almost impossible to move past the hurt. Unforgiveness not only keeps us in a loop but also blocks good things from flowing to us and through us. We are meant to be a channel through which grace flows, but grace won't flow where unforgiveness is present. Unforgiveness is like a roadblock to all the blessings and goodness God wants to channel through to us. We must reprogramme our minds to shift the focus away from those things that appear to have control over our emotions.

The practical way of applying this is to observe a thought or a memory without attaching your emotion to it and without judging it. Let it just sit in your mind for a moment; don't react to it or allow it to affect the way you feel. If you start to feel uncomfortable, remind yourself that it's not happening at present. Remind yourself that you are safe right now. You can look around and find something to be grateful for and say out loud that you are grateful for it. You are grateful that you are not in that situation in the present moment, and you are still standing in spite of it.

Some people find that taking a deep breath helps to shift the focus back to 'now'. Past traumas cause fear and anxiety, but once you remind yourself that it is just an emotional reaction and not a truth or a reality of the present moment, you can move past it and continue with your life uninterrupted. There is a fear that is normal and natural, but it doesn't have to control you. It's the self-preservation kind of fear, the fear that tells you to run from danger. It has its place. It can act as a guide, to tell you when to remove yourself from a situation.

You do not have to wait until it's too late to remove yourself from a situation. When you are in tune with your inner self, you will know when it's safe to stay and when to observe or even love from a distance. People have had their lives permanently scarred (Physically) and others have even lost their lives for not knowing when to remove themselves from a situation. You must always tune into the frequency you want to be in and align with it. Align yourself with what supports your purpose and detach from those that derail it.

You cannot serve two masters; you must decide what you want and align with that. Don't let fear keep you from moving forward, aligning your energy with the desired outcome is an essential discipline to embrace. We have already seen how our thoughts and emotions create a powerful force that influences our reality; it is equally important to understand how energy works. The vibrational frequency you emit is an energy that determines what you attract into your life. Like attracts like.

Have you ever noticed that when you're happy,

everyone you meet seems happy? if you walk around smiling, the people you meet will smile even if they don't say a word to you? If you look grumpy, the people you meet will look serious or grumpy. People pick up your frequency and reflect it. Nature does, too. Whatever you want from life, you must be it. You must embody the qualities you desire in others, if you expect kindness from others, you must practise kindness in your life.

You cannot expect others to be honest with you if you're not honest. Be what you seek from others. It is simply tunning your energy to match your ideal reality and to stay in alignment, even when external circumstances are challenging, and to sustain this high-vibrational state over time so you can consistently attract the experiences you desire. We are energetic beings, constantly emitting waves of energy based on our thoughts, feelings, and beliefs.

When we feel emotions like joy, gratitude, love, and excitement, our frequency is high. We are vibrating at a frequency that is in harmony with the abundant nature of the universe. When we experience emotions like fear, anger, anxiety, and sadness, our frequency drops, and we align more with lack, scarcity, and survival. This when people begin to wonder what the point of living is as they feel trapped and unable to move forward.

You must feel worthy of what you desire and know that you are worthy because you already know who you are. Do not allow yourself to stay in the frequency of fear and insecurity as it is the survival frequency and does not align with the abundant nature of the universe or the will of your creator. The secret to elevating your emotions is finding something to be grateful for. When you are joyful, you are expansive and hopeful. You open the door to possibilities and positive experiences.

Guilt, shame, and frustration may seem innocent, but they are also low vibrational emotions that attract negative experiences by closing the door to possibilities. They are connected to survival mechanisms that keep you locked in the past, unable to step into the future you desire, and the future God wants you to have. He wants you to always have hope as the one who lives in you is the 'hope of glory'.

When you are caught in low vibrational states, you attract more situations that perpetuate these feelings, thus reinforcing the cycle of negativity. Rather than let your circumstances dictate your life, align yourself with the will of God for your life. His plan is to prosper you and to give you a future. A good one. A future full of misery is not a future. We must not fear for our future as it is in His hands.

'Fear not, little flock; for it is your Father's good pleasure to give you the kingdom.' Luke 12:32

It gives Him joy when we discover the kingdom within because it is in that that we break the chains that bind us. His word says, 'The knowledge of God is the beginning of wisdom.' One of the mistakes we make is to wait for conditions to change so we can feel better. We say things like, 'I'll be so happy when this happens'. What if we practice being happy before it happens? We can teach ourselves to feel happy as we wait for it to happen.

We can also teach ourselves not to attach our happiness to that thing happening because if it doesn't, we get disappointed and feel unhappy. We can practice elevating our emotions regardless of our current circumstances by counting our blessings moment by moment. Gratitude automatically elevates emotions and mood, and when you are grateful, you get more things to be grateful for. The more we practice staying in these elevated emotions, the more they become engraved in our system, eventually becoming our default state of being.

We become happy people without a reason. I learned this from my son; he's always so happy, I'd find him laughing or smiling and ask, 'why are you so happy?' He'd say, 'Do I need a reason to be happy?' After getting that answer a few times I got the message. We really don't need a reason to be happy. Being alive is reason enough to be happy. Meditation is a good practice to train ourselves to elevate our emotions, first by quieting the mind and then focusing it on the positive things in our lives.

David meditated regularly on the word of God. Paul also talks about 'thinking on' those things that are noble and of good report. Thinking on something is meditation, some translations say, meditate on those things. 'Whatever things are of good report, if there is any virtue and if there is anything praiseworthy—meditate on these things.' [Phil. 4:8] It is therefore a good practice to think on all the good things in our lives.

When you meditate, you enter a state of deep relaxation and focus, which allows you to disconnect from the stress of everyday life and into your higher consciousness. It allows you to connect with the infinite source of all possibilities, enabling you to feel the energy of your desires even before you see them. This is where, instead of saying "I'll believe it when I see it," you believe it before you see it. Let one of the major takeaways from this book be, *I believe therefore I shall see*. In the realm of the spirit, you see it when you believe it. You see the answers to your prayers when you believe your prayers have been answered.

That childlike faith brings your desire into manifestation. Matthew, Mark and Luke all talk about childlike faith. [Matt. 18:3, Mark 10:14, Luke 18:17] Children do not try to analyse everything or use logic to disqualify what they do not understand. They believe without seeing. They use their imagination to visualise the impossible. Once they can see it in their mind, they do not need convincing or evidence. Doubts steal what is rightfully yours. When you're quiet in meditation, your thoughts may begin to wander. Focusing on your breath helps to stay in the moment. It helps to release any negative or limiting thoughts that may arise, including doubts.

There are different ways you can meditate regardless of where you are. The style does not matter; you could be walking or on a bus or train, in the office, at home, etc. Visualisation meditation, for example, involves holding a mental image of things the way you want them to be, or living your desired life. If your desire is for a sick relative or friend to be healed, you hold a mental image of them looking well and healthy, may be doing things they cannot currently do, but those they love to do. In other words, you assume or imagine your prayers have been answered and act it out in your mind.

By meditating regularly, you strengthen your ability to stay in alignment with your desire and the best version of yourself. It does not help if you are in that state for a day, and the next you are complaining of lack or illness. Once you assume your prayers have been answered, begin to act as if they actually have in real life. Be grateful for being in this state. When you focus on what you are grateful for, you are telling your Creator that you have everything you need and are happy and grateful. He, in return, gives you more, and you are more grateful.

Does that ring a bell? *The parable of the talents* – to the one who had, more was given. To the one who had not, even the little he had was taken away. [Matthew 25:29] Gratitude shifts your focus from what is lacking or missing in your life to what is present. It helps to keep a journal of all the positive aspects of your life, or just a mental record. When you appreciate the positive, the negative aspects lose power over you. Nothing is too little, even opening your eyes in the morning and being able to breathe freely is something to be grateful for.

Having worked in a hospital and seeing people struggle to breathe on their own taught me not to take the simple joy of breathing freely for granted. Even something as simple as hearing. One day, not too long ago I woke up with my ears blocked. I couldn't hear anything. I went to the bathroom and turned on the water, I couldn't hear the usual noise of water running down the sink. I panicked and just then realised how much I had taken it for granted. For hours that morning I could not hear. In the kitchen I turned on the kettle and didn't hear it boil, tried opening and closing drawers with a bang, nothing. I thought I would never hear again.

Be grateful for the little things, and greater things will follow. This is the message communicated in the parable of the talents. The one who lives with a consciousness of abundance receives more, while the one who lives with a mindset of lack sees the little they have slip away. It is a spiritual law that teaches us to utilise what God has given us and be grateful no matter how insignificant it may seem, knowing it replenishes itself such that the one who gives never lacks.

'Thou hast been faithful over a few things, I will make thee ruler over many things' Matthew 25:23

Talking about the power of gratitude, an author whose work I revere, Dr Joe Dispenza, who is also a neuroscientist, posits that gratitude strengthens neuropathways for positive thinking. He further tells us that the brain can 'rewire and create new circuits' at any age as a result of input from the environment and our conscious intentions, meaning we can create a new level of mind. We can learn and unlearn things at any age, allowing us to rise above our current limitations and 'be greater than our conditioning or circumstances'.

That is science proving what the scriptures say about renewing of mind. Neuroplasticity proves that the brain is not rigid but alive, responsive and adaptable. That it has the ability to form new neuropathways and to change its structure based on our thoughts and experiences. This, unlike popular belief, happens throughout our lives and not just when we're young. I have always heard people say you can't teach an old dog new tricks, or old habits don't die.

According to Dr Dispenza, we can learn new tricks and break old habits no matter how long we have been doing something or how old we are. We can influence the body through the power of belief. Belief, he says, is one of the most powerful forces we have. It shapes how we see the world, how we show up in it and ultimately, the reality we create. We can reprogramme our mind at any age, he says. If you are advanced in age and begin to realise, you're becoming forgetful or you're losing memory, your cognitive function is declining, you are not doomed. It does not have to be permanent.

You can affirm boldly that you have the mind of God. If you are physically sick and your body is weak, boldly affirm that as Christ is, so are you in this world. Keep saying it with conviction until it becomes real in your mind (until you believe it). Begin seeing yourself in this new state. It must feel true to you. If doesn't feel true it will just be empty words and no matter how many times you repeat them, they will have no effect. They only have effect when you believe them.

Nothing is permanent; all we have to do is fill our minds with life-giving patterns of thought, and all negative and traumatic hurts, pains, and discomforts will be obliterated. We also must shift our attention from 'evil conscience' as the scriptures say:

> *'Let us draw near with a true heart in full assurance of faith, having our hearts sprinkled from an evil conscience and our bodies washed with pure water. Let us hold fast the profession of our faith without wavering; (for he is faithful that promised;).'*
> Hebrews 10:22-23

Like other scriptures we have read, it is stressing on faith, focusing on the good and being steadfast or firm in what we confess. This is what makes our thoughts, words and affirmations a reality. You can spend hours repeating the words, 'I am healed, I am rich, I am whole', but if it doesn't feel true or it if one moment it feels true and the next you're doubting it, it will not have an impact. It is like planting a seed and digging it up every now and then.

You must be consistent and stick to what you are affirming or declaring regardless of the outward appearance. You must realise that riches are of the mind. Everything you desire, be it good health, good relationships, confident expression, soundness of mind, material wealth or whatever success is to you, is all in the mind. You are rich when you know you can tap the intelligence and wisdom within and bring your desires to pass.

> *'You are rich when your mind is full of peace, love, confidence and faith in the goodness of God in the land of the living.'* **Dr Joseph Murphy**

You can change the present, and your future will be the present conviction made manifest. Consider the past dead and realise that nothing matters but this moment, the present moment. Change your present thoughts and keep them renewed moment by moment. The future will be a perfect projection of your new habitual thinking based on the premise that, what you sow in the garden of our mind is what will show up as a harvest. Some laws of nature cannot be changed or broken, and this is one of them.

Harbouring resentful thoughts, striking back at others or seeking revenge neutralises your best effort to create a positive change in your life. It destroys you physically and mentally. I witnessed this in the hospital wards where I saw people in their twilight years suffering from dementia and other challenges related to the mind. Most of them could not remember much, but what was surprising is that they endlessly talked about things that caused them pain, like betrayal, loss of money and negative incidents witnessed even if they had nothing to do with them.

They seemed to remember them in detail; some even remembered the abuse they went through as children but couldn't remember what happened a few minutes ago.

Currently, there is no medical cure for dementia, though there are treatments and medications that help with the symptoms; not the problem itself. This moment you have right now is the best time to deal with those negative emotions. You may not know it, but left unresolved, they remain in the subconscious mind to resurface when least expected.

'Behold, now is the accepted time; now is the day of salvation.' 2 Cor. 6:2

Resolve issues of the day before you retire to sleep. Forgive and ask for forgiveness. Do not allow frustrations and disappointments to be impressed upon your subconscious mind, which is likely to happen if you go to bed carrying these emotions. We were created perfect and valuable; it is time we reclaimed our birthright. There is a reason why scriptures tell us not to go to bed angry. [Eph. 4:26] We create when our minds are resting, when our conscious mind is asleep.

What we go to bed thinking about is likely what we end up creating. It is vital, therefore, that we clear our minds of all negativities before going to bed. Your thoughts are the bricks you use to build your life. When the conscious mind is resting, the subconscious mind takes over, providing answers to the dominant thought of the day. Job, the man the devil sought permission to tempt according to the scriptures tells us that God speaks, but man hears not. He adds:

'In a dream, in a vision of the night, when deep sleep falleth upon men, in slumbering upon the bed; Then he opens the ears of men and seals their instruction.' Job 33:15-16

No matter what you did or did not do before, no matter what your circumstances are right now, when you begin to fill your mind with life-giving patterns and align yourself mentally with infinite love, infinite life and infinite healing presence, the negative patterns slowly fall off, and the past is forgotten, to be remembered no more.

This promise is repeated several times in the scriptures, both in the Old and the New Testaments. If your Creator promises not to remember your past mistakes, why do you torture yourself with their painful memories? Just let go!

> *'This is the covenant that I will make with them after those days, says the Lord, I will put my laws into their hearts, and in their minds will I write them;* And their sins and *iniquities will I remember no more.'*
> Hebrews 10:16-17

There is no need to carry burdens of the past that weigh you down. It's a new day. You cannot fully embrace today while holding on to the failures of yesterday.

Grace Wairimu

CHAPTER EIGHT

The Sleeping Giant

Do you not care that we are drowning?

Have you ever felt like you are drowning, and nobody seems to notice? You could be drowning in the sea of fear, anxiety or depression. You could also be drowning in a lake, like these men crossing over to the other side of the lake in a small boat. They were frightened. There was a lot of wind tossing the boat from one side to the other. It began to fill with water. Suddenly, they realised that someone who had been in the boat with them was missing. I can imagine the fear that gripped them, worrying he might have been tossed into the troubled water.

They called out to Him. He had been sleeping, completely oblivious to the conditions outside. 'Teacher, don't you care that we are about to drown?' They were simply asking, 'What's wrong with you? How could you possibly be sleeping when such winds are blowing, threatening to sink the boat? Do you not hear the commotion?' 'Quiet! Be still!' He commanded. He wasn't talking to them; He was speaking to the wind and the waves. The wind stopped, and the water was calm. In their distress, they cried out and awoke the sleeping giant. The first thing He asked them when all was calm was, 'Why are you afraid?

Do you still have no faith?' [Mark 4:40]

I heard these words in my mind not too long ago. I was sitting at my desk writing when a message came through about my mother's health having deteriorated. My heart immediately began to race. My mind started to do what the mind does best, then I heard these words, 'Why are you afraid, do you still have no faith?' They were a reminder to quiet my mind. It's amazing what a difference it makes when you purposely and consciously silence the noise in the mind. You block the fear, the worry and anxiety from coming in and stealing your peace.

When your mind is still, it is easy to direct it where you want it to go, but when you are anxious on the other hand, it's a different story. Your thoughts take you wherever they want. You begin to imagine the worst. Have you ever wondered why the automatic response to news is always the worst possible outcome? Why do we not impulsively imagine the best possible outcome? Having been reminded to adjust my reaction, I rephrased the question and asked myself, 'Why are you afraid? What are you scared of? What do you think will happen?'

That put the power back in my hands, why? Because whatever you think will happen is your faith — and it's done to you according to your faith. Why did Jesus ask the people He healed if they believed they could be healed before He healed them? None of them said they did not believe. They all got healed. Even in the valley of dry bones, God asked Ezekiel if he believed the bones could live. Imagine looking at dry skulls and bones of people who died ages ago and someone asking you if you believe they could live again.

It takes a lot of faith. I guess it also depends on who is asking. Ezekiel was very smart about it. 'Only you know Lord,' he replied. God then asked him to prophesy to them; would he have prophesied if he didn't believe they could live? Was God testing his faith? He had to see its possibility in his mind before he could see it physically. By asking him to prophesy to them, he was enabling him to visualize it, and once he formed that mental image in his consciousness, it became possible.

In the boat, Jesus 'spoke' to the problem. He used 'words' to calm the wind and the waves. He did not use any power. Ezekiel also used words to prophesy to the dry bones. There are some similarities in the two incidences. Jesus commanded the wind and the waves to be still. Ezekiel prophesied to the winds to come and breath upon the now dead bodies lying where the scattered bones laid. [Eze. 37] We are told that in the beginning was the Word, and the Word was with God, and the Word was God. Then the word became flesh and dwelt among us.

God used words to create the universe. We use words to create our reality because we are made in His likeness, and we have the word (Jesus) living in us. We can use our words to speak to our problems with the same authority Jesus used. We can prophesy to our past and change the course of our future like Ezekiel did with the dry bones. We have the same authority, but we lack faith.

Before the disciples got in the boat, Jesus had been telling them and the multitude who had come to listen to Him about His Kingdom (the Kingdom of God), comparing it to a mustard seed. A mustard seed, He said, is smaller than any other seed that can be planted. When it grows, it becomes bigger than any other plant in the garden. It creates shade and a home for birds to build nests, where they are protected from the sun.

In another teaching, He compares a mustard seed to faith, telling us that we can grow our faith from a little speck, the size of a mustard seed and achieve great things through it. One of the greatest things we can achieve through faith is becoming a support system for others like the tree that creates shade a home for birds.

I was thinking about all this with my mother in mind. I like to imagine her in perfect health, with no symptoms whatsoever. Isn't that what faith is about – the substance of things hoped for, and the evidence of things not seen? Faith also means, not stressing over something when we commit it to God, because stressing indicates lack of trust. We know all these things theoretically, we know what faith is and what it can do, but how to cultivate it eludes us. How do we cultivate faith and trust? The answer I got then, was to imitate Jesus.

Now that we know who we are, that we have His power working in us, all we need is to exercise it by doing what He did. He spoke to problems. We can speak to our problems starting with the minor ones. As we start to see small things change, our faith grows and as we continue to use our words to change things around us, our faith gets stronger just like our muscles when we exercise them. As things around us change, our reality changes, and as our reality changes, our faith continues to grow, just like a mustard seed. It may not take a day, a week or a month, but it certainly grows stronger and stronger as we exercise it.

This is the sleeping giant within you at work. Start affirming dominion over anything that contradicts this. Rearrange your thoughts to conform to the belief that you are one with all the power and all the presence there is, and that, what He can do, you too can do. By that, you will be declaring His word which cannot lie, nor be added to or removed from.

That statement may feel wrong because it sounds like we are comparing ourselves to God or claiming to be equal with Him. Jesus Himself said it, that we can do the things He did and even greater if we believe. He imitated His father, and we must imitate Him. Though He was fully God, He lowered Himself and served as a servant and did not consider it 'robbery to be equal with God'. Paul tells us to have the same mind.

'Let this mind be in you, which was also in Christ Jesus: Who, being in the form of God, thought it not robbery to be equal with God: But made himself of

124

*no reputation, and took upon him the form of a
servant, and was made in the likeness of men ...'*
Philippians 2:5-6

We too should not think that we are robbing God by declaring truths about who we are and what we are capable of through Him. We should humble ourselves and serve others since we are imitating Christ, evolving to be more and more like Him. We do not achieve this in a day, but our faith grows as we continue to imitate Him and to live in this consciousness.

His power is always flowing through you as health, success, peace, happiness, and harmony—anything you desire. Bless everything you do, take the restrictions off your efforts and declare them good and perfect, just as God declared creation before resting upon completion. Declare yourself healthy, prosperous and happy. Whatever you pray for yourself, pray also for others and not just your family and friends. Remember, prayer is not just when you kneel down to ask of God; declarations, affirmations and thanks giving or gratitude are prayers, too, as they align with the will of God. Remain in the consciousness of wish fulfilled.

When you realise the person you are praying for has the same power within them, it does not matter the distance between you. This power is not restricted by distance, space or time, nor is it restricted by the size or magnitude of the problem. It is not some power; it is ALL power. It is the power that made everything, big and small. It knows no difference. There is no difference between healing cancer and healing a common cold; we are the ones who see the difference because we are limited – because we live in a sense of disunion with Life.

We must consciously remove ourselves from the darkness of unbelief. We do not have to beg God or beseech him. What He has is rightfully ours, and He has everything, healing included. All we do is receive and be grateful. We just need to use the authority given to us by faith and use our words to make declarations.

'You shalt also decree a thing, and it shall be established unto thee: and the light shall shine upon thy ways.' Job 22:28

Keep every channel open, alive, awake and aware. Live, think, speak and act as though the entirety of life was delivered to you individually. The more you give of your gifts and talents, the more you will receive. You cannot outgive nature. Science tells us that electricity is everywhere and not just on earth. We, however, must follow certain rules and guidelines to enjoy its benefits. If the stream flowing into your home becomes disconnected, no light will be delivered to your house even though the universe is filled with electric energy.

If the water pipe connecting your house to the reservoir is disconnected, there will be no water in your house. That doesn't mean that the reservoir has dried up. It just means you have no connection and therefore no means of receiving water. If you go to draw water in the ocean with a small container, you will only draw a small amount of water. It does not mean the ocean has dried up or could only give you that small amount. The ocean does not care how much you draw from it; you are only limited by your container. The air we breathe is also available in abundance, it does not care how much of it you take in when you breathe.

The source of life is an infinite sea of energy, power, love, and wisdom. What connects us with this source is our inward life, the thoughts and emotions that make up our consciousness. Our consciousness is our connection to the source of all life. Two people could be in the same room, but one may be in absolute bliss while the other is in torment. Depending on the consciousness in which we live, we can see beauty, order and harmony where others see disorder, chaos and disharmony. We can have peace amid a storm just like Jesus when He slept comfortably through a storm.

It is possible to live every moment being conscious of our union with good. Someone might think they are being religious or too spiritual trying to live this way, but there is no other way to be for someone who wants to see good in the land of the living. Some people do not care much how they live here on Earth as long as they have hope for a perfect life in Heaven. They await a kingdom to come that will erase all misery, a paradise sometime in the future. But Jesus explicitly said that the kingdom is here and now as it is within us.

Remember it is God's plan and desire for you to live a full life and to see good in this life, the land of the living. He did not put you here to be in limbo until you get to heaven. He is a just and loving God. He want you to enjoy life and to learn from it. We are living in uncertain times; storms and thunders are raging, and people are losing the will to live. We are promised that our sun will never set again, and our moon will wane no more, that the Lord will be our everlasting light, and our days of sorrow will end. [Isaiah 60:20]

The sun represents the inner spiritual principle, the illumination of Truth. When it shines, all obstructions are removed, it's symbolic of pure consciousness; the Christ consciousness, the light of I AM. This promise represents the embodiment of God within us, which the Bible calls the Christ:

> *'Thou art the Christ, the son of the living God.'*
> Matthew 16:16

This was Peter's answer when Jesus asked them who people said He was, and who they themselves thought He was. Jesus confirmed his answer telling him that flesh and blood did not reveal it to him but the Father in heaven. Only God could have revealed that to him. Notice he did not say Christ but 'the Christ'. What difference does the simple word 'the' make? We tend to think that Christ is Jesus' second name, but it isn't. Christ is a state – a state of consciousness, which we embody when we acknowledge the God within and become one with Him.

He becomes our everlasting light spoken of in the verse above (Isa. 60:20) illuminating everything, casting away the shadows that hinder our sight. It is the pearl of great price which we spend our lives seeking. It makes us perfect in the eyes of our Creator, our Father – just as He is.

'Be ye therefore perfect, even as your father which is in Heaven is perfect.' Matthew 5:48

It is important to realise that we are not being asked to strive for perfection; we are told *to be,* to rest in knowing that we are. We do not strive or claim to be holy, perfect or righteous. We just rest in the presence of Him who is Holy, perfect and righteous. We realise that when we are joined with Him, what is true of Him is true of us. We bask in His glory:

'But we all, with open face beholding as in a glass the glory of the Lord, are changed into the same image from glory to glory, even as by the Spirit of the Lord..' 2 Cor. 3:18

All His power flows through your words. When you still your mind and rest in that secret place of your consciousness (a place where no one can intrude), in prayer, meditation, or just being in conscious awareness of the presence, you sense an inner stillness. You feel energised and inspired to act. You feel a sense of peace 'that passes all understanding'. This peace guards your heart and mind. [Phil. 4:7]

If you have a thought or inspiration to do something, don't ignore it. Have absolute faith in it and act as directed or guided. Remember you are not entering this silent space to seek power, the infinite presence is already power. You are instead recognising this power and permitting it to flow into action through your word. Your word is your conscious intention, faith and acceptance that because of the inspired action you're taking, the power will flow in the direction you give it.

Having faith alone is not enough, acting as directed is what produces results. You are simply speaking something into being. What you see comes from what you do not see. The visible is the invisible made manifest as demonstrated in the story of Ezekiel and the dry bones. When Ezekiel obeyed God and prophesied to the dry bones, he witnessed what our brains cannot process logically to this day. The scattered bones started to come together, and flesh appeared on them, then skin began to cover them.

Step by step, everything that had been eaten away came back and when he prophesied to the winds to breathe life into the now dead bodies, they started to breathe. They stood up and he was standing in the midst of living people where dry bones lay. [Eze. 37:1-14] Whether this happened in a dream, a vision or in real life, what is evident is the supernatural power of words.

Every time you speak, you are giving form to an invisible power. Thought is always involved when we speak, even in Ezekiel's case. He had to engage his mind to declare whether he believed it was possible or not. This is a gift given to all of us, let use it constructively. Lay aside all sense of unworthiness; yes you may not be a prophet, an apostle or strong in faith, but it is not about you. It is all about the power within you; the power of creation is within every man, and it is the same power Ezekiel used to bring the dry bones to life.

The fact that we are not aware of it does not mean it is not there. The fact that we cannot see air does not mean it's not there. We are always using our words, our thoughts and emotions to create, whether we know it or not, which means we are always altering the course of our lives, creating new possibilities and demolishing others. When I was little, we used to sing a song in Sunday school, saying that we're building an invisible temple every moment of our lives, brick by brick. Of course we didn't know what that meant. Our words and thoughts are the bricks we use to build our lives.

A parent who keeps telling their children they are stupid or useless creates that reality for them, it creates a belief of inadequacy in them. The one who uses empowering words empowers the child. Idle words uttered by people against themselves produce results in due course. Let us, therefore, use our words to bless ourselves and others. In speech or in prayer, always use your words positively. God is not moved by desperation, He is moved by faith. The scriptures tell us to come boldly to the throne of grace. [Heb. 4:16] It means to have confidence and trust.

There should be a sense of calm, peace and joy: a deep realisation of the divine presence. Begging and beseeching denote anxiety and fear that your prayer might not be granted. Our prayer must be specific and affirmative, with the result in mind. This is what praying from the end means. It is important to realise that the creative power within us is neutral. Like a parent who unknowingly uses it to harm their children by using negative words against them, it can be used to cause harm to others. Let us not be ignorant but consciously choose to use it only for good.

> *'Oh, that men would praise the Lord for his goodness, and for his wonderful works to the children of men! And let them sacrifice the sacrifices of thanksgiving and declare his works with rejoicing.'*
> Psalm 107:21-22

Awaken the sleeping giant within.

CHAPTER NINE

Divine Love

There is no fear in love, perfect love casts out fear.

Not too long ago, I had a dream that I was walking on the side of the road, and within sight was a beautiful view of a coastline. I wondered where I was. I began to look around for clues; there were other people around who looked like tourists. They were looking down what seemed to be a valley, taking pictures. I seemed to be on a cliff. I kept walking and suddenly realised I had company. As we walked and enjoyed the view, my companion, an old friend I had not seen in many years, kept talking, but my mind was on what was happening down the coast.

The view got more and more beautiful as we walked on. I wondered if we were all seeing the same thing. We were not walking towards it but parallel to it. We would soon lose it if we kept walking. It was so captivating, almost unreal. It appeared to get brighter and more spectacular with every step. There was a beautiful aura of love and warmth filling the atmosphere. I stopped to soak it in. I wondered if my everyone else felt it, but as I turned to my side where my friend was, there was no one, just a stillness and calm.

It felt so serene. It made my heart vibrate. When I woke up, my hands were across my chest like I was holding on to my heart, which was still racing. I was a little disoriented. I sat up in bed, looked around and soon realised I had been dreaming. Rather than go back to sleep, I started to analyse the dream in my head. It had seemed so real.

I have seen coastlines in real life, but never have I seen such beauty, it was mind blowing. The experience felt almost like the warmth and love I felt when I saw the sun smile and mountains and trees dance. I tried to make sense of it and get some meaning from it, but nothing significant was forthcoming except that it was an absolute beauty, like I was in a magical place.

The next day as I was driving to work, listening to an audiobook as I often do, a similar thing happened. I was listening to Joseph Murphy, an author and spiritual teacher I have quoted in an earlier chapter. I discovered Dr Murphy's work while dealing with anger issues. It was a time in my life when I could not control my emotions, and it was ruining my life, from work to relationships.

In his books, lectures and videos, he uses prayer and affirmations to help his audience transmute their negative tendencies into something constructive. That day, as I listened to the audio, these words caught my attention, *'I claim now that the infinite intelligence is guiding and directing me, and that divine love fills my soul...'* as the words 'divine love fills my soul' were pronounced, I had the same feeling I'd had in the dream.

It was so bizarre. I tightened my grip on the steering wheel, willing myself to focus on the road. It was as if the words were being animated. I was fully awake and alert. There was nothing out of the ordinary, no beautiful scenery on the side of the road and no one in the car with me. I realised then that it was not the scenery, the cliff or the company I was in that had triggered the feeling in the dream.

The words that followed said, *'I am inspired and illumined, my hidden talents are revealed to me. I radiate love, peace and goodwill to all men and women.'* At that moment, I realised that the whole meaning of the dream was about indiscriminately allowing the love in me to flow through me to others and seeing beauty in everything. It just came to me like an epiphany.

The very first experience where I had experienced that love and warmth emanating from the sun was about letting the light shine, and the one from the dream, whose meaning was revealed through the audio was about radiating love to everyone, indiscriminately. The message was to see everything as beautiful and everyone as God sees them, perfect beings whether they appear so or not. My job is not to judge but to love and do whatever I am guided and inspired to do, regardless of the circumstances or prejudices.

That's a tall order, but when God directs you and inspires you to do something, He provides what is needed to do it—the strength, the courage, the confidence and the resources. Divine love is perfect love. It casts out all fear. It helps us to see good in everything and God in everyone as we are all sons and daughters of the Most High. I set out to put it into practice, constantly reminding myself to see God in the people I met. That day at work, I found it very challenging. Some people are naturally annoying and as if by design, I met several of those that day.

That night as I reflected on the events of the day, something came to my mind. It was about the temple of God, reminding me that our bodies are temples, and the covering of the temple is a garment [clothe], that when removed, there is no difference between one person and the other. It came to my mind that nothing really matters but what is inside as garments can be taken off, they are not permanently stuck on people. What's on the inside is what I should address when interacting with others no matter how 'annoying' they may be.

We are all children of the same father who does not discriminate; a saint and a murderer are both His children, hard as it is to believe. We are to see them both as God sees them—perfect because He is perfect. A day will come when the murderer hears the voice within and acknowledges it. He then discovers the light within him and sees it light up his whole being as he opens himself to it.

The human nature is to look on the outside, but God looks on the inside. He sees what we cannot see. We see only in part, but a time will come when we shall see and know fully. We do not need to know everything, we just need to trust.

> *'For now, we see only a reflection as in a mirror; then we shall see face to face. Now, we know only in part, then we shall know fully, even as we are fully known.'*
1 Corinthians 13:12

Like a father knows his children, God knows us by name. He goes before us, straightening the crooked places and lighting up the path for us. This is divine love.

'Divine love is a miraculous healing power. This infinite healing presence is flowing through you now. It watches over you, guides you, and clears the path for you. Devine love surrounds you, upholds you and enwraps you.' Dr Joseph Murphy

We are bombarded with information every minute we're awake in the form of news, gossip or propaganda. Most of it produce nothing but fear. It discourages rather than give hope. It is, therefore, important to surround ourselves with empowering words and statements. Positive words and affirmations neutralise negative ones. Reminding ourselves that there is a miraculous healing power within us that is flowing through us all the time puts us in a state of gratitude and relaxation.

We realise that we are continually being energised, vitalised, and purified. Dr Murphy emphasizes the need to bless ourselves before we fall asleep at night, from the crown of our heads to the soles of our feet. To declare everything in between whole and fully functional as it's meant to be.

There are eleven systems in the body (respiratory, digestive, skeletal, muscular, cardiovascular, reproductive, urinary, lymphatic, endocrine, integumentary and nervous system), which must function at their best for a healthy and well-balanced life. You don't have to mention them or know how they work.

The short declaration of health covers everything, including the brain and the functioning of the mind. When you declare wholeness of body, from the crown of your head to the soles of your feet, you are simply blessing the whole body, mind and spirit. When all these are functioning harmoniously and coherently, you are dancing in the rhythm of your Creator. He created you to be whole, fully functional, and to fulfil your days. When divine love fills your soul, what you want for yourself, you also want for everyone because you realise that we are all one.

We are told that love is the fulfilment of the law [Romans 13:10-14], and that we cannot claim to love God if we do not love our neighbours. Our neighbour in this context is not the person next door to us. It is every person. The everyday person, the one we see on the bus, on the train, in the office or in the street, even the ones we see on the news going through something. We can love them by wishing them blessings, protection and peace, and doing whatever else we can to relieve or ease their suffering. We are our brothers' keepers. This is the highest form of love, the agape love.

It is divine love, the love that keeps on giving even when it is not acknowledged or rewarded. At the appointed time, everyone will come to see the transcendent glory and Love which is God. It is all there is—He is all in all. No one is lost, there is no lost soul. Every knee shall bow, and every tongue confess that He is God. He does not give up on his own. We sometimes give up on ourselves, but he never does. We are reminded that when completeness comes, what is in part disappears [1Cor.13:10].

When man truly finds God, he becomes serene, harmonious and happy. In other words, he becomes complete. He is created complete, but as long as he is unaware of the God within, he remains lacking and thus incomplete. When he finds his true self, he finds freedom and grants it to others; he does not deny them the right of expression.

Love is kind; it does not dishonour others. It is trusting, it protects, it always hopes and perseveres. We are told that love never fails; everything else does. This is the nature of God, and we are here to grow and develop our love nature, to be more like Him. We are still immature in our love and emotional nature. We must cease to be vain, arrogant and ignorant. If we see faults in others, if we are jealous, envious, resentful or in any way unkind to others, no matter what they have done, our love is wanting. The Word tells us that even if we speak in the tongues of angels and have no love, we are only 'a resounding gong or a clanging cymbal.' [1 Cor. 13:1]

Love is God's invention and God himself. In romantic relationships, family or friendships, work relationships or in whatever way we relate with others, we must demonstrate love in all its attributes, i.e. non-judgement, kindness, selflessness, understanding, etc. In marriage, for example, if we truly love our partners, we want the best for them. We want to see them happy and prosperous.

There is an urge within us all, constantly seeking to express itself at higher levels of consciousness. We must never limit or put chains on people we claim to love. It is mostly in marriages and romantic relationships that we see all sorts of chains like possessiveness, mistrust, judgment, control and restrictions of all kinds.

To limit someone based on the assumption that they should only concern themselves with your needs is to mock the union and the purpose of marriage. It is selfish and immature. It is based on fear and insecurity as opposed to love. People always lose what they will not give room to expand, grow and unfold. It is every human's mandate to grow and develop. The sense of freedom held by husband

and wife portrays the real spiritual marriage wherein each is wedded/married to Christ and is one with Him.

Husbands and wives should, therefore, learn to free each other. It is no wonder the word tells husbands to love their wives as Christ loved the church and gave Himself for her. [Ephesians 5:25] The love of God in their hearts (thoughts, words and deeds) should guide them in all their ways. There should be no need for insecurity. Let us broaden our vision in thought, words, and deeds so that our love gradually becomes the love that Jesus has for His bride, the church—the church spoken of here is you and me, not a building.

When He walked among men in physical form, his love was not limited to his father, mother, siblings and followers; he loved all humanity, Jews and Gentiles alike. This love includes the saint and the vilest sinner—even the thief on the cross. God is the impartial giver who gives to all men, regardless of creed and colour. You may wonder why, if that is the case, do we not all have the same fortune.

He, the giver, gives to all that which they feel is true of themselves. There are people, for example, who would have a hard time imagining themselves as millionaires, and there are those who have no problem seeing themselves as such; there is no struggle or conflict in their minds about it. Both receive according to their conviction. There are those who cannot imagine themselves healed. I met one such person at the hospital once. He had Leukaemia. He could not entertain any possibility of being cured or miraculously healed. He was comfortable with the thought that he could never recover inasmuch as he was seeking treatment.

God is the giver and the gift itself; we are the receivers. He is the gift in the sense that He has given the capacity to create the outcomes we desire using His creative power. What we create is up to us, there are no rules. What you conceive in your mind you create. His word tells us that He has made everything beautiful in its time:

'He has set eternity in the human heart, yet no one can fathom what He has done from beginning to end'
Ecclesiastes 3:11

Natural marriage (husband and wife) versus Spiritual marriage (Christ and you)

The Bible talks about the union between Christ and His church (us) as a marriage. He is the groom, and we are the bride. When we acknowledge Him, and are joined with Him, we are married to him. The marriage between a man and woman is an illustration of the spiritual marriage between Christ and His people.

It is also an illustration of the function of the conscious and the subconscious mind, because of the objective nature of the husband and the subjective nature of the wife. When a man and a woman marry, they become one, just as we become one with God when we are married to Christ. The act of marriage strengthens the bond in both the natural and the spiritual marriage, also called the supernatural marriage.

Just like in the natural marriage, there must be a conscious decision to wed. The conscious mind is referred to as the male, and the subconscious mind, the female aspect of creation. These two also marry and create. The conscious mind is personal and selective; the subconscious is impersonal and nonselective. As discussed earlier, the conscious mind has the power to impress ideas and concepts on the subconscious mind through feeling.

The subconscious mind receives all ideas felt as true and gives form and expression to them. The children birthed or brought into existence by the subconscious mind result from our conscious thoughts. It is not different from a physical marriage, where the female receives a seed from the male and incubates it for nine months, after which she births a child or children.

The children birthed by the union of conscious and subconscious minds are our lives' conditions, events and circumstances. Children possess the qualities of their parents, likewise, our lives' conditions, events and circumstances will have the qualities of our conscious thoughts and feelings.

Since we have discussed this in the previous chapters, so we are only looking at the relationship between our consciousness and the marriage between a man and a woman. Just as a pregnant woman is advised to check her feelings and mood, what she does and what she consumes lest they harm the unborn child, we must always check our feelings and mood, the thoughts we entertain, etc, as they all affect the 'children' we bring into existence every moment of our lives as experiences.

'For this cause shall a man leave his father and mother, and shall cleave to his wife, and the twain shall be one flesh.' Genesis 2:24

A man must leave behind his old beliefs, superstitions and unconstructive thoughts. He must no longer have 'false gods' such as fear, doubt, worry, resentment, anger, etc. He must not look to the world for peace, guidance, enlightenment, supply or strength. He must look to the God within, the source of all supply who is ever present.. His faith must not be in his father, mother, brother, sister or friend. His faith and reliance must be on the Indwelling Christ, Emmanuel—the God in us/God with us, the I AM.

Only then is his faith well founded, for 'He that loves his father and mother more than me is not worthy of me.' [Matthew 10:37] Man likes to cling to his old beliefs and dogmas for sentimental reasons. Though he has outgrown his old concept of things, he may find himself attached to them for social, political or family reasons. These are his father and mother, and he must be willing to leave them behind and cleave to his 'wife' instead – his ideal.

He may feel a sense of betrayal walking away from them even though he knows they no longer serve him. He suffers a conflict of consciousness – it is what the Bible calls a double-minded man, 'a double minded man is unstable in all his ways.' [James 1:8] Such a man (or woman) cannot have a full realisation of the presence of God. His false pride causes him to refuse the truth that sets him free. Man shall cleave to his wife – he must be true to his ideal or his desired objective.

He must consciously claim himself to be what he longs to be (cleave to his ideal/wife) and feel the reality of his desire. He must not allow himself to react negatively or to accept suggestions of failure, fear, lack or doubt. He must remain faithful to his wife (his ideal/desire). 'The two shall become one flesh.' When man withdraws from the world and contemplates the joy and happiness brought by his realising his objective, he becomes one with his ideal, meaning he has embodied his vision.

If he abandons his ideal, he becomes unfaithful to his wife. Man's wife is his concept of himself. She is a bride of the Lord, a noble, dignified Christ-like state of consciousness. To realise our desires moment by moment, we must sustain this state of consciousness until we are united as one. As we grow from strength to strength, we begin to live from our soul outward, where who we are, what we do and how we show up reflect our inner truth.

In this state, 'what God has joined together, no man can put asunder.' When man reaches the absolute conviction that he is who he was meant to be, that he has embodied his ideal, God has joined them together as one, and the two cannot be separated.

'No power in the sky above or in the earth below; 'Indeed, nothing in all creation will ever be able to separate us from the love of God that is revealed in Christ Jesus our Lord.' Romans 8:39

Jesus addresses the topic of divorce

Concerning the issue of divorce, the Pharisees asked Jesus if it is lawful for a man to put away his wife. He answered that no man should separate what God has joined together. They asked him why Moses commanded them to write a 'letter of divorcement' and to put her away.

To that, He answered, "Moses, because of the hardness of your hearts suffered you to put away your wives: but from the beginning, it was not so. And I say unto you, whosoever shall put away his wife, except it be for fornication, and shall marry another commits adultery: and whoso marries her which is put away does commit adultery".

Let's look at this from the perspective of consciousness – the wife being our ideal or desired objective. Moses represents the written law, which the Bible calls 'letter'. 'The letter kills, but the spirit gives life.' [2 Cor. 3:6] Jesus, who is now expounding the topic, represents the spirit (grace), which is the fulfilment of the law. The worldly, materialistic individual wedded or married to his past does not know that God is within him and that his own unconditioned consciousness or awareness of life is God, neither does he know that the solution to all his problems is within him. This is because he is not married to God/Christ yet, he's not even aware of His existence within him.

Inasmuch as his desire for peace, happiness, security, and integrity comes from within himself, he seeks the fulfilment of these desires outside of himself. If he knew that the law of life that puts these desires in him has whatever he needs to fulfil them, he would trust the infinite intelligence to bring them to pass. But he doesn't. He's not aware of such power within him. This would be the solution he seeks. But, not knowing the law written in his heart, he rejects the ideas that come to him.

'I will put my law in the inward parts and write it in their hearts ... and they shall teach no more every man his neighbour, for they shall all know me, from the least of them to the greatest of them.' Jeremiah 31:33-34

By rejecting the ideas and aspirations put in his heart, he 'divorces' his 'wife' (ideal) and puts her away. This rejection is due to ignorance. He ignores this power within and looks for solutions outside in the world. Asleep within him, awaiting recognition and claim are inspiration, divine guidance, and enlightenment. He puts them all away and seeks guidance from the world. That is adultery. By so doing, he commits adultery.

Man's concept of God hardens his heart. When he awakens and finds out that the subjective self of life in him is God, then he leaves the Moses state of consciousness, which represents the law of sin and death, judgement and damnation, and embraces the law of grace—his own higher self, the God within, the I AM.

If man conditions the realisation of his desires to external conditions, he is adulterating his thoughts. If he conditions the realisation of his desire to money, other influences, or his own intellect, he is adulterating his thoughts. He is implying that what God put in his heart is not enough. When we put away our highest ideal and marry another, such as dependency on external influences or people instead of the God within, we commit adultery.

The belief in a distant God, a God who watches from a distance as His people suffer and cry out to Him with no response, is an adulterated concept of God. It hardens our hearts. Embracing grace is a shift from fear-based religion to the freedom that Christ came so we may have. [Gal. 5:1] The belief that we must beg God as though He is withholding good from us is also an adulterated concept of God. It does not yield much. God does not withhold anything from us.

'For the Lord God is a sun and shield: The Lord will give grace and glory, no good thing will he withhold from them that walk uprightly' Psalm 84:11

We walk 'uprightly' when we have the right concept of God and know where we stand with him. We are sons to him, and everything he has is ours. He calls us to 'come to the waters and drink freely'. He gives of himself to us freely and fully, without price:

'Come ye and buy wine and milk without money and without price.' Isaiah 55:1

The only price for divine gifts is the right concept of God and the right belief—faith. If you have the wrong concept of something, your faith in it will false or blind because you do not have full awareness of what you believe in. The disciples, hearing Jesus' answers to the Pharisees said to Him, "If the case of the man be so with his wife, it is not good to marry." The disciples here are our attitudes of mind, our twelve faculties. These are not disciplined in most cases and are governed by our worldviews.

So, the natural man (worldly man) cannot understand that what he marries is a state of consciousness, his own mental concept. 'But the natural man receives not the things of the spirits of God, neither can he perceive them, because they are spiritually discerned.'

Spiritually, man's wife is that which he is conscious of being, his dominant mental attitude. The conscious state in which man dwells is his wife or the mother of his children. The children are his affairs, finances, health, and all that pertains to him.

When he looks out into the world and sees dysfunction — the divorce rate, the separation and the unhappiness, the lack, the economy, etc and says it is better not to marry, he fails to understand that he attracts to himself a wife conditioned exactly upon his inner conviction. Jesus then said to them, "All men cannot receive this saying, save they, to whom it is given." [Matthew 19:11] Not all people can see this truth.

Many people believe in luck, good luck or bad luck, confidence or lack of it, etc. To them, life is a game of chance. Jesus, in conclusion to His answer, talked about eunuchs. Eunuchs represent our desires, concepts and ideals that are asleep or dead within us. We are eunuchs when we fail to realise them. God put them in our hearts and knows we have what it takes to realise them. When we come to the end of our lives having not realised our ideal, which simply means to bring our vision or highest goal into reality, we die like mere mortals as we saw earlier. [Psalm 82:6-7]

We are here to radiate love, peace and joy, not just at Christmas but at all times. As sons and daughters of the Most High, we are here to express Him in thought, words and deeds. We must let our light shine before all men, that they too may come to the realisation of the truth and be made free [Matt. 5:16]. Because of fear and false beliefs, many people lose the capacity to create spiritually and to realise their God-given desires. They become slaves to conditions, traditions, and wrong beliefs. We are told to 'come out from among them', to know who we are and to shed the radiance of the light within, all around us.

Marriage on the physical plane symbolises the spiritual union of two souls seeking their way back to the heart of Reality, which is Love. God is Love, and the Reality of us all. Love gives. It frees. It forgives, and it does not condemn or keep a record of wrong. We must not blame God for the attack we are witnessing on marriage around the world. Instead, let us discover the true impersonal love, the divine love, so marriage will be a happy union.

As the subconscious mind is subjective to the conscious mind, the wife whose husband's love is lavished on her naturally subjects to him. In the same way, when we acknowledge the power that works in us and live in that consciousness, our lives are naturally transformed.

Knowing we are all one and more importantly who we are, let us be careful not to despise God in human form. He is the person you walk past every day in the streets, the homeless man or child in the streets who is always hungry or that patient in hospital who no one visits, or even the scruffy looking old man or woman in prison. Consider these statement, 'I was hungry, and you gave Me something to eat, I was thirsty, and you gave Me a drink. I was naked and you clothed Me." [Matt. 25:35] When did you see God hungry, thirsty or naked? Think about it.

Man's Mind versus Christ's Mind

What comes to your mind when you see these words by Jesus, 'Be ye perfect even as your Father is perfect?' [matt. 5:48] Our natural thinking sees this as a call to be flawless in conduct, which then becomes a contradiction as it is impossible for anyone to be flawless or to live without mistakes, but Jesus was not talking about human perfection but spiritual.

He was not talking about doing everything right but thinking from a higher realm, seeing with the single eye of the spirit, which sees all things as perfect and good. He was talking about living from unity with the Spirit within and acting from compassion and not judgement. Being perfect in his eyes is to think with the mind of Christ.

We saw earlier that the single eye sees no duality, meaning it does not see as the human eye sees. The human eye sees things as good or bad, but the spiritual eye sees all good. This perfection is spiritual vision. It is to look at other people and see beyond their physical form, their history or past mistakes. To look at what the natural mind perceives as disorder and see order. To not be bothered or perturbed by external conditions or physical appearances.

Ephesians 4:23 tells us to be renewed in the spirit of our minds, to put off the former conversations, the old man, which is corrupt and put on the new man, which, after God is created in righteousness and true holiness. That new man is the inner man, the spirit of God within. [Eph. 4:20-24] Perfection is not earned or built, it is recognised. It is already within us, we just recognise it and align with it.

When Paul talks about renewing our minds so that we may know what God's perfect will is [Roms. 12.2], he is not talking about changing the superficial ideas but elevating the entire consciousness. To cease from thinking from limitation and start thinking from abundance and power. To cease from identifying with the physical and start identifying with the spirit. To think, speak and act from our union with God.

When he says that we have the mind of Christ [1 Cor. 2:16], he means that we have the consciousness of Christ, and that consciousness is what makes us perfect because our spiritual vision purifies the physical form (body). As our inner vision is the cause of our outer experience, we must choose which eye we want to see through because what we see we believe, and what we believe we bring to life.

The human mind is full of contradiction, we trust and doubt at the same time. We love and hate, we desire peace and cause conflict, we claim to have faith yet feed fear, which attracts doubts negating the very faith we claim. We have a divided mind which the Bible calls carnal mind; 'For to be carnally minded is death; but to be spiritually minded is life and peace.' [Roms. 8:6] To choose life and peace, all we need is to choose or decide to see through the single eye.

Your life experience is very much dependent on the eye through which you are seeing, hence the words, 'You will know them by their fruits'. [Matt 7:16] Jesus used the single eye, that is why He could look at a lepper and see a healthy and clean man despite them being regarded as unclean. He could look at a tax collector and see a disciple, and the woman caught in adultery and see a dignified, forgiven and whole being.

He looks on the inside while the human eye looks on the outside. [1 Sam 16:7] When our eye is single, the body responds. When you see only good, tension ceases, the body systems are ordered i.e., the nervous system relaxes, digestion improves, and vital energy is restored. This is because the body no longer reacts from hurt or perceived threats but responds from love and peace. The mind is relaxed and at peace.

The energy that was lost in the internal battle and

conflict now flows like a river without obstruction. Your life becomes more harmonious and health flows freely because the gifts of God flow where the mind is at rest. This rest enables you to remain calm in high pressure situations because you now perceive things differently. Your composed energy allows you to navigate complexities with ease and face challenges without being consumed by them.

You begin to realise that life is not random but a reflection of the mind. Rather than live anticipating threats, you live with a consciousness that is clear, loving, secure and grateful. You trust more, instead of holding on to control. Everything in you becomes an expression of the union with the spirit within.

The carnal mind cannot sustain this state. It tires, distrusts and fragments. It starts to fall back into the old habits of comparison, fear and anticipating threats. The Christ mind can remain in this communion effortlessly because it does not depend on willpower but on surrender, and one who has surrendered to the will of the Spirit within lives in communion with God even without saying a word.

Jesus lived in continuous prayer, not because He was always on His knees or asking from the Father but because he was one with Him, acted from divine inspiration, and did nothing that was not born from His union with the source. He did not think of faith as something to be activated only in extreme cases but lived in this state of mind continuously. His faith was His way of seeing, feeling, acting and interpreting things.

He spoke and did everything in faith, not as a belief in the results but as certainty in the presence. It is this faith He invites us to embrace, not to admire from a far, but to live from within. This is what He is teaching us by asking us to be perfect, a call to express what is already perfect. This is the faith that transforms lives and transcends limitations.

CHAPTER TEN

Beauty for Ashes

The power that binds up the broken and proclaims liberty to the captives.

There will be difficulties and troubles in life, and sometimes disaster and heartbreak. Yet by calling upon the power within, it is possible to rise from the ashes stronger, wiser and better through experience. We are destined for greatness. We may not see it when there are obstacles obstructing our view in the form of challenges, but we have a deeper 'knowing' that needs no proof, that what we see now is not all there is.

Our five senses only allow us to see half the reality. There are infinite possibilities in the spirit realm, which can only be perceived or seen through the eyes of the spirit — the ability to see through this eye is the power to overcome. It helps see that there is a solution to every problem, that nothing is fixed or permanent. We attain wisdom and character through overcoming, what Isaiah calls beauty for ashes in this scripture:

> 'The spirit of the Lord is upon me because the Lord has appointed me to preach good tidings unto the meek; to bind up the broken-hearted, to proclaim

149

liberty to the captives and the opening of the prison to them that are bound... To give them beauty for ashes.' Isaiah 61:1-3

Happiness and true success depend on how we meet or deal with the troubles and difficulties we encounter. Adversity comes to us all; no one is immune to them, not even the richest or the greatest, but if it's met correctly, even the worst of them can be the stepping stone to success and freedom. It can be the doorway to something magnificent. The ultimate aim of life is to attain wisdom through experience. This cannot be achieved by giving in to the challenges and difficulties and letting them break us, but by overcoming them.

There are no promises that life will be smooth and without obstacles, but there is a promise that we shall overcome and move past them. No matter what comes our way, we always find strength that comes from within to overcome. We get frustrated when we fail to realise or to remember that our help is within and look outside for it.

In the book of Psalms, David says, 'I will lift up my eyes unto the hills, from whence my help comes.' One may then argue that our help comes from the hills or mountains or even the skies. But we must remember that David lived in the days of the Old Covenant. Hills and mountains were seen as places of strength, refuge and divine encounter. On Mount Sinai, Moses received the law and Mount Zion symbolised God's dwelling.

Because the Old Covenant was physical, a high ground represented physical safety in times of danger. He however makes it clear that his help comes from the Lord, the Creator of everything including the hills. David, as we saw earlier, foreshadowed the New Covenant in that, though he lived in the Old Covenant, his relationship with God went deeper than merely law keeping; there was intimacy and unwavering trust.

Many people today are seeking an easy life, free from suffering and care. They have not found it and will probably not because they often look in the world. They look for security in high paying jobs thinking that securing enough money will give them security. Life is a paradox. As much as we all want happiness and spend a lot of time and resources in its pursuit, its attainment is not the object of life. When we attain the object of life, we find happiness.

The object of life is the building of character through which we obtain wisdom. This only happens through experience; how would you appreciate safety if you never experienced insecurity? How would you appreciate good health if you never knew sickness? Rather than seek a life free from difficulties, it is more beneficial to learn to overcome them. Those who realise they have the power of the infinite within them by which they can rise above any challenge, overcome their weaknesses, and, through victorious experiences, gain wisdom and character are the ones who receive the promise.

The promise is to overcome and not to never have problems. What used to be a challenge becomes beauty, what once caused you pain becomes a source of strength and courage to go further — courage to withstand whatever comes your way and to have the assurance that you will rise above it stronger and better for it.

> 'And they shall build the old wastes; they shall rise up the former desolations, and they shall repair their waste cities.' Isaiah 61:4

This is the promise. It is not possible to sail through life without any difficulties whatsoever. It would defeat the purpose. Those who are ignorant of life's true purpose and seek happiness and pleasure fail to find it. On the other hand, those who recognise the true purpose of life and follow it, find happiness and pleasure, without necessarily looking for it. It comes to them when they are busy living their life joyfully, with gratitude and purpose.

God is, to many, a go-to when the going gets tough, in times of sadness, loss, mourning or when disasters strike. They go to Him when they want something; they will even ask for prayers, but when all is calm, and there is no need or want, God becomes something they are ashamed of. There is no easy life except for a strong soul who has overcome. His life appears easy because he draws strength from within. He has gained wisdom and character from his experiences through overcoming.

He has also learned that real happiness comes through service, that when he serves others, with or without reward, he finds happiness and fulfilment. Happiness, therefore, comes through service and overcoming. Serving others doesn't have to be for free. Many people are paid to create products that make other people's lives easier or better. They use their skills, talents or knowledge to serve others, and they are rewarded for it.

There is joy and satisfaction in being of service to others, joy is a higher form of happiness. It is the next level of happiness. It comes with the conquest of one's nature. If you were short-tempered or judgemental, for example, and have overcome the habits (traded your ashes for beauty), you have conquered your nature. The conquest of one's nature is a climb to higher and better things, where old habits die and weak points in character are strengthened and rebuilt.

It is a road to liberty and freedom, and there is no limit to the upward climb. The notion that those who serve are lesser beings, for example is something to overcome or conquer. Even Christ, being God, humbled himself and served others. [Phil. 2:6-7] This high road leads to realisation that behind this world of shadows is the real spiritual world of splendour and joy. That joy comes through realising our oneness with the Divine Source.

When a soul finally finds its way back to its Source, it becomes aware of this intense joy, a joy too marvellous for description and too wonderful for comprehension. It not only realises that the reality of life is love and joy but also that the universe is filled with tremendous love and quiet joy, only to be experienced in stillness and in confidence. [Isaiah. 30:15]

The one who possesses this quiet joy can never be defeated in life's battles and challenges. He has something within him that can never be quenched, and which will lead him from victory to victory. He begins to see the supernatural working of God in his life and miraculous synchronicities. His intuition becomes sharper and more reliable as he gives up all selfish striving.

To finite reasoning and logic, yielding to the will of the Infinite may seem foolish or an act of weakness, yet it is the door to a life of boundless power, peace and joy. No man is separate from his Divine Source, nor has any man ever been. Man has always been one with the Infinite right from the beginning. The separation that he feels and experiences is mental, it is only in the mind.

It is important therefore to emphasise strengthening our mental faculty with right believing, right thinking, and right expression. Man can never be separated from spirit, for he himself is spirit. He has a soul which makes him an integral part of one complete whole: the Divine. He may feel alone from time to time, but he's never alone. This feeling is only in his thoughts and beliefs and not in reality, but so long as he believes he's alone, he will be weak and helpless, just as though he was alone and separated. As soon as he realises the truth of his relationship with the Infinite, he regains his power.

If a man thinks he is a mere material being, he lives the limited life of a material being and can never rise above it. His whole life becomes about the pursuit of material gains, but if, he believes he is a spiritual being, then he finds that he possesses all the powers of a spiritual being. He neither gets disqualified for the time he spent chasing things that were meant to follow him, nor does he lose his right to what was always his.

This truth is beautifully captured in the parable of the prodigal son. The younger son took his inheritance and ran after everything he thought would make him fulfilled — wealth, freedom, pleasure. But when it all turned to ashes and he found himself empty and alone, he made his way back home. Instead of punishment, he was met by a father who run toward him, embracing him like he had done nothing wrong. He may have anticipated rejection, but he was met with restoration instead.

He did not lose his sonship because he wandered. His father didn't revoke his inheritance because he wasted it. He reinstated him fully, adorning him with a robe, ring, and a big feast to celebrate his return. This is what happens to us when we find our way back home. Back to our source, our Father. He reminds us who we are. The prodigal son's story is not about how far we fall, but about how deep the Father's love runs — a love that refuses to disqualify us, even when we disqualify ourselves.

Life's challenges can cause us to forget who we are, or even disqualify ourselves. Elijah the great prophet of the Old Testament, whom God used to do mighty things in his time, including raising a young boy back to life and calling down fire from heaven, found himself in a cave having run away because someone had threatened to kill him. In the cave, he asked God to take his life. He had had enough. God fed him and asked him to go on a journey that took him many days and nights. He wanted to speak to him at Horeb, 'the mountain of God' — Mount Sinai.

This is the same mountain where Moses had received the commandments. On this mountain, God had presented Himself in fire, thunder and lightning, and a thick cloud that made the mountain tremble. This time, a powerful wind tore through the rocks, but God was not in it. It was followed by an earthquake, but God was not in the earthquake. Then came fire, but He was not in the fire. Finally, after all that had passed, 'there was a still small voice'. [1 Kings 19:12]

Elijah was used to God appearing in dramatic manifestations, but this time He was in the stillness. He reassured Elijah, who had felt alone when he went into hiding. He led him to connect with others who shared his vision, and his life changed from that moment. He no longer feared the woman he was running away from, Jezebel, instead, he prophesied her death, and it happened just as he had prophesied. He did not have to kill her or hide from her. God gave him beauty for ashes, the oil of joy for mourning.

Some years back, during lockdown, an agency I was working with as mentioned earlier sent a number of us to a neighbouring country to support vulnerable people in a residential home. Most of the staff had contracted the virus (Coronavirus) and had to isolate. The home had converted a section of the property to cater for staff, enabling us to lodge there.

Among the residents we looked after was a lady called Lorna. She was eighty years old, partially blind and had been diagnosed with dementia. She repeated the same thing over and over about her brother and his wife, who had been found dead in their house, and a large amount of money found buried in the backyard. It sounded like something you would see in a movie. There was no way of telling whether it was true or not, but she got very emotional when she talked about it, which was every few minutes. It broke my heart.

We tried to distract her with activities, but she could not concentrate on anything for long. She was always on her feet. The residents were all vulnerable in different ways and our job was to ensure they were safe and slept well throughout the night. One night, Lorna would not sleep despite our best efforts to reassure her, and did not want to be left alone in her room. We alternately sat with her in her room encouraging her to go to sleep.

Realising that she wasn't going to sleep, we invited her to join us in the lounge where we sat watching a TV show. Within no time she was on her feet. I walked with her back to her room and sat with her for hours talking about her childhood, which she vividly remembered like it was just yesterday. We looked at pictures of her family, some of whom she remembered and others not. She had no memory of her children and grandchildren.

She remembered growing up, her parents, her only brother and childhood friends. Her latest memory was about her only brother and his wife, who were found dead in their house. She had known the brother's wife since they were young as they all grew up together. It was very sad that she had no recent memory past the brother's tragic death. I wished I could magically or miraculously wipe out that memory and replace it with those of her children and grandchildren. I remember silently praying for her.

When she wasn't talking about the brother, she was a very happy and pleasant person to talk to. We talked about a lot of things, including my children. Sleep was nowhere in the horizon for Lorna. It was 2 am and I was beginning to feel sleepy and tired. I turned her TV on and hoped the noise would lull her to sleep or at least tire her out. I then tried to sneak out of the room as she wouldn't let me leave.

As I gently closed the door behind me, I heard her call out to me. 'Is your mother alive?' she asked. She wanted to talk a about my mother at 2 in the morning. We talked a little about my mother who was in perfect health at the time. She asked where she lived and what she did. I told her that she was a teacher and had retired and opened a school, not far from where I grew up. We then talked a little about my growing up and that seemed bring more memories of her own childhood. She told me about her favourite teacher before I insisted that I had to leave, and she must stay in bed.

Several years later, I was walking with my mother, then walking with a walking stick after suffering a stroke when suddenly my conversation with Lorna that night came to mind. I had not thought about her or the conversation since leaving the residential home. I remembered how I had tried to sneak out of her room and how I had eventually left. I wondered about her, a part of me feeling bad that I had left her when she did not want to be alone.

I wondered why she couldn't sleep that night and why she had asked about my mother in particular. That brief moment allowed me to see what I had not seen back then. Though I had compassion for Lorna and the other residents, I lacked empathy. I could never have known what it felt like to be in their position but seeing my mother walking with a stick as Lorna did brought her memory to my mind. With the memory came lessons I should have learned back then. It opened my eyes to something I had been blind to all those years. As far as I was concerned, I was there to do a job, which I did to the best of my ability.

Sometimes we may think we are where we are just to make a few bucks and pay the bills, but that is not always the case. Sometimes we are strategically placed there to learn things that we need to learn or to gain experience we might need in future. Empathy was the lesson for me. Empathy is not just about feeling sorry for someone or trying to fix things for them like I wished I could help Lorna erase her painful memory. It's recognising what others are going through and offering comfort, what Jesus called rejoicing with those who rejoice and weeping with those who weep. [Romans. 12:15]

He was not only talking about compassion, but compassion with empathy as opposed to sympathy. It is about setting aside assumptions and stepping into someone else's experience, to see through their eyes or walk in their shoes. Sometimes we judge when we ought to show empathy. As a poet would say, the eyes that squint once sparkled with childhood wonder, and the hands that now tremble once held babies.

Life is a cycle, and we must honour every cycle, learn from them and prepare for them, just as a farmer prepares for planting and harvesting. All seasons are equally important though different. Everything that happens in life comes with a lesson or lessons, which we must be open and receptive to rather than feel helpless or victimised. Rather than ask God why, we should ask ourselves, 'What lesson is here for me?' The sooner we learn the lesson, the quicker the issue is resolved, freeing us to move on to the next.

For every lesson learned, no matter how difficult, no matter how painful, there is beauty beneath the ashes. We do not always see it, but when we transcend the challenge, we understand the meaning of the words 'Joy comes in the morning'. Morning is daybreak when the darkness is gone, and we can see clearly. A farmer never mourns the dry season because he understands it's a cycle.

We must not feel powerless even in the darkest hour of the night because 'weeping may endure for a night, but joy comes in the morning.' [Psalm 30:5] Joy is the beauty that replaces the ashes. What looked like a waste can become a place of new growth and purpose. Our pain is never wasted, like Elijah in the cave, we find our strength when we disconnect from the noise and into that quiet place where we can hear the still small voice.

Thoughts can Make us Sick, and they can also Heal us

I read a lot of books in a space of about ten years — a time when I was struggling to control my emotions, something I have mentioned in a previous chapter. After a whole decade of trying to manage anger, I came across one of my old journals of dreams. For years I have kept journals of my dreams because I realised quite early that I dream more than most people and I wondered why. Though I write them down, rarely do I ever go back and read them.

At the beginning of 2023, I was moving house and as I was packing, deciding what's important and what's not, I came across this old journal going back to 2010. I opened it and noticed that some writing was highlighted, which made it easy to scheme through. They were all dated, showing the time as well. There was one dated 16 March 2012, which could have saved me so much anguish had I taken it to heart. As recorded, 'I heard a voice telling me that God had given me peace, but the devil was trying to steal it because his work is to steal, kill and destroy'.

It said I needed to guard the peace that was already in me. As you might already have guessed, I never give it much thought. It was shortly after that things happened that I could have controlled had I guarded my peace, as warned in the dream. I could have saved a decade worth of stress had I learned to be still and not allow the external noise to influence my internal state. It was in this space of time, doing everything I could to regain my balance that I came across the work of one of my all-time favourite author, Dr Joe Dispenza.

It's not every day you see a scientist who believes in God. Dr Dispenza is a neuroscientist, who has studied the brain for years. He believes in God's supernatural power to restore health without medical intervention. He believes the body has what it needs to heal itself because the intelligence that created it endowed it with everything necessary to sustain itself. Being a scientist, this might sound absurd, but he does not just talk the talk, he walks the talk. At age 23, he had a fatal accident during a bike race where he was knocked off his motorbike, bounced on the pavement and rolled for almost 20 feet.

He refused to undergo surgery. As a doctor, he knew exactly what needed to be done for him to ever walk again but decided against it, choosing to let his body heal itself. He believed in the power of mind and the body's ability to heal itself, and he was going to prove it. He strongly believed that the power within is greater than any other power outside. His family and educated friends, most of whom were doctors could not understand what was going on in his mind.

In one of his books he says, 'We simply have to get our educated minds out of the way and give a greater intelligence a chance to do what it does.' He continues to say, 'I call this intelligence God. Some people call it the universe, others divine consciousness, but I call it God.' The power of God that works within us. 'This innate intelligence runs through the central nervous system from the midbrain and the lower subcortical regions of the brain to the body,' he explains. This, according to him happens all day every day. With this conviction, his body took only three months to heal itself without medical intervention which was shorter than it would have taken to heal from surgery.

Dr Dispenza has written several books about the brain and has tried to answer some of the questions people ask, like why we remember things we don't want to remember and forget the important things we want to remember. During the time I was struggling with anger, I would forget important things like appointments and things I needed to do, but I could not get some things out of my mind that caused me pain. Having had this experience helps me relate with Lorna's struggle and also have a little understanding of what that might feel like. It never crossed my mind at the time.

Today Dr Dispenza holds seminars and conferences teaching people how to use the power within them to heal their bodies. Many times, we wait for God to do for us things that he has already given us power and authority over. This is not because we're lazy or ignorant, but because we do not know we have this power or that we can do these things. The greatest lesson we can learn when it comes to healing our bodies is to guard our minds and learn to block anything from the outside world that threatens to steal our peace.

Peace of mind is our most valuable treasure and the only way to maintain it is to ignore anything that does not align with our ideals. To resolve all issues as they come and to never go to bed angry. Anger is a destructive emotion. Nothing good comes from it. To heal our bodies, we must heal our emotions and to heal our emotions we must heal our thoughts.

CHAPTER ELEVEN

The Power of the Spirit

This is the victory that overcomes the world.

The power of the Spirit is far greater than the power of the subconscious mind. It is the power of the spirit of God, the superconscious mind or the supernatural power that is God's. This power is also man's as it works through him as love, joy, peace and all the things we know as the fruits of the Holy Spirit. It fills all space and is yet spaceless. It is the Infinite life.

The joy of the infinite life increases in proportion to the measure of expression of that life in the consciousness of those who partake and manifest it. Our willingness to express what is within opens doors to greater things, as the power of the spirit can never be quenched or depleted. The soul perpetually seeks to express its all-sufficiency. As we align ourselves with our soul's purpose, we become so deeply conscious of that desire that we begin to appreciate the true purpose of life.

We then realise that we do not secure power from things but can give power to things when we live in the Spirit. Through the same Spirit, we can manifest power in the external, in agreement with our consciousness of that power within. Rather than live our lives being controlled by the conditions, we control the conditions of our existence. In other words, instead of merely being alive, we begin to live life.

There is a difference between being alive and living life. When we are simply alive, we are conscious of life only in its passive or inactive state, but when we begin to live life, we discover that there is no limit to what we can be or become; life can go forth in many different directions. Life then becomes more interesting and purposeful. Almost every ambitious person is constantly looking for external advantages or better opportunities. We search for greater accomplishments, and to some extent, we find these accomplishments, albeit in a measure.

If we would first search for the greater power within, that is, the all-sufficiency of power, realising that every opportunity exists potentially in the life of the soul even now – the power desired would arise in the consciousness. Through this power within, every individual can create his own opportunities, privileges and channels of greater and richer expression. This is what seeking the kingdom of God first is all about. Everything we could ever want is available.

So long as we live in the world of things believing that we are subject to things and dependent on them, or that we can secure happiness, wisdom and power, or a richer life through acquiring material things, we cannot access this power. We secure certain desirable combinations of things in the external world only as we gain consciousness of the ideal of that combination in the internal world of the Spirit – the Real and the True. In other words, what we become conscious of, we bring forth in the visible world.

Being true to ourselves is of paramount importance because the inspiration to act comes from within, from the real and the true. You cannot fool your own conscience. It is only when we are true to our inner being that we become conscious of the all-sufficiency of the soul. On the contrary, we cannot be true to the self as long as we keep looking outside of ourselves for those things that the self alone can provide. By so doing, we 'grieve the Spirit'; we deny higher power, believing that we can find what our souls want in the world.

However, when we arrive at that higher consciousness where we realise that the 'All-in-All' is in the Spirit only, in the spiritual life of the supreme self, we no longer deny the Holy Spirit, (the Christ/the Infinite) we realise that this is the source of all life, the power that animates our being. The All in All.

When we accept the idea that the human soul, having everything necessary for life can need or lose nothing, we cannot be depressed or disappointed with external conditions, no matter how bad they may seem to be for the time being. The practical value of such an attitude, in the beginning, is to give us peace of mind no matter what transpires, but the taking of that high ground works wonders with time.

If we continue to live with the conviction that we have it all and that all is well, we will continue to create the perfect and the ideal in our consciousness, scaling it higher and grander every day, and whatever we create in our consciousness we will eventually experience or have in the external world. We have everything to gain by taking this higher ground now. When we enter the Spirit of all life, we find a state in which all being is as it is for all time, and in that state, we find the All in All – a state to which nothing can be added or taken away.

Everything existing in or pertaining to the spirit is in itself complete. The soul is spiritual and, therefore, contains within itself everything necessary to the life and external existence of the soul (a soul needs a body to exist externally, a host/temple). Our body and mind are incomplete, and this is true of everything finding expression in the external world. It is necessary, therefore, to go to the inner or spiritual source of everything, health, wholeness, vitality, life, power, etc. as there, we secure the finest and most perfect conceivable quality.

Though the external expression may be incomplete or imperfect, the inner source is complete and perfect. The external can continue to draw from the internal for an endless period, constantly receiving without exhausting the source of supply. You can never exhaust the Spirit, no matter how much you take from it. This dynamic is demonstrated by Elijah and the widow who had very little to sustain her and her son. [1 Kings 17:7-16]

The poor woman was out gathering firewood to cook their last meal as there was a famine and had only a little flour and oil in a jar. The prophet asked her for water and bread, and she responded saying she had only enough for herself and her son, after which they would both starve to death. Elijah promised her that neither the flour nor the oil would get used up. The poor woman did as the prophet asked, she made bread for him with the little flour and oil she had left, and it so happened that it never got used up. The oil kept running and so did the flour. The more they used them, the more they had left.

It took faith for someone with no source of supply to take the word of a stranger, especially concerning food during a famine. She prepared bread for him using the last bit of flour and oil, having no proof that it would not run out except the prophet's word. Her faith paid off. No matter how much or little we may have, whether in material wealth, spiritual or even emotional, we can always receive more from the Spirit within and continue to receive more without an end. The same spirit that worked through Elijah is working through us today when we allow it.

In those days, it was at work only through a handful of chosen people, the prophets, but today, it is available to everyone who cares to tap into it. We just need to look within and not without. The outer life is always incomplete, always growing, developing and advancing, while the inner life is constantly giving from its inexhaustible supply to increase the perfection, richness and worth of external life for any individual who's constantly bringing forth from the spirit within, the abundance of the life of the Spirit.

Such an individual is on a spiritual path that has no end. As he draws more and more from the spirit, he is transformed from the inside out, from 'glory to glory'.

> *'But we all, with open face beholding as in a glass the glory of the Lord, are changed into the same image from glory to glory, even as by the Spirit of the Lord.'*
> 2 Corinthians 3:18

We are all destined for greatness. We are destined to become conscious of the Spirit in due time and thereby begin the expression of the spiritual life through every phase of the external life; but as this is an endless process, no individual soul will come to a place of full expression of the spirit in external life. Though the word says we are gods, no one can fully express themselves as God in this physical life. If we should reach such a state, then life would stop, there would be nothing further to live for in the future. We would have nothing to learn, no hurdles to overcome and no more growth necessary.

There would be no purpose to life as the whole purpose of life is to evolve and become more like God. This process is an ongoing process. It's a journey most people discover towards the end of their lives. When we realise the full significance of life and its development, we find that we live in two worlds. These worlds constitute the great within and the great without.

The great within is the spiritual life, which is inexhaustible perfection and the great without is the external life, which is eternally receiving a greater and greater degree of expression from the spiritual, the great within. When we continue to live in the spiritual as much as we live in the physical, every moment becomes magnificent, more wonderful and harmonious because we are constantly drawing on the richness of the spiritual for a perpetual increase in the external.

There cannot be a greater joy than the consciousness of continuous ascension into the richer, the higher and the greater in life. This, I presume, is what Jesus prayed for when His human experience was coming to an end. He prayed to the Father, saying,

> *'I am coming to you now, but I say these things while I am still in the world, so that they may have the full measure of my joy within them.*
> *I have given them your word and the world has hated them, for they are not of the world any more than I am of the world... Sanctify them by the truth; your word is truth. As you sent me into the world, I have sent them into the world. For them I sanctify myself, that they too may be truly sanctified.*
>
> *I pray not only for them, but also for those who believe in me because of their message.'*
> John 17:13-20

We can choose to live in the spiritual world consciously, even though we are physically in the world. This is what it means to be 'in the world but not of the world'. The spiritual world is a state of consciousness. It can be accessed anytime, anywhere. In this state of consciousness, we enter the realisation of a world where all things are perfect and inexhaustible so that we may receive an ever-increasing measure of not only life but all the elements and qualities of life.

The key to the spiritual world is what we become conscious of in that realm of being, where all things are eternally perfect, absolute and divine. If, for example, we have ill health physically, we can go into our consciousness and access perfect health, perfect joy, or anything we may describe as full expression of harmony. When we feel overwhelmed and want to feel peaceful and calm, we should turn our attention towards the spirit within, which is our consciousness and realise the internal calm within.

Whenever we want harmony, we turn our attention to the spirit of harmony within and experience more and more of that state until it becomes our default state. For good health, instead of thinking about the body as it currently is, we turn our attention to the spirit of health, which exists in the soul within. Everything exists within in perfect expression. Because the soul is fully spirit, it cannot be sick.

We must know that health does not have its origin in the body. It is good to care for the body as best as we possibly can, but real health has its origin in the Spirit. Before the symptoms of a disease appear in the body, they have been cooking inside for a while. It all starts on the inside, in the mind. The deeper we go into the consciousness of wholeness, the more perfect and powerful its expression will be.

We must always remember that whatever we become conscious of in the inner world (within), that very thing we will manifest in the outer world (without). When searching for power, we must realise that its source is not found in the physical world or the mind. Its source exists in the spiritual world. As we become more and more conscious of real power in the spiritual world, we will not only grow in power but also in the consciousness of the spiritual world itself, which is our purpose in life.

Our continuous aim should be to find more of the wonderful gifts and qualities that exist within or at the source of all things — the supernatural world itself. This is where we find life in all its fullness. Life in all its fullness is the state where life is so perfect that nothing could be added to make it fuller or more complete. A state where peace is beyond all understanding [Phil. 4:7]; light is so brilliant it cannot get any brighter, and harmony is so perfect it could not get any better.

When we consider the real meaning of life in all its fulness, joy in all its fullness or health in all its fulness, we realise we are in the presence of unconceivable ideals, and the more deeply we enter the consciousness of these ideals, the closer we get to experiencing the supernatural.

CHAPTER TWELVE

The Heart of Surrender

My strength is made perfect in weakness

In everything we do, there is a power working behind the scenes. That does not mean we should slack off because someone is working behind the scenes. Our efforts and struggles are important, but there is a truth that there is something greater behind the scenes. If you have ever found yourself overwhelmed by life, wondering if you can keep going or if you will ever make it, it's important to know you are never alone, you never were. The truth is, there is a divine hand guiding you, and your part is to do your best.

Surrendering your plans to this hand can unlock a life filled with peace, purpose and provision. The world tells us that we must do everything ourselves, that we should make things happen by any means necessary. While there is truth in the importance of hard work and dedication, there is also a deeper truth that no matter how much we strive, no matter how much we achieve on our own, we cannot accomplish everything by our own strength.

The real key to success, fulfilment, and peace in this life is understanding there is a divine partner, a force beyond our understanding who is willing to work with us if we choose to do our part and trust him with the rest. We are all called not only to do our best but also to surrender the outcome to God. The great people we know from the past whose stories are recorded in the Bible did their part with all their hearts, and God stepped in and made the impossible happen.

He took their efforts, multiplied them and brought about results far greater than they could ever have achieved on their own. When we understand this, we realise that our best is enough, but only when we let God do the rest. This is the essence of faith, believing in his power, trusting in his timing and resting in his perfect will. When we look at the lives of great figures in the Bible, Moses, David, Daniel, Esther, Joseph, Gideon and many others, we see a pattern. They did not just sit back and hope for divine intervention. They took action. They did their best and when it came to the impossible, they relied on God's strength, wisdom and timing to bring them through.

We saw earlier how Moses delivered the Israelites from slavery. He only had to do his part and leave the rest to God. They all understood that they were not in control of every outcome, God was, and he was the one who would bring them to the place they needed to be. It is so easy to be caught up in the idea that we must do everything on our own, make every decision, push through every difficulty and fight every battle by ourselves.

The truth is, there is only so much we can control. We can control our actions, attitudes, and obedience, but we cannot control the world, the people around us or the future. That's why it is crucial to understand the power of partnership with God. When we do our best, he does the rest. Even Gideon, only had to do his part, God caused confusion in the camp of his enemies which resulted in them killing each other before Gideon's army of three hundred men arrived. He did not lift a finger to fight them.

It's okay to surrender. It's okay to know that you are not carrying the burden alone. You don't have to have all the answers. You don't have to have everything figured out or to fix everything. The God who works in and through you has the power to intervene, to open doors and to close others, to change circumstances and to bring you through situations that seem impossible.

But you must trust him. You must let go of the fear that says you have to do it alone and step into the freedom that comes from knowing God is with you every step of the way. When we talk about doing our best, it is not just about striving harder or working more, it's about being faithful with what God has given us. Sometimes our best might not look good enough in the eyes of the world. It might not bring immediate success or instant results, but when we are faithful in the small things, God sees our hearts and multiplies our efforts in ways beyond our comprehension.

In the parable of the talents, Jesus reminds us that God rewards faithfulness, not necessarily hard work. If we do our best and offer it to him, he is faithful to take what we give and make it more and bigger than what we could ever have imagined. Gideon, if you remember his story was not a very brave man. He was hiding when an angel appeared to him. Because he obeyed, he won the battle and secured freedom for his people without having to fight or kill anyone. His enemies' army of more than a hundred thousand soldiers killed each other.

The struggle many of us face is that we think doing our best means achieving perfection, but God never asks for perfection. He asks for our best. Our best comes from a heart that is surrendered to him. We may fall short of our goal, but when our efforts are offered with faith, they become part of God's plan. The story of the widow who gave an offering of two small copper coins shows us that it is not about how much we give but how much of our heart is in it.

When we give our best, no matter how small or insignificant it seems, God can multiply it and use it for his glory like he multiplied five loaves and two fish to feed a crowd of over five thousand people. The story of David and Goliath is another good example. When David was called to be king, he did not have any qualifications that could have been considered in that situation. He was just a shepherd boy. He spent his days in the field looking after goats, no one paid him attention. But he gave his best in the field, protecting his father's sheep with all he had.

He learned to trust God in the quiet moments when no one was watching. When the time came for him to face Goliath, he did not hesitate. He did not try to do it in his own strength. Instead, he said the battle was the Lord's. 'You come to me with a sword and a javelin, I come to you in the name of the Lord of hosts.' He placed his trust in God's power. He did his part. He slung the stone, but it was God who brought down the giant. David knew that his best was enough because he trusted that God would do the rest, and He did.

In the same way, God is asking us to give our best in everything we do, whether it's in our jobs, relationships, ministries or our daily activities, and once we have done our part, we must release the rest into his hands. There is peace that comes from releasing control and not being attached to the outcome. We cannot control the outcomes, but we can trust that God who works through us will work everything together for our good. This is the peace that the Apostle Paul talked about when he said,

> *'Be anxious for nothing, but in everything by prayer and supplication, with thanksgiving, let your requests be made known to God; and the peace of God, which surpasses all understanding, will guard your hearts and minds through Christ Jesus.'*
> Philippians 4:6-7

This peace comes when we stop trying to control everything and allow God to take over. When we do our best and let God do the rest, we enter a divine partnership that brings peace, hope and confidence. It is not about doing more, striving harder or being perfect, it's about doing what we can and leaving the results to God. This is where true freedom is found.

The story of the apostle Peter walking on water provides another profound lesson in doing our best, being obedient and trusting God with the impossible. When Jesus asked Peter to get out of the boat and into the water, Peter did not ask how; he stepped out of the boat and into the water with his eyes fixed on Jesus. He began to walk on water. It was only when he took his eyes off Jesus and looked around that he began to sink. His mind moved from focusing on object of his desire to the conditions around him.

Jesus did not condemn him for his failure to focus. He reached out and caught him saying, 'You of little faith, why did you doubt?' Doubt, as we saw earlier, is the thief who comes for no other reason but to steal our faith. So, in asking why did you doubt, Jesus was simply saying, you allowed the thief to steal your faith. The absence of faith is unbelief, so in that moment, Peter failed because of unbelief. The moment he began to doubt, he blocked the gift that Jesus wanted him to have, the experience of walking on water as He did, reinforcing His statement, 'If you believe, you can do the things that I do'.

What's sad is that Peter believed. But, like any of us, once he focused on the 'problem', the thief seized the opportunity to do what he does best. The lesson here is clear. When we take our eyes off God and focus on our abilities or the circumstances around us, we become disempowered. But when we do our part, maintaining the awareness that it is not us, but the power of God working through us, we will sail through.

Our faith is strengthened when we do our best and perfected when we rest. This partnership requires trust, and trust is built over time. As you continue to do your best in every area of your life, God continues to work behind the scenes, orchestrating things you cannot see yet. He makes ways where there seems to be none. Just as he made a way in the dessert and provided for the Israelites in the wilderness, he will do the same for you. You can rest in the assurance that your efforts are never in vain. He that promised to take care of you is faithful and will hold his end.

There is power in surrendering your plans, your dreams and your efforts to him. It is only then that you will experience his provision, his timing and his blessings in ways you never could have imagined. He never sleeps. He is able to do 'exceedingly, abundantly, above all that we ask or think', and he does it all according to the power that works in us. [Eph. 3:20]

Notice the last few words of the above statement, 'according to the power that works in us.' His power is already in us. The decision to surrender to this inner power is not a one-time decision but a daily choice, a lifestyle that we must adopt if we are to experience the fullness of God's provision and peace. This is why we must cultivate a heart of surrender, a heart that continually trusts God in every situation.

The world expects us to be self-sufficient, to take control and to trust in our abilities alone. We are constantly pushed to perform, to be independent and to prove ourselves worthy of success, but in God's kingdom, true strength is found in surrender. We must adopt Jesus' attitude. Even though He was the Son of God, he knew he could do nothing on his own,

> *'I can of mine own self do nothing: as I hear, I judge; and my judgment is just because I seek not mine own will, but the will of the Father which hath sent me.'*
> John 5:30

The more we try to hold on to control, the longer we carry unnecessary weight and burdens that God never intended for us to carry. The more we insist on doing it all ourselves, the less we make room for God to move in our lives.

This is why the call to surrender is not a sign of weakness but rather a sign of strength, a sign of trust in the one who is far greater than us. It is human nature to want to take matters into our own hands and to control the outcome. We want to make sure everything works out exactly as we envision it, but the Bible teaches us that our thoughts are not God's thoughts, and our ways are not His ways. His plan for us is far greater than anything we could ever imagine, greater than anything we can ask or think.

We are limited by our understanding, but God is not. He knows things we do not have a clue about. He knows what the future holds; we don't. When we let go of the need to control every situation, we allow him to do something far beyond what we could ever achieve on our own. Our best is never wasted when we entrust it to God. No effort, no act of faith, and no prayer is ever in vain. God sees it all, and He works behind the scenes in ways we cannot always comprehend.

Take the story of Joseph in the Bible, for instance; Joseph did his best to remain faithful even in betrayal, slavery and imprisonment. He did everything right, and yet his circumstances seemed to go in the opposite direction. We see that happening all the time, it does not mean that God has forgotten about us or is not aware of our efforts and good intentions.

He saw everything that Joseph was going through. He saw him remain steadfast in faith, not allowing his circumstances to dictate his inner state. He saw him refuse to give up on His promises or his own ideals. Even in prison, he continued to do his best. Ultimately, God elevated him to a place of great influence.

His story of betrayal and elevation is a powerful reminder that our efforts are never in vain even when they seem to go unnoticed. Even when nothing seems to make sense, God is working all things together for our good. Nothing in Joseph's early life made sense. He was sold as a slave by his own brothers, who made his parents believe he was dead. He later spent years in prison for a crime he did not commit, all for being a dreamer. His brothers hated him because he was a dreamer.

Joseph's life teaches us that sometimes, our best may not immediately lead to success or recognition, but it is always a part of God's greater plan. We may not see the immediate results of our effort and hard work, but God sees it, and in his perfect timing, he will make a way for us. This is where trust comes in, trusting that God is always at work even when we can't see the outcome. Trusting that he will take our best actions and make them greater than we could ever have imagined.

The challenge is not in doing our best but in trusting God with the results. We are good at doing what we do, but not so good at releasing control. Another important aspect of this truth is the understanding that God's timing is perfect. We may think we know when something should happen or how it should happen, but God's timing is always better than our own. His ways are higher than our ways and his timing always perfect, never early or late.

There may be times when we are impatient or frustrated, but we must hold on to the truth that He knows exactly when to bring things to fruition. The key to peace in the waiting is understanding that we are not in control of everything. There is a peace that comes when we learn to be grateful in the waiting, not from knowing everything will work out exactly how we planned it, but rather from knowing that God is in control, and he is good.

Being convinced of his goodness, we know that the outcome will be for our good. It may not always be what we expect it to be because he knows better than we do, and he sees what we cannot see. This peace is a result of fully surrendering to his will and trusting that he knows what is best for us. Most people struggle with anxiety because of the need to control every aspect of their lives.

This need for control makes them worry about what they cannot control like the future, the economy, what happens in the world, to their families or loved ones etc.

They feel like they need to hold things together all the time lest they fall apart. But Jesus tells us not to worry about tomorrow, for tomorrow will worry about itself. [Mathew 6:34] Also, worrying doesn't add any value to us or make anything better. 'Which of you by taking thought can add one cubit unto his stature?' Mathew 6:27.

Each day comes with enough trouble of its own, but we choose to live in the present by doing what we can at that moment and leaving the results to God. We don't need to carry the weight of tomorrow; God will take care of it when tomorrow comes. This is the freedom that comes with surrender. Today, people are worrying about everything: disease, politics, economy, and the future of everything, which is causing a lot of stress.

Stress, in turn, causes 'dis-ease', which negatively affects a lot of things, even the economy. It becomes a vicious cycle with no apparent solution. Instead of going down that path, it is better and wiser to learn to trust God more each day and to rely on his strength, his timing, his plan and his guidance.

In this life, we will face challenges, we will experience setbacks, and we will encounter difficulties. There is no escaping that, but if we hold on to the truth that God is always with us and that He is always working on our behalf, we can face these challenges with confidence and peace. We can trust our inner voice of intuition more and act on inspirations from within rather that look to the world with anxiety.

Paul, though a great man of faith and one who God used greatly, had his good share of troubles. He talks about a particular challenge, which he refers to as a 'thorn in the flesh'. Three times he asked God to take it away, God said to him, 'My grace is sufficient for you, for my strength is made perfect in weakness.' [2 Cor. 12:9] It is in our weakness that God's power is made perfect.

That may not make much sense, but it is in our weakness that God's greatness shines through the most. Look at it this way, if you light a candle in the day no one will see it, but if you light it in the dark, its light will shine so brightly

177

everyone will see it. It is in our darkest moments that we have the best insights and clarity. It is also then that we realise that our own wisdom and ability are not enough. It is usually in those dark moments when we sit with ourselves long enough to discover that inner strength we never knew we had, the power of God within us.

It's in those moments that we are most likely to withdraw from the busyness of life and the noises around us and be still. In that stillness, we are told, is where we find strength. 'In quietness and in confidence shall your strength be.' Isaiah 30:15. In letting go, we allow God to take control and do what only He can do. This is not about passivity; it's about actively participating in God's plan while trusting Him with the outcome. It's about doing everything we can with the resources and abilities God has given us and leaving the results in his hands.

When we embrace this truth, we experience a deep sense of peace and freedom and no longer carry the heavy burden of trying to hold things together or controlling the outcome. We instead trust that God will bring about what is best for us in his time, and we rest in this promise. This is the kind of life that God desires for us: a life of faith, trust, and peace, knowing that we are not alone in our efforts.

As we live this life, let us remember it's not about striving for perfection but being faithful with what God has given us. His plans are greater than ours, and his power is more than enough to bring about the transformation we need.

Choosing faith over fear

A surrendered life is a life of faith, and faith is not simply a feeling or a belief but an active stance we take in our lives. Faith is something we choose to walk in every day, especially when it feels like the world is pushing us to hold on tighter to what we have, to control every detail and to find our own way out of the challenges we face.

When we choose faith, we choose to trust God, not because we understand everything or because we see the end from the beginning, but because we believe in the one who knows all things and holds all things in his hands. Our role is to do our best and rest, knowing God will bring to pass what we have committed to him. The story of Abraham in the Bible is one of the most powerful demonstrations of this principle.

Abraham had faith in God, he trusted him fully, and for this, God called him his friend. He was called by God to leave his homeland and go to a place he did not know. God promised to make him father of many nations. The path to that promise was not easy. He faced uncertainties, challenges and had moments where his faith was tested, yet he chose to do his best in following God's instructions. He also trusted him with the outcome. He had no idea how God would fulfil the promise, but he walked in faith, trusting that God would take care of the details.

God responded faithfully and did everything He had promised to do. His story encourages us to trust God even when we don't have all the answers. It tells us that faith is not about understanding every step or knowing every outcome. It is about believing that God is good, that he is faithful, and that he is more than able to deliver on his promise. When we give our all, we are not relying on our strength but on his.

This is where the power of God is revealed in our hearts. The process of surrendering control can feel uncomfortable but when we release our grip on things, we open ourselves to the possibilities we never knew existed. This requires humility and openness to God's plan, and a willingness to let go of the need to know how everything will unfold.

The Book of Proverbs tells us to trust in God with all our hearts and not to lean on our own understanding. 'In all your ways, acknowledge him and he will make your paths straight.' [Proverbs 3:5-6] When we do this, we are acknowledging that his wisdom is greater than ours. We may not always understand how he is leading us, but we can trust that his path is the best one. When we let Him guide us, we invite his supernatural power to work in our lives.

This is where God takes our small, imperfect efforts and turns them into something extraordinary—it is when miracles happen in our lives. The paradox of Christian life and letting go is that we receive more when we are resting, having done our best. When we are striving and holding on, nothing happens. It is in the 'rest' where we begin to see the transformative power of faith.

When we rest in surrender, we become vessels for God's power. Our efforts, no matter how small, are magnified by his grace. This is not just a principle; it is a way of life, a way of living in harmony with God's plan for our lives, but even then, we must remember that our journey with God is not always going to be easy. There will be moments when we question why things are happening the way they are. We may face challenges that seem insurmountable and wonder if we're doing enough. But it is in those moments of uncertainty that we are encouraged to press on and continue trusting in him. In those moments, our faith is tested and refined.

It is easy to think or feel like God has forgotten us or that He is not working with us, but He is always working even when we cannot see the evidence. He is orchestrating everything for our good. He is with us throughout the entire process and will continue to the end. As with Abraham, He does not work according to our plans but according to his own divine purpose for us. This is why we should not rush to see results but instead have the patience that Abraham had in waiting for the promise.

The Bible is full of examples of people who trusted God's timing and received the rewards of their patience and faithfulness. Joseph, for example, had a dream where he saw his brothers bowing down to him. This dream was a prophesy, a glimpse into God's plan for his life. But Joseph's journey to that promise was neither easy nor straightforward.

We have seen how he was sold into slavery by his brothers, accused of a crime he did not commit, and imprisoned for many years.

He could have given up and become bitter and disillusioned. He didn't. He chose to do his best regardless of the circumstances. He did his best as a servant in Potiphar's house. He did his best in prison and never lost sight of the fact that God was still at work in his life, even when the situation seemed hopeless. In God's perfect timing, he was elevated to a position of power in Egypt. His brothers came to him for help, just as he had seen in his dream years before.

He could never have imagined that his faithful service in prison would lead him to a place where he would save not only his family but his entire nation from famine. He did his part, and God did the rest. He brought it together at the perfect moment. The same principle applies to our lives today. When we are in the midst of trials, when it feels like we are doing everything we can but seeing little to no results, we must not forget that God is faithful. We may not understand how He is working or how long it will take, but we know he is working, nonetheless.

The reality is that our faith is often refined in the waiting. Our patience is also put to the test in the waiting. As a farmer waits for the fruit of the earth and has long patience for it, so should we be patient. Nature does not rush its harvest. The farmer sows the seeds and waits for the harvest; we must also wait on God's timing.

If you want to understand the workings of God, study nature. No matter how hungry you may be, you cannot plant a seed today and harvest its fruits tomorrow. God does work miracles though, but He alone knows when to deliver. In the waiting process, we build perseverance and character. In other words, we build spiritual muscles that prepare us for the blessings God has in store for us:

> *'And not only so, but we glory in tribulations also, knowing that tribulations produce perseverance, perseverance character, and character hope.'*
> Romans 5:3-4

We come to see that God's purpose is bigger than our own plans. He transforms the waiting process into something that shapes us for eternity. He is not just concerned with the outcome, but with the work He's doing in us as we wait. Trusting God in the waiting process refines our character, strengthens our faith, and prepares us to receive the promises he has for us. It is important to understand that God does not measure our success by the world's standards.

He measures our success by our faithfulness and trust in Him. He knows us and knows what He has given us. No one can say they have nothing because everyone has something that God has given them freely. This could be in the form of qualities, talents or natural abilities, wisdom, ability to learn and retain information, etc. Some are things we take for granted, not everyone learns easily or retains information. What seems small and insignificant to us can be mightily used by God when we utilise them and trust him with the outcome.

Our best is enough when it is in God's hands. There will be moments when this fact will not feel true, moments when the weight of the world will feel heavy, and the burden of your efforts will seem overwhelming. In these moments, you might question whether your sacrifices and hard work will ever lead to the desired outcome. It is in these seasons of uncertainty and struggle that God's faithfulness is most evident.

The Bible tells us that He is close to the broken-hearted, He is present in our pain, and that He will never leave us. When you find yourself at the edge of your strength, remember that it's not about your strength or ability alone. God has always used ordinary people with limited resources to do extraordinary things.

There will be times when it feels like others are succeeding, even those that do not have the advantages you have, and you wonder why your best hasn't led to similar results. Remember that God's plans for you are uniquely designed for your life. What may seem like a delay in your life is God preparing you for something bigger and better than you could have imagined. He knows the future, and He knows exactly what you need to shape you for the calling He has placed on your life.

We do not all have the same calling, just as we don't all have the same qualities, talents and skills. We are individuals and unique but equally important and valuable. Imagine if you wanted to build a house and everyone you recruited for the job had the same skills. The job requires different skills, and so does the collective purpose we are all serving in this life. Don't look at your friend with envy, realise that we can't all be the same.

Keep doing your best where you are, and do not judge by outward appearance. Always have a quiet knowing that something is happening behind the scenes. Even when praying for a sick person, do not look at the physical appearance and say nothing is happening, that there is no change. There is a lot happening in the background, behind the scenes.

Grace Wairimu

CHAPTER THIRTEEN

Your Inner Dialogue

Keep your heart with all diligence, for out of it are the issues of life.

This short verse of the Bible found in Proverbs is all that we need to know about life. [Pro. 4:23] We know that there is power in our tongue, that the things we think and say mould our lives and that by changing our minds, we can change our lives, but how often do we think about the things we tell ourselves that no one hears?

Do you ever listen to your inner conversations? What do you tell yourself when you cannot seem to get things going your way? When you fail at something you pegged your hopes on or worked so hard on? What do you say to yourself when you wake up in the morning, when you look at yourself in the mirror, or at the end of the day when you have missed an important appointment or forgotten something important?

The silent conversations we carry within ourselves every day, the inner talk, whether we are aware of it or not, is the architect of our reality. The question is, are they filled with hope and expectations or doubts, fear, and frustration or self-condemnation. Do you catch yourself saying things like, 'you're so stupid, how could you do that? How could you

185

forget something so important, or something you've been looking forward to with such anticipation?'

Life is a mirror, reflecting back to you the dominant tone of your inner dialogue. It is one thing to have thoughts come in and out of your mind, and quite another to hold conversations in the mind. When you're filled with enthusiasm and optimism, good things come your way, and when you're filled with self-criticism and judgement, things tend to go wrong. It is not a coincidence but a direct result of what is happening within your inner world.

We often speak to ourselves in ways we wouldn't speak to others or allow them to speak to us. We criticise ourselves, assume the worst and rehearse scenarios of failure, rejection and disappointment in our minds. To our dismay, we see these very things materialise in our lives. Once you understand what Solomon, the author of the book of Proverbs and the wisest man who ever lived meant by these few and profound words, you can begin to take control of your inner dialogue.

You can consciously direct your inner speech in ways that align with the life you truly desire because your inner talk shapes your world: 'Guard your heart above all else, for it determines the course of your life'. We have covered the thought and words part of it, but the tone of our inner conversations say what we think of ourselves. The first step in correcting the tone is becoming aware of the content of our inner conversations.

Pay attention to the words and images that dominate your thoughts throughout the day. Do you affirm your desires, or do you negate them with worry and doubt? Do you see yourself as successful and capable, or do you belittle your abilities and potential? This awareness is critical because your habitual inner talk is like a script directing the course of your life. If the script is filled with conversations that tear you down, the play of your life will reflect that.

As you continue to monitor your inner conversations and notice their content, depending on whether it is empowering or self-defeating, you can take the next step to deliberately make the changes required to steer your life in the direction of your desires. You can do this by consciously reversing the negative talks to affirm your desire. Whenever you catch yourself thinking, 'I'm a failure, I don't think I can do this', for example, reverse it and say the opposite, 'I am confident and capable; I will find a solution'.

Notice that you don't have a solution yet, but you are hopeful and expectant. Aim to always have great expectations. You feel hopeless when you lose hope, always remind yourself who lives in you, Christ the hope of glory. You don't have to struggle to convince yourself or dwell on it. See yourself having achieved what you are trying to achieve and speak to yourself as you would in that situation.

You don't have to monitor every thought, but you must practice consistently returning your focus to the kind of inner conversations that support your dreams. Imagine for a moment that you were already living the life you desire; how do you talk to yourself? There's nothing wrong with congratulating yourself. Begin to adopt this new inner conversation as if it were already true. Speak to yourself in ways that reflect the fulfilment of your desires. Your tone when you speak to yourself, just like when you speak to others carry a vibration, which attracts corresponding experiences into your life.

Speak to yourself with kindness and compassion as you would a friend in need of encouragement. Imagine a friend confided in you that they are struggling with an addiction and can't seem to get anywhere with it. Would you tell them they will never beat it, that it's a waste of time? I doubt it. Why do we say demoralising things to ourselves? Your inner talk is a creative force. Nothing happens in your life that has not been contemplated in your mind, either consciously or unconsciously.

Your mind is like a garden, your inner thoughts and conversations are the seeds you are planting in the garden. Just as the gardener tends to the soil, waters the seed and nurtures their growth, so too must you tend your inner garden. If you neglect it and allow weeds of negative thinking and speaking to take root, you will reap a harvest of unwanted experiences. But if you carefully choose and cultivate a self-talk that is in harmony with your highest ideal, you will see them blossom into the reality you desire.

This is a law of consciousness, and it is as reliable as the laws of physics – just as gravity pulls objects towards the earth, your inner dialogue pulls experiences into your life that match their tone and content. This is what some people call the law of attraction. The thoughts and conversations you have in your mind become the blueprint for the reality you live in. The more you dwell on certain ideas, the more power they gain to shape your world.

This creative process goes on continually shaping and creating your life. The question is not whether you are creating, but what you are creating because whether you're aware of it or not, you are creating every moment of your life. The good news is that once you become aware of this creative power, you can harness it to create the life you want or to create the reality you want to experience. Instead of allowing your mind to run on autopilot, you can choose to engage only in what supports your ideal. This is where true mastery begins.

'By becoming the deliberate creator of your inner world, you become the deliberate creator of your outer world as well.' Neville Goddard

This proves that we are not at the mercy of external circumstances, nor are we victims of fate. We are the masters of our own destinies, shaping our lives, not only through the thoughts we hold but also the narratives we tell ourselves. The power to create is always within us, and that is what makes us co-creators with God, a privilege we abuse when we use it negatively. What you say in the privacy of your mind becomes the substance of your life — It becomes physically visible. Let your inner conversations affirm the good, the beautiful and the true.

> *'That which ye have spoken in the ear in closets shall be proclaimed upon the housetops.'* Luke 12:3

Exercising your creative power

This is the essence of creation: Your inner dialogue is the seed, and your reality is the fruit. By consciously directing your inner talk, you are exercising the creative power that is inherent within you. You are aligning yourself with the flow of life, and life will respond by bringing to you the experiences, people, and opportunities that reflect your inner state.

To create a new reality, the first task is to observe your inner talking and bring those conversations to the light of awareness. The main problem with our inner talking is that most of the conversations are negative, limiting and self-defeating. They are based on old beliefs, past experiences and conditioned patterns of thought.

These negative thought patterns become so ingrained that they operate almost unconsciously over time, shaping your reality without your direct input. Many of us are our worst critics, engaging in constant self-judgment and criticism. This is very damaging because it reinforces feelings of inadequacy and unworthiness. For example, you might find yourself thinking, nothing good happens to me, I cannot seem to get ahead, things will never work out for me, everybody else seems to be getting on alright, but I feel stuck etc. These are things we tell ourselves but never say out loud.

Never say you can't do something you wish to do. When you say you can't, let it only be in the case where you wish not to do something, otherwise, if you want to do something but confess the opposite, it becomes a self-fulfilling prophesy. We often think that the devil is a creature with horns who runs around carrying a gigantic fork, but our self-defeating language is the actual devil. These kinds of thoughts, beliefs and self-talk, though subtle, are powerful creators of our experiences, reinforcing the very limitations we wish to overcome.

Speak to yourself with kindness and compassion. Instead of criticising yourself for perceived failures and shortcomings, speak to yourself words of support and encouragement. You cannot change what you do not acknowledge; you must be aware of this self-talk before you can begin to change it. Once you are aware of your self-defeating inner dialogues, you have taken the first step towards changing them.

Reflections on your habitual thoughts reveal the deeper beliefs and assumptions that are running the show behind the scenes. If you think you are not good enough, for example, it may suggest that you hold a core belief about your inadequacy, which, reinforced by habitual inner talking manifest in your life as experiences of failure and rejection. The next step is to question these inner dialogues. Are they true, are they serving you, and most importantly, are they aligned with the reality you wish to create?

Ask yourself, is this true, or is it just a belief I have accepted? In most cases, they are not true. By questioning them, you begin to loosen the grip they have on your mind and create space for new and more empowering conversations to take root. It is also helpful to become aware of the triggers that typically lead to limiting inner talk. By identifying the triggers, you can prepare yourself to respond differently the next time you encounter a challenge.

Instead of automatically falling into a pattern of self-doubt, you can silently engage in a mental dialogue that supports your success. You can say to yourself, I'm perfectly capable of overcoming this obstacle. I can handle this, I have what it takes. Always remember the I AM, when you say, 'I am capable', have the conviction of a greater force backing you up.

By being mindful of your triggers and deliberately choosing your inner conversations, you are breaking the cycle of negativity and creating a new pattern of empowerment. Any time you feel like you are failing or are unable to complete a task, tell yourself that you are doing your best, which you are if you are not giving up. That is enough to shift the inner dialogue. It not only helps to change your mental state but also fosters a sense of inner peace and self-acceptance.

Changing your inner dialogue is not about denying reality or pretending that challenges don't exist. It is about choosing how you respond to those challenges in your mind. You can acknowledge that a situation is difficult while still engaging in an inner talk that empowers you to overcome it. Instead of saying it is impossible, you can say, 'It is challenging, but I'm capable of finding a solution'. This keeps you in a positive and proactive mindset even in the face of difficulties.

Changing your inner dialogue requires commitment. The more you practice, the more natural it will become to engage in positive, empowering inner conversations. Over time, it becomes second nature. Your life then begins to reflect the changes you have made in your inner world. You will find that you are more confident, resilient, and capable of achieving your goals. Opportunities will start to appear, and your relationships will improve. Your overall life experience will be more aligned with the positive inner dialogue you have cultivated.

You will discover that your inner world is a powerful tool for creating the life you desire. When you introduce new patterns of thinking, you are forging new neural pathways. These new pathways are initially weak and require repetition to become strong and automatic. In the early stage when you are beginning to make these changes, it might feel like a constant battle to maintain your new inner dialogue. You might catch yourself slipping into old patterns of self-doubt or self-guessing, it's completely normal. What matters is how you respond when this happens.

Instead of becoming frustrated or giving up, gently bring your attention back to the new inner pattern you are cultivating. If you have thoughts of inadequacy, acknowledge them and replace them with affirmative ones that put you in a position of power, like 'I can handle any challenge'. This is the key to building new mental habits and neural pathways. It's more like walking on a path where no one has walked before. You won't create a visible path in a day; you might even struggle to find it for a few days. You will need to walk the same path several times to create a visible path.

Over time, it will become a way that others can follow without you guiding them or needing to show them where the path is. In the same way, your new inner conversations will start to feel natural and will eventually take over as your default mental patterns. Consistency is what leads to lasting changes. Incorporating the new pattern into your daily routine will help maintain it so it becomes ingrained in your system.

You can do this by using daily affirmations; this is where you set aside time to consciously affirm some truths about yourself that you want to see manifest in your life, like I am confident, I am worthy, I am successful, etc. Affirmations are positive statements that reinforce our desired beliefs and outcomes. Repeating certain affirmations daily helps rewires our minds to embrace positivity, productivity and possibility.

When we consistently affirm our worth and potential, we lay the groundwork for success. It is important, however, to realise that using affirmations without taking any action is not going to produce results. You must take inspired actions to complement the affirmations. Saying I'm successful a thousand times a day while doing nothing will not make you successful. Examples of inspired actions include distancing yourself from negativity, whether it is toxic relationships, harmful media or pessimistic environments.

The more we expose ourselves to positive influences, the more our thoughts align with our desires. Another practice that can help maintain our new healthy self-talk is mindfulness. Mindfulness is a moment-by-moment awareness of our thoughts, feelings, surrounding environment and bodily sensations. This helps shift any negative thoughts or feelings. If the environment is not conducive, it allows you to change it where possible.

Lastly, you can engage in visualisation exercises where you mentally rehearse your desired reality. This exercise involves seeing yourself living your desired life and allowing yourself to feel the emotions you would feel in that position. Make these practices a regular part of your day, keeping your focus on the desired outcome and being grateful — for everything.

CHAPTER FOURTEEN

Emotional Resonance

As a man thinks in his heart, so is he.

It is easy to confuse emotional resonance with emotional intelligence. While both are important, they are quite different. Emotional intelligence involves recognising, understanding and managing our own emotions while also being attuned to the emotions of others. It helps navigate relationships with greater empathy and compassion because it enables us to actively listen to others, to validate their feelings and to respond thoughtfully without judgement. Emotional resonance, on the other hand, is about the energy we emit through our emotions.

When we are sad, angry or unhappy, we resonate with negative emotions, which sometimes cannot be avoided but in so doing, we invite more negative emotions and events, unknowingly making our lives more miserable. It is closely tied to the law of attraction and manifestation in that the energy we emit attracts similar energies. It is one of the laws that govern the universe. When we resonate with positive emotions, we invite positivity into our lives. We attract positive people to us, positive events and opportunities. The cycle of positivity goes on and on, and so does that of negativity.

You may have heard people say things like, when it rains, it pours, or misery loves company. That's because misfortune rarely comes singly. It attracts more miserable events. Cultivating a mindset of gratitude, joy, and love can lead to greater fulfilment and abundance, where misery has no room to generate more misery.

By focusing on uplifting emotions even in the face of difficulty and misfortune, we align ourselves with higher vibrations, the vibrations of our desire, creating a fertile ground for manifestation; not of more misfortune but those in alignment with our emotions. It is crucial to harness emotional resonance and develop emotional intelligence as well. When we create environments where emotions are acknowledged and respected, we foster emotional resonance within ourselves and in our interaction with others.

We become aware and mindful of other people's feelings, and rather than be quick to judge, we show empathy and compassion. Empathy is the ability to feel what someone else is feeling, to step into their shoes, to understand their emotions and respond with compassion. We can do the same for ourselves. Mindfulness is, therefore, an important aspect of emotional resonance. It helps us to become more aware of our emotions as they arise, enabling us to respond rather than react impulsively.

Observing our feelings without judgment creates space for exploration and understanding, enabling us to identify patterns in our emotional responses and consciously make choices that align with our intentions. Have you ever responded to someone hastily and later wished you had taken time to think it over? Sometimes we react instead of responding to things. Reacting gives you no time to think, you act impulsively only to realise what you reacted to was not what was implied or meant.

If only you had taken the time to listen and fully understand what was meant or intended. In addition to mindfulness, self-reflection is a valuable tool for deepening our understanding of emotional resonance. When we self-reflect, we see areas in which we fall short while interacting with others. Are we too quick to respond? Do we allow people to express themselves fully in conversations? Are we judgemental or prejudiced? Do we hear people out, or are we busy crafting a response while they speak? Engaging in any retrospective practices can help us process our emotions and uncover underlying beliefs and prejudices.

By examining the root causes of our feelings, we can identify areas for growth and healing, fostering emotional resilience. Our emotional well-being is influenced by various factors such as environment, relationships and daily habits. Consciously choosing our environment, the people we spend time with and what we do daily can strengthen our capacity to resonate with positive emotions. In our quest for emotional resonance, we must embrace the full spectrum of human emotions.

While it is easy to seek out positive emotions or feelings, it is essential to acknowledge and process negative emotions as well. Suppressing or ignoring challenging emotions can lead to emotional dissonance, creating internal conflict. You cannot fool yourself, being aware of negative emotions and accepting them as part of our human experience rather than denying them can help us deal with them and transcend them without dwelling too much on them.

By allowing ourselves to feel and process emotions like sadness, anger or fear, we can release their hold on us and create space for healing and growth. Emotional resonance is a vital aspect of our journey towards self-discovery and empowerment. Understanding the interplay between our emotions and experiences, can help cultivate deeper connections with ourselves and others, enabling us to navigate life with authenticity, purpose and joy.

Our emotions are not just feelings; they are powerful signals guiding us towards our true selves. It is important, therefore, to be in alignment with our emotional resonance because our emotions, thoughts and beliefs shape our experiences and the world around us. That simply means that we have the power to create our experiences through our thoughts, beliefs and emotions. It is out of these three that we speak, and words can build or break, give life or kill:

> *'Life and death are in the power of the tongue, and*
> *they that love it shall eat the fruit thereof.'*
> Proverbs 18:21

Words originate from a thought or thoughts, and thoughts are influenced by beliefs. Thoughts evoke emotions, good or bad, and these emotions create our reality. What reality are you experiencing? Much as we may want to blame someone or something outside of ourselves, we must learn to take responsibility and understand that we have created these realities through our thoughts, beliefs and emotions.

Reality creation asserts that our perceptions and interpretations of reality are not fixed but fluid and malleable. This understanding invites us to take an active role in creating our lives rather than simply reacting to external circumstances. We are not meant to create our reality by ourselves, we co-create with the creator of life. He has given us the power and authority, see Luke 10:20; even spirits are subject to us.

To grasp this concept, we must first recognise the relationship between our thoughts and our experiences. We must fully understand that our thoughts are powerful manifestations of our beliefs, and they play a crucial role in shaping our reality. When we think empowering thoughts, we create a mental environment that aligns with abundance and possibility. On the contrary, when we have limiting and disempowering thoughts, they lead to a reality that feels constricted and limiting.

No one desires these outcomes in their experiences, but often, we have negative experiences and wonder why they keep showing up in our lives. Spiritual things are not easily understood as most people are more interested in things that can be proved or argued out logically. Scriptures say they are 'foolishness' to them. In another scripture we are told that they have been 'hidden from the wise and prudent and revealed to babes'. [Luke 10:21] Educated minds try to analyse everything, but some things cannot be analysed intellectually or by use logic.

While logic disqualifies what it cannot explain, children or babes don't. We are spiritual babes because we're learning. This is why we are told to be like little children. Our beliefs act as the lenses through which we see the world. Children have no beliefs until they get to a certain age when they start questioning everything. A shift in our belief system can dramatically alter our experiences and open new pathways for growth.

We have talked about consciousness in the previous chapters, and this really is the place where it all happens. It is where we exercise this great power that has been given to us and the authority to tread on serpents and scorpions. These are metaphorically the daily challenges we face, including sickness and lack. They are all subject to the power that work within us, and all solutions are found in our consciousness.

'Whenever you are faced with a problem, regardless of its nature, seek the solution within your consciousness.' These are words I have found to be true and very helpful. It is a statement by another author I revere, Joel Goldsmith in his book *The Infinite Way.* Joel hailed from a non-practising Jewish family living in New York around 1900. When he was 19, he heard a voice telling him to *'find the man Jesus, and he would have the secrets of life'.* He knew nothing about Jesus except that Christmas was a celebration of his birth.

He did as instructed and devoted the rest of his life to learning and teaching the truth about Jesus. Concerning health, he says that our consciousness is the 'all-power and the only power acting upon our affairs', controlling and maintaining our health and revealing the intelligence necessary for our healing.

Our consciousness is the secret place of the Almighty, where we go to find everything necessary for our success in every area of our life. It is the God-consciousness or Christ-consciousness discussed earlier. To access it, we just need to relax and feel the constant assurance of the presence and power of God within us. A practical way to realise this is to visualise or imagine those things that we desire, such as health, joy, wholeness, success, etc. as a reality that has been made available to us and just waiting for us to pick like you pick fruits from a tree.

Imagine a tree of life with everything in their perfect form as fruits. See yourself picking what you want, if you're sick, pick health; take your pick and see it in your imagination. The body acts from the stimuli coming to it from within. Little do we know the depth of the riches within us until we come to know the realm of our consciousness, the kingdom of our soul.

Joel reinforces the idea of stilling our minds saying, 'when we still our minds and go into the temple of our being for solutions or answers to problems, it is important to silence our thinking mind, so we do not formulate ideas or outline a plan.' He emphasises the need to listen instead, for inner guidance and let the God within us (the Christ) provide the solution. Let him reveal to you 'the riches of the glory of this mystery, which is Christ in you, the hope of glory'. [Col. 1:27]

By vividly imagining ourselves experiencing the kind of life we want to experience, good health, success or even wealth, we engage our subconscious mind and signal to the universe our intentions. The universe is abundant. Everything you need or want is out there in the universe. Have you ever wondered how many minerals lie beneath your feet? Metals like gold, silver, uranium, and copper have always existed, created by God, discovered by man, and still being found in new places. Plants of all kinds in different parts of the world and salt in the ocean among many other wonderful things.

Visualising helps us create a mental picture of what we want to achieve, be it a personal goal, a career aspiration or a fulfilling relationship. When we immerse ourselves in this imaginative process, we evoke emotions associated with those desires, reinforcing our belief that these outcomes are attainable. If you can see it, you can achieve it. You just need to see it in your mind.

Just close your eyes and see it in your imagination; don't concern yourself with how to get there. This emotional connection is vital as it helps align our energy with our intentions. Not filling in the details leaves room for inner guidance or intuition. You may not have a plan or even know how to get where you want to go, but when you see yourself there in your imagination, ways to get there are revealed to you through intuition or inspiration. Trust this inner guidance and take inspired action.

Much of our inner growth is accomplished by letting go of anything that no longer serves us, including beliefs, habits, points of view, perceptions and opinions. We must let go of anything that blocks the next stage of our development and set clear intentions. A good example of these beliefs or perceptions is that desiring riches is evil and worldly. If that was true, why would God place minerals in the earth if not for our benefit? Why would he give us the wisdom and power to acquire wealth? His word clearly says he gives power to get wealth. [Deut. 8:18]

Living with intention is essential for effective reality creation. It involves consciously making choices that align with our values and goals and requires us to be aware of our thoughts, emotions and actions, ensuring they are in harmony with our desired outcomes. This approach empowers us to take responsibility for our lives, recognising that we are active participants in shaping our own realities and not passive observers. We are not passengers in our lives; we can consciously steer the wheel in the direction of choice.

Many people, not realising this, allow the wind of life to blow them wherever it may. They see themselves as victims of life and blame God for every misfortune and negative experience. When we live with purpose and intention, we create a clear pathway towards our aspirations, which leads us to the life we were created to live, no matter how many years later.

Some people have this realisation quite early on in life. It does not matter how far along in life you are, how old you are or how many years you may have wasted not knowing which way to turn or what your life purpose is. The Bible tells us that 'right now is the acceptable time'. [2 Cor. 6:2] Set your intention if you haven't already, and let your inner guide take you where you want to go. You can no longer leave it to chance. Don't let self-judgement or shame stand in the way of you living the life you were created to live.

You were created to live in abundance, drop the resistance and let that life unfold. Just don't neglect the inner guide, it is your compass leading you to the abundant life you were meant to live. Simply living your ideal could be your purpose. If you can see it (visualise or imagine), you can achieve it. This life is not in the future. It has always been there, waiting for the fertile conditions to manifest outwardly.

You must see yourself being what you want to be now. If you see it in the future, it will always be in the waiting. In everything you do, remember that your emotions are the language through which you communicate with the creative force of the universe. Do it with passion and a deep feeling of joy and gratitude; the stronger the emotion, the more powerful your communication.

CHAPTER FIFTEEN

Grace

The law was given through Moses, but grace and truth came by Jesus Christ.

Everything we have been talking about from the very first page points us to the grace of God, the undeserved favour upon our lives, the gift of God to mankind, the amazing grace. It is very common to hear people say, 'What goes around comes around'. It's a reminder that life has a way of giving back what you put in. In other words, 'You reap what you sow'.

This is a Biblical principle, which, like all principles and natural laws, cannot be challenged. Some people call it karma. They say there is good and bad karma, if you do good, good things happen to you and vice versa. It's the law of cause and effect.

Would you believe it if I told you there is a higher law than the law of cause and effect/karma? It is the 'law of grace', the law that frees man from karma, the unmerited favour. Under grace, the gifts of God are poured out upon us freely, and all that the kingdom offers is freely accessible, not because we have done anything to deserve it but purely because of the goodness and kindness of God.

That goodness is grace, the whole point of this book. We have access to this grace by faith. It is the amazing grace famously sung about, the super abounding grace that sets us free, reconciling us back to God through faith in Jesus Christ. We do not earn it, we just receive it.

We were all once estranged from God because of the transgression of one man, and because of the obedience of one man, we are now reconciled back to God:

> *'By the offence of one, judgment came upon all men to condemnation; even so, by the righteousness of one the free gift came upon all men unto justification of life.'* Romans 5:18

The two men described here are Adam and Jesus, Adam being the first man, and Jesus the last man. [1 Cor.15:45] Through the act of one, we were all condemned, and through the act of the other, we were all made free. We are no longer under condemnation. This law of grace is unlike any other; above it, there is no law.

> *'For sin shall have no dominion over you, for you are not under the law but under grace.'* Romans 6:14

Grace is not a law written on a piece of paper or a slab, it is written in our hearts. It is the conviction in our hearts. We are not perfect, nor can we, on our merit, be righteous or claim to be, but by the grace of God, through faith, we are justified and made righteous. It is not by our ability to do the right things or to be good or holy. This grace that fulfilled the law of Moses cancelled all the curses that were put in place due to the disobedience of one man, Adam.

Jesus took our place and became the cursed one by hanging on the cross, redeeming us from the curse that was meant for us.

> *'Christ hath redeemed us from the curse of the law, being made a curse for us: for it is written, cursed is every one that hangs on a tree.'* Galatians 3:13

He broke all curses, including generational, by hanging on the cross. In the Old Covenant, there was no remedy for curses. The remedy only came after Jesus' death on the cross. He rose from the dead with victory over death and all evil (curses included), thus fulfilling the Old Covenant.

Before his death and resurrection, people were guided by the Law of Moses and before the Law was given on Mount Sinai, God protected his people from the consequences of their sins and transgressions by declaring some things forbidden. Grace took care of all that. Today, nothing is forbidden except that which your conscience or conviction tells you to stay away from; it is an individual decision and not a law:

> *'Unto the pure all things are pure: but unto them that are defiled, and unbelieving is nothing pure, but even their mind and conscience is defiled.'* Titus 1:15

Paul had this to say out of his own experience. 'All things are lawful for me, but not all things are expedient/beneficial.' [1 Cor. 10:23] This is to say that just because things are lawful does not mean they are beneficial or edifying. Some things may be lawful but dangerous or harmful to oneself or others. It is up to us to use our good judgment and wisdom.

The law of grace is a law of liberty. Someone may ask, does that mean people are free to sin then? The simple answer is that there is also wisdom and discernment in this liberty as it is the spirit of God. It guides people and counsels them because the Holy Spirit is a counsellor. Paul addressed this issue in a letter to the Roman church, saying:

'What shall we say then, shall we continue in sin that grace may abound? God forbid. How shall we, that are dead to sin, live any longer therein?'
Romans 6:1-2

It takes us back to 'sin shall have no dominion' over those who are under grace. Let me add this sneaky point that just came to mind, just because there is no law against taking rat poison does not mean we should take it. However, if you took it by accident and believe it will not harm you, it surely won't. Don't try! It won't be an accident if you did. It'll be intentional and ignorant.

When David, the King of Israel and Judah committed sins against God so many years after the initial curse of Adam and before the birth and death of Jesus, a curse came upon him even though he was a friend of God and had obeyed and pleased Him all his life. There was no remedy for him. He repented and asked for forgiveness, and he was forgiven. He, however, could not escape the curse because once it was pronounced, it was put in place and activated by the act of sin. It did not matter who committed the sin; it automatically activated a curse.

David was spared death, but the curse terribly affected his family. All this is recorded in the second book of Samuel, chapter twelve. David's advisor, who was a prophet of God, delivered a message from God, telling him what would happen to him. He used an allegory of a rich man and a poor man, to break the ice (I guess). The rich man had committed a very serious crime against the poor man.

David was angry at the rich man and swore by the name of God that he must die for the cruel thing he had done. Being the King, he had the authority to ensure that this 'criminal' was punished appropriately. According to him, the befitting punishment was death. He did not know that Nathan knew what he had done. But God knew, and David must have known that he could not hide anything from God.

'You are that man, David!' Nathan said to him. God had sent the prophet to tell him what the consequences of his actions would be. He had a man killed in battle and made it look like an accident. He then took the poor man's wife for himself. He was the rich man who took advantage of a poor man in the allegory. This is what God said to him through Nathan the prophet, 'I made you king of Israel and rescued you from Saul. I gave you his kingdom and his wives; I made you king over Israel and Judah. If this had not been enough, I would have given you twice as much. Why, then, have you disobeyed my commands? Why did you do this evil thing?'

It pained Nathan to pronounce his sentence according to what God had instructed him just as it pained God himself, because David was a good man. They had a good relationship, God called him a 'man after my own heart'. [Acts 13:22] 'Now, in every generation, some of your descendants will die a violent death because you have disobeyed me,' God said through Nathan. Because David had chosen to do evil, the curse was inevitable in as much as he was a good man. Nothing could have been done about it, not even by Nathan the prophet. Once a curse was pronounced, it could not be reversed.

Today, because of the grace of God, curses have no power over us. Some of the things we imagine or assume are curses are simply consequences of our ignorance or bad choices. If you put your finger on a hot plate or fire, for example, it will burn, and you will feel the pain. That is a consequence and not a curse. If people from the same family fell in an open well at different times and never think to cover the well. It doesn't matter how many times or how many people die in the well, it's not a curse. It's carelessness.

Curses still exist, but they have no power over someone who is under grace. Curses affected people many generations down the line, just like they did David's family. You could be suffering an ailment due to something that someone in the family did many generations back. Thank God that is not the case anymore.

Because of the finished work of Jesus, we are free from such things. You have to be aware that you are free though, otherwise if you hold the thought that you are cursed or bewitched in your consciousness, it will be your reality. Your consciousness is your reality. Some people still believe they are enduring unfavourable conditions, not limited to diseases, poverty and misfortune because of their ancestors. The good news is, we have power and authority to break those curses. No child of God should suffer because of something his father, mother, grandparents or great, great grandparents did.

It is, however, important to understand that even though 'the fathers' sins are not going to set the children's teeth on edge' [Old Covenant metaphor for generational curses], the children must accept it for themselves and act on it. You must be aware of the fact that you are free, to free yourself mentally. [Jer. 31:29-30, Eze. 18:2-3]

Jesus offered us a gift, and until we accept and receive it, it is of no use to us. The authority given to us to 'trample on serpents and to overcome all the powers of the enemy', [Luke 10:19] is not going to act on its own. We must assert it, and to assert it, we must be aware of it. According to Deuteronomy 28:61, every sickness and plague is a curse. Christ purchased the right for us to live free of all curses as well as sin.

So many times, we hand things down to our children due to ignorance, by the way we think, speak and act. It is time we realised that under the new covenant, we have been redeemed from sickness, plague, calamity, disease, premature death, poverty, failure, and sin. and that we not only have power over them but also the right not to experience them.

As we receive all these blessings that have been given to us freely, we must also give freely [Matt.10:8]; we must learn to forgive freely without making demands for apologies or reconciliation. Forgiving is a decision consciously made without any conditions, having chosen to believe God's word over our fears. One of the reasons we are unable to forgive freely is the fear that someone will take it for granted and never learn from their mistakes.

Forgiveness is a gift you choose to give to someone without expecting anything in return otherwise, it wouldn't be a gift. Whether or not they know you forgave them is not important, forgive anyway. In everything, be grateful and joyful even when you forgive. Don't do it grudgingly. Gratitude and joy are God's love language.

> *'And whatever you do, whether in word or deed, do it all in the name of the Lord Jesus, giving thanks to God the Father through him.'* Colossians 3:17

What Jesus did on the cross is more than we can fully comprehend. He created a bridge for us to cross from one territory to another. The territories are the kingdom of darkness, which is Satan's domain, and the kingdom of light, which is God's domain. We have been delivered from the kingdom of darkness and translated to the kingdom of light [Col. 1:13]. The kingdom of Christ.

This kingdom is full of love, peace, joy, and liberty. It is not a hard choice to make. The secret lies in discovering our real identity and purpose. Beneath the layers of our human existence, the race to fulfil our obligations in this life, who we truly are deep down is a soul that longs for connection with its source, just like a baby longs for its mother. Our personalities, egos and all the labels we have become so accustomed to are all part of the layers. Beneath them all is our soul, the spark of God, which is our true identity.

A time has come for us to embrace our identity, to embrace grace and access the power to transcend our limitations. A lot is going on in the world today; there is so much fear of what might come next, and people don't know where to turn. It reminds me of some scriptures I used to see in tracts many years ago when I was little, 'How shall we escape if we neglect so great salvation?' the tracts read. I used to read them, but I didn't quite grasp the message spiritually, I was very young. They however left an imprint in my mind; and I still see them clearly. I see the words 'Herald of His Coming' in large print. I was surprised to find that the ministry is still in operation. Here is the full scripture the words were taken from:

> *'How shall we escape if we neglect so great salvation, which at first began to be spoken by the Lord, and was confirmed unto us by them that heard him; God also bearing them witness, both with signs and wonders, and with divers miracles, and gifts of the Holy Ghost, according to his own will?'*

Hebrews 2:3-4

In my understanding today, it's more like how shall we escape if we deny such an awesome gift, the power to transcend our limitations, what other plan do we have? How are we going to deal with the strange diseases, financial and political insecurities we face today and in the future, the climate change etc?

Transcending limitations

The ability to transcend limitations may sound like a myth, but it is the divine plan of the master planner and the purpose of grace. The secret lies in embodying our declarations of truth and having them engraved in our consciousness. It is one thing to know something and to believe it, and it's quite another to embody it. When you embody something, you become it.

Grace is not just about spiritual gifts. We now know that we are spiritual beings having a human experience. We are in the world but not of the world. What does that mean? It means that even though our life is spiritual, and we should concern ourselves more with spiritual matters, we must not ignore physical matters because they affect us. They also affect our ability to be fruitful, which is one of the greatest principles of the universe. Everything should bear fruits, multiply and evolve.

When God created man and woman, he blessed them and said to them, 'Be fruitful, and multiply, and replenish the earth, and subdue it: and have dominion over the fish of the sea, and over the fowl of the air, and over every living thing that moves upon the earth.' [Genesis 1:28] He was not just telling them to produce children and provide for them, and to use animals as their food. He was asking them to do what nature does. Nature knows these principles and does exactly that. It keeps on giving. It gives from its abundance.

Look around and see the infinite supply of the universe. The stars in the sky, the sand on the seashores, the leaves on the trees, the sun, the air etc. They are all reminders that abundance is the nature of creation. They all replenish themselves from the abundance of the universe, from within themselves. The sun never stops shinning, the air never runs out no matter how many billions of us are taking from it every second of every day. The power that replenishes them is the same power that is within us. The same power that we, too, must use to ensure that we have enough for ourselves and to share with others.

When the sun shines, it shines for everyone. When it rains, it rains not just for a few good people but for everyone. When you plant seeds, the soil brings forth a harvest for you as it does for anyone else who planted, according to what you planted. You don't all plant he same seeds, you plant according to what you want to harvest. The God who ensures that rivers flow for years and decades without running out of water is the same God who supplies you.

'My God shall supply ALL your needs according to his riches in glory by Christ Jesus.' Philippians 4:19

All His riches are available to you by grace. Anything you could ever want is out there in the universe. He wants you to draw them from the abundance within, not to beg Him for them. He has already given you the power, the wisdom and the ability to do all things. There is no scarcity in the universe. The same force that created the stars, the oceans and the mountains has provided for your every need, replenishing your supply as you draw from within. Like the river flows, so should your supply.

The wealth you desire is ready for you to draw forth, and it's not taken from someone else; it is created anew in the infinite abundance of the universe. There is more than enough for everyone, including you. Even if everyone in the world had everything they wanted, it would not run out. It is therefore not selfish to want things for yourself. We are here to live life and to enjoy it. It's a little sad that we spend half of our lives avoiding it [living a life fully].

We make the mistake of thinking that supply is going to run out, so we hold tight to what we have. We are meant to let it flow. Whatever comes to you should have an outlet just as it has a source. That's the only way it can flow and replenish. That's the way the universe replenishes itself.

> *'And God is able to make all grace abound toward you; that you, always having all sufficiency in all things, may abound to every good work.'*
> 2 Corinthians 9:8

That means you will always have enough for yourself, to share with others, and to invest in making the world a better place for everyone, which may include giving to support ministries or projects that serve others, especially the needy.

Another mistake we make is harbouring negative beliefs and thoughts about wealth and money, resulting in subconscious negative attitudes toward them. Many people criticise wealth and money, and even speak negatively of those who have it. They hold the wrong belief that lack is synonymous with humility. Some believe that money is evil, not realising that you repel anything you don't appreciate. If you don't appreciate money, it will always run from you.

The belief that money is evil is a false belief out of ignorance. Money is a medium of exchange, just as the cattle and goats that God blessed Abraham were. If you want food, you go to the supermarket with money, without which you cannot get the food you want. People back then exchanged what they had for what they needed. It is all wealth, and Abraham, David, Solomon, and many others had it. If wealth was evil, why would God give it to them and call it a blessing?

The Bible talks about the love of money being evil and not the money itself. Money is neutral, just as water, fire and many other things are. Water can quench your thirst, and it can also drown you, fire can keep you warm and cook your meals, it can also burn your house down to ashes. That does not make them evil. Our positive or negative use of things is what produces either positive or negative outcomes.

The love of money the Bible talks about is not appreciation of it but more like hoarding. When you hold so tightly on to it not wanting it to flow as it ought to, you signal a lack mentality. This mentality holds the idea that something is scarce and must be held on to in case it runs out. Love of money may also mean valuing money above everything else.

When we do these things, money becomes an idol instead of a tool. We should see it as a tool to move us forward and to support others and help them do the same. Money should not be the sole aim in life but a resource to help us contribute to the growth, success and happiness of, not only our families but the wider community.

You can have all the money you want and still have peace of mind, wholeness and serenity. You can do a lot of good with it. In both Testaments, there is a great emphasis on helping the needy, the orphans, the widows, and the afflicted. Prophet Isaiah said this about supporting the needy [prophets spoke on God's behalf, they were his voice to the masses].

> *'Is not this the kind of fasting I have chosen: to loose the chains of injustice and untie the cords of the yoke, to set the oppressed free and break every yoke? Is it not to share your food with the hungry and to provide the poor wanderer with shelter; when you see the naked, to clothe them, and not to turn away from your own flesh and blood?'*
> Isaiah 58:6-7

When we pray for ourselves, it is important to remember the needy, not just in prayer but practically also. Psalms 82, the verse that tells us we are gods has some very insightful points for us to consider. It talks about justice and compassion.

> *'How long will ye judge unjustly and accept the persons of the wicked? Defend the poor and fatherless: do justice to the afflicted and needy. Deliver the poor and needy: rid them out of the hand of the wicked.'* Psalm 82:2-4

God sees everything; he sees when we close our doors to the needy and turn a blind eye. He sees when we see injustice and do nothing, when we act like it is has nothing to do with us or it's none of our business, as we often say. We turn the other way when others are being mistreated or ignored.

According to the scripture, this is what God judges when he says we will die like mere mortals. He judges our inability to empathise with the needy and the afflicted. But we are not mere mortals when we have the consciousness of grace. We are compassionate and empathetic. In this consciousness, we see others as part of us and consciously wish them what we wish for ourselves. We use what we have; our resources, our time, our words, our talents and skills to support those who need support in whatever way we can. Then this Old Covenant promise, which is already fulfilled comes alive because we have aligned ourselves with it:

> *'Then shall our light break forth as the morning, and our health shall spring forth speedily: and our righteousness shall go before us; the glory of the Lord shall be our reward.'* Isaiah 58:8

Money in the hands of an elevated mind becomes a powerful force for creation and growth—a means of serving humanity and enhancing the wellbeing of others. Never hesitate to offer support where there is need; you may be entertaining an angel without knowing it.

CHAPTER SIXTEEN

Staying on Purpose

Blessed to be a blessing

Wealth is not just about money in God's kingdom. It's about influence, purpose and responsibility. The wealth released in our lives is not just for us but for God's glory and the advancement of his kingdom. The blessings about to be poured into your life as you open yourself up to the possibilities discussed in this book are tied to your willingness to walk in alignment with God's will and plan for your life. In this kingdom, nothing is random; everything is strategic, including the wilderness season [the desert].

You may be in that season right now, but it's just a season and seasons are temporary. Nothing is permanent. What you must understand in this season is that wealth without purpose is empty, and so is success without significance. God's intention is not just to make you wealthy but impactful. He wants you to be a beacon of his glory—a testament to his goodness. He blesses us so we can be a blessing to others. He provides for us so we can provide for others. His will for us is to be our brother's keepers, to do to others as we would have done to us.

His desire is for us to love our neighbours, not just with words but actions, and to serve each other with the resources he has given us. He pours into our lives so we can pour into others. This is why the trials in the wilderness phase are so intense; they are not meant to break us but to build us. The trials we have endured so far have given us a heart of compassion, a deeper faith and a vision for a greater good, not just our own.

Consider David, we've discussed him quite a bit. He was appointed king long before he wore the crown. When God blessed him, anointing him as King when he was just a youth, he understood that he was a channel through which God would bless others. It is the same today; you may not think you have a part to play or what it takes to make an impact simply because you are not a preacher or a minister of the word, but just like the shepherd boy, David, you carry a gift to share with the world. We all do. That gift, no matter how insignificant it may appear is what God wants to bless so we can bless others.

In his kingdom, wealth is not just about accumulating material possessions or the numbers in our bank accounts. True wealth is a state of being. A consciousness of abundance that comes into every aspect of our lives. As you step into this season of abundance, don't forget the lessons of the wilderness. In the wilderness or the days of struggle, you learnt to depend on God for your daily provision. You learnt the value of faith over fear, obedience over convenience and worship over worry.

Those lessons will be your anchor in the season you are getting into. The wilderness was not just a season of struggle but of preparation. It prepared you for the weight of influence, the responsibility of leadership and the discipline required to handle abundance with humility. The trials you have endured have given you resilience, clarity and perspective. They equipped you for the journey ahead. You now understand that success is not about what you can achieve but what you can steward or carry forward.

God is not blessing you so you can hoard his blessings but so you can impact other people's lives. His plan for you is far greater than you can imagine. All He requires from us is faith and patience, always being conscious of his grace. He has orchestrated every step, every challenge and every breakthrough to prepare you for this exact moment. His plans for you have always been intentional.

When bike riders are going through training, they have to learn riding manoeuvres, some of which are very challenging. Some are frustrating for new riders especially when it comes to swinging the bike around staggered cones. The exercise teaches them to control their speed, steering input and lean angle. The cones are intentionally staggered and the distance between them can be modified for an even greater challenge or level of difficulty. The greater the challenge the more rewarding the outcome.

The challenges are meant to force the learner to turn their head, look where they want the bike to go and get through the cone weave without missing a single apex. It can take several lessons to do this, but once they master it they become great riders. They can weave through traffic with confidence that leaves motorists amazed. The training is tough but intentional.

In the same way, God has always intended for a day to come when you would walk in the manifestation of a promise that was spoken over your life long before you could imagine. It has always been His plan for you to walk in confidence, expressing him in all aspects of life, from spiritual to financial. It may have taken a long time and even a few blows and scratches but what may have felt like random circumstances or disconnected events were part of a divine plan. It was part of the training.

You were being equipped, shaped, and moulded to handle what is now unfolding. In this season, you must guard your heart and mind with even greater diligence, knowing that success and abundance bring their own set of trials. They test your humility, priorities and allegiance to your source.

219

Though success and abundance elevate you, they are not meant to isolate you from the one who made them possible. You must keep your eyes fixed on Him, for He is both the one who gives and the one who sustains every good thing in your life. The gift should not overshadow the giver.

In this season, God wants your life to be a beacon of hope and inspiration to others. People will look at you and wonder how you overcame, how you rose above the trials, and how you found the strength to keep going. Your testimony will be a living sermon, a testament to the power of faith, perseverance and grace. There is no need to question whether you are worthy or capable, as everything you have been through is proof enough.

Each time you choose to believe in your purpose, to step forward with unwavering faith, the universe conspires with you to support your vision. Being one with the creator, you have the conviction that everything you need is already provided. You understand that to live in divine purpose is to live with intention, to move with conviction, and to rest in the knowing that He, the creator of the universe commands the universe to serve you as you serve others. He ensures that you never lack. As you give of yourself, so shall you receive.

Being convicted of this, you must allow yourself to move beyond the limits of the physical world, to move beyond the noise and distractions, and into the quiet certainty that your destiny is unfolding in perfect timing. Hear the words, 'Be still and know that I AM God,' coming from within. Believe them; they will help you let go of fear and doubts when they try to creep in as they will from time to time.

You must realise that these two, fear and doubt will always be lurking around, waiting for an opportunity to steal your treasure, the gift God has given you. You must remain strong and courageous.

> *'Be sober, be vigilant; because your adversary, the devil, as a roaring lion, walketh about, seeking whom he may devour.'*

1 Peter 5:8

'Have I not commanded you? Be strong and of a good courage; be not afraid, neither be thou dismayed: for the Lord thy God is with thee wherever you go.' Joshua 1:9

Fear and doubts are the thief that comes at 'night'. They come for no other reason but to steal, destroy and kill. [John 10:10] Night, in this context, is when you are off-guard or distracted. The devil is not this powerful being we imagine, he has no power whatsoever; he is a representation of the tricks our minds play on us. He comes to us in the form of fear and doubts, which paralyse us causing us to lose faith. Once we lose faith, we become vulnerable. We are then easily manipulated in whichever way that will have us believe a lie that eventually takes away the blessing or the good things meant for our good.

It can happen to the best of us, it happened to Peter when Jesus asked him to step out of the boat and walk on water to meet Him. The moment he took his eye off Jesus and looked at the waves, he began to sink. What did Jesus say, 'Why did you doubt?' He got distracted by the wind and the waves. In that moment of fear and doubt, his faith was stolen. It doesn't take much to let the thief in. Fear makes you forget who you are. It made Peter forget who was calling him.

It makes you forget you are powerful, that you have the power to crush the 'serpents and scorpions' spoken about in this verse:

'Behold, I give unto you power to tread on serpents and scorpions, and over all the power of the enemy: and nothing shall by any means hurt you.'
Luke 10:19

Serpents and scorpions represents such things as fear, doubts and other things that appear to have power over us. The circumstances of our lives have no power over us when we step fully into the truth of our being. You were crafted with the resilience, courage, and grace required to uplift others and to lead them to the *awareness* of what you are now aware of: the power within.

You must allow your life to be the proof of what is possible when one aligns with divine purpose. You are the light that leads others to their purpose. You must step into this role with faith, love and clarity. The world awaits your light. You will, however, encounter resistance, for the world may not recognise the divine spark that burns within you yet, but you need not seek approval. Just let your light shine. At the appointed time, the world will see the light and acknowledge it:

> *'For the vision is yet for an appointed time, but at the end it shall speak, and not lie; though it tarry, wait for it; because it will surely come.'* Habakkuk 2:3

Your vision is supported by forces unseen, the divine energy that flows through all creation. It can only be perceived through discernment and not seen through physical eyes. It requires faith, so be patient if the world rejects your vision at first. The world rejects what it does not understand. It [the world] is always looking for something, but it does not know what that is. By the world, I mean the general population, the people of the world.

We are all seekers. It is only when we realise who we are that we stop seeking, and it is then that we know what we have been seeking. We are assured that anyone who seeks will find, so those who have not found what they are seeking yet will do at some point.

> *'Ask, and it shall be given you; seek, and ye shall find; knock, and it shall be opened unto you; For every*

> *one that asks receives, and he that seeks finds; and*
> *to him that knocks it shall be opened.'*
> Matthew 7:7-8

So long as they continue seeking, they will find. Jesus calls it hunger and thirst. We hunger for something that only God will fill and thirst for something that only the knowledge or realisation of our oneness with Him will quench. Jesus knew that as people hunger for bread and meat and thirst for water and wine, so is there an equal hunger and thirst for the bread of Life and the water of the Spirit. It is only when this yearning is deep enough that the consciousness turns within and receives this bread of life, fulfilling the desire of the soul to return to its source so it can be whole in God.

The yearning is for completion. When the soul is separated from its source, there is always going to be a feeling of something missing no matter how much you have. That is what drives people to acquire more and more of the things they think will satisfy them, only to find themselves feeling empty and lost after they have acquired them all and yet remain unsatisfied.

Let us for a moment think about what is happening in the world today. We all read the news. What is currently happening with the richest and the most powerful men in the world? They have it all, yet they want more and more. The richest man in the world is doing whatever he can to acquire more wealth, and the most powerful [leader of the most powerful nation on earth] is doing whatever he can to acquire more power. Nothing in this world can satisfy the hunger within.

One of the principles and teachings of Jesus is that, just as physical hunger can be appeased, so can our spiritual hunger be gratified. The kingdom is always at hand. Some people ask how come they have heard this for ages and ages and the kingdom has not come yet. The kingdom is always here. It has always been within us. He said that to the people who asked him when the kingdom would come as we have seen in the previous chapters. When He said it is at hand, He meant it is within reach for those who seek it. About spiritual hunger, he said:

> *'I am the bread of life: he that cometh to me shall never hunger, and he that believeth on me shall never thirst.'* John 6:35

All these statements tell us that these things he speaks of are not in the future but now. His kingdom is already here for those who realise it or recognise it within them, and he who lives within us is the bread of life. His teachings also make it clear that it is only when we accept this gift of life that it can be received. If we deny it, we choose to live with limitations, denying the power that overcomes the world:

> *'For whatsoever is born of God overcomes the world: and this is the victory that overcomes the world, even our faith.'* 1 John 5:4

Faith is belief in the unseen. There is no power quite like the power of belief.

The Power of Belief

The power of belief is the foundation upon which our life is built and the driving force behind any manifestation. I use the word manifestation to mean the visibility of the invisible, in other words, bringing those things we hold in our consciousness as imagination into reality.

Paul describes faith as the substance of things hoped for, the evidence of things not seen. When you hope for something, it only exists in your mind. It is not a reality that is physically visible, but it is a reality in your mind, in your imagination. If, for example, your vision involves providing service to people who need it, and you are struggling to move from point A to B or to deliver the service required effectively, you can hope for a better means of transport than you already have.

Let us assume you are hoping to have a vehicle; you can imagine yourself driving it and doing the things you need to do efficiently without having seen the vehicle. Even if you do not know how to drive a car, your imagination is unrestricted. It does not need a license to drive a car. You can however, go a step further and learn how to drive in anticipation for the vehicle you hope for. That is faith. It is the bridge between your imagination and your reality.

Jesus, on many occasions, taught us that it is done to us according to our faith. With belief, we open the door to limitless possibilities. When you believe in something with all your heart, it creates a powerful force that directs the universe to bring that belief into reality. It is as though the universe is waiting for you to make up your mind, to commit fully to your desire and to trust without a doubt that it will come to pass. Once you get to that point, the universe begins to align the circumstances, the opportunities or the people who will help bring your vision to life.

This alignment is only possible when belief is strong and unwavering. Unwavering belief overrides doubts and fear, the greatest obstacles anyone will ever encounter in life. Doubts and fear create resistance. It is like wanting something, seeing it in front of you and then putting up a wall between you and that something, your ideal. When you doubt that it is possible, you are sending mixed signals to the universe. You are asking for something, and at the same time you are saying you cannot have it, it is impossible.

Remember the universe is abundant, it has everything you could ever want. The universe is God's bank. There is nothing you could ever want or desire that is not available in this bank. Your only job is to align in thoughts, emotions, words and action with it. Mixed signals are sent when these are not in alignment. This confusion and double mindedness delay the manifestation process, but when belief is strong it dissolves doubts and fear. It sends a clear signal that you are ready to receive.

A double-minded person, we are told, is unstable. An unstable person is one who does not know what they want or are not clear on their position or intention. We must be clear on what we want to receive it.

> *'For he that waver is like a wave of the sea driven with the wind and tossed. Let not that man think that he shall receive anything of the Lord. A double-minded man is unstable in all his ways.'* James 1:6-8

What we hold in our consciousness is the only reality, everything else is fluid. We can change it with the power of belief. It is just an appearance that doesn't have to be our reality. Think about when you have a strong feeling that something bad is going to happen, you are gripped with fear. You begin to see it as real, if you stay in this state of consciousness long enough, the fear will become a reality.

Belief also changes the way we see the things. When you believe in the possibility of something, no matter how hopeless the situation, you start to notice signs and opportunities that you might have overlooked otherwise. Belief is not something you can fake; you either believe or you don't. When Jesus healed the people that he healed, He told them that their faith had healed them. He never claimed to be the healer, but their own faith. He even asked beforehand if they believed they could be healed.

You can tell yourself a thousand times that you believe something, but if deep down you have doubts, your energy will reflect that. True belief comes from a place of knowing. It is a quiet confidence that what you desire is already a done deal, even if it physically looks impossible. True belief is the inner peace that comes from trusting the process, knowing that God is working behind the scenes, driving your desires and bringing everything together even when nothing visible supports it.

This inner peace helps you to remain calm, patient and persistent, not in asking but in knowing; you do not keep asking for something you believe you already have. That would indicate doubt, which is counterproductive. Belief is a self-fulfilling prophecy. What you believe about yourself, and your capabilities shapes your actions, and your actions shape your results. If you believe you are capable of achieving something, you will take the necessary steps to make it happen. You will be willing to take risks, to put in the effort and to stay committed even when things get tough.

If, on the contrary, you believe that something is out of reach, you will not even try, or you will give up at the first sign of difficulty. Your belief or lack thereof, determines your level of persistence, and persistence is key to realising your desires. One of the most powerful aspects of belief is that it creates momentum. Once you believe in something, every thought, action and emotion starts to align with that belief. This goes both ways, whether the belief is right or wrong. It creates a ripple effect, where each step you take brings you closer to your goal.

The more you believe, the more momentum you build and the faster you move toward your goal. This is why people who have strong belief in their goals often seem unstoppable. They are fuelled by the power of belief, and that power propels them forward even in the face of challenges. Having a strong belief is not something that happens overnight. It is something you cultivate over time.

It requires practice and reinforcement. Every time you take a step towards your goal, you reinforce your belief in its possibility. Every time you overcome a challenge, you strengthen your belief in your ability to succeed, and every time you see evidence of your progress, your belief grows stronger. This is why it is important to celebrate small wins along the way, as each win is a confirmation that your belief is valid and that you are on the right track.

It is equally important to be mindful of the beliefs you hold as some beliefs may create invisible barriers that hold you back from reaching their full potential. The good news is that those beliefs can be changed at any time or age by becoming aware of them and choosing new, empowering beliefs.

CHAPTER SEVENTEEN

Your Consciousness is Your Only Reality

Let this mind be in you, which was also in Christ Jesus.

In the life of Jesus, the boundary between the physical and the spiritual realms seemed to not exist. The story of the woman at the well who Jesus asked for water to drink is a good example of the many occasions where the space between the physical and the spiritual appeared to effortlessly collapse.

When Jesus saw this Samaritan woman drawing water from a well, He did not care that Jews were not allowed to mix or even speak to Samaritans. He was thirsty and asked her for some water to drink. As a Samaritan, she did not expect a Jew to speak to her, let alone ask her for a drink. She was surprised, did he not know the rules? She must have wondered. She did not know who he was except that he was a Jew.

Before she could figure out whether to indulge or ignore Him, He said to her, 'If you knew the gift of God and who it is that is asking you for a drink, you would have asked him to give you the living water.' [John 4:10] The woman was puzzled. One moment, he was asking her for water to drink and the next, he was offering her 'living water', where was he going to get this 'living' water from?

He went on to tell her that whoever drank the water he was offering would never thirst again. His disciples had gone to buy 'meat' so they could all have a meal after a long day speaking to the multitude. When they returned, they were surprised to find Him speaking to a Samaritan woman. Without questioning Him, they invited Him to eat with them. They knew He was hungry when they left Him to go buy the food but that didn't seem to be the case anymore. 'I have meat to eat that you do not know about.' He replied. [John 4:32]

'Has anyone brought Him something to eat?' They whispered amongst themselves. Perhaps the Samaritan woman had given Him some food. But that couldn't have been the case as normally, the two (Jews and Samaritans) did not mix. Like the Samaritan woman, His disciples had no idea what He was talking about. First, He had water that the woman could not see, now, He has meat that the disciples did not know about. 'My meat is to do the will of Him that sent me, and to finish His work.' He told them.

Spiritual water quenched His physical thirst it'd appear, and spiritual 'meat' satisfied His physical hunger. You could say He lived in his own world, and quite literally He did. He lived in a world even the disciples did not fully understand. This world was His consciousness. This world was more real to Him than the physical world He was in. That is how He was able to say to the dead, 'rise up', and they rose like they had been sleeping.

The difference between Him and His disciples was the states of consciousness in which they lived, and this is what He was teaching them. In His mind, everything He needed or desired was already done. He completely embraced the concept that we already have what we ask for. When we pray, we must believe we already have what we pray for. That's His teaching about prayer, and He was living it. [Mark 11:24]

Naturally, we wait to see so we can believe, we even say, 'I'll believe it when I see it'. Jesus believed before He saw it, then He saw it. Paul tells us to be like Him, to have a mind like His. He knew he was one with the Father, and though He was in a human form, he did not see Himself as anything less than the Father. He knew that what the Father could do, He too could do. He 'thought it not robbery to be equal with God.' [Phil. 2:6]

We humans are so judgement conscious that even to say we can do greater things than He did feels like we're calling judgement upon ourselves by claiming to be equal with God, yet Jesus Himself said those words. Our human nature is threatened by anything that appears stronger or better than us, but that is our ego and God is not man. He is not threatened by what we can do as he gives us the strength and ability to do it. There is nothing we can do by our own strength.

As we have already seen, He works in and through us. How could He possibly be threatened by His own strength? The worst that can happen is us being proud and thinking we did it by our own power. Still, it would not change who He is. It would not take away from His power. Jesus never saw Himself as separate from God, or as smaller or less powerful. He knew who He was yet humbled Himself to the level of a servant to do the work His Father sent Him to do.

He served without complaining, even to death. We are told to have the same mind. To operate from the same state of consciousness as He did, the consciousness of 'wish fulfilled'. He did everything from the end, from healing to raising the dead even when He died on the cross. He had the end result in mind, that being liberation for mankind. This is what His Father had sent Him to do. With His blood He bought our freedom.

It was not easy for Him. At some point He wished He did not have to go through with it. He prayed to the father, saying, 'Father, if you be willing, remove this cup from me: nevertheless, not my will, but yours be done'. [Luke22:42] An angel appeared and strengthened Him. This demonstrates to us that He was fully man, just like us, and fully God by realization of His oneness with the Father. Physically, He was fully man and in consciousness fully God.

We cannot realise our oneness with God through our physical body or mind [1 Cor.15:50], we can only do this through consciousness. As long as we identify with the body, we are mere mortals. Christ consciousness is our natural state. It is within us, hidden in layers of identification with self. Identification with the body, family, careers, beliefs, traditions etc.

The Christ in us does not need to be activated, it needs to be realised and aligned with, we cannot do this unless we create space for it. We create space when we let go of what we're not. We are not all these things we identify with. If all the things we hold so dearly were taken away, and we don't wish for them to be taken away, what's left is what we are. Christ consciousness is not about facts but truth, and truth is already settled in heaven; nothing can be added or taken away from it. It is eternal.

Living from the end/wish fulfilled

Jesus lived from the end. When He saw a physically lame person, He saw him whole in His consciousness. All he did was declare what already was. When He raised Lazurus, the boy who had been dead for four days, He gave thanks to God first, saying, "Father, I thank you that you have heard me." Before that, Lazurus' sister had tried to warn Him that the boy had been dead for too long and there would be a bad odour. She was simply saying, "If I were you, I wouldn't disturb that grave. The body's rotting by now, there's no way he can come back to life."

I can only imagine what Jesus was thinking listening to her. He calmly replied, "Did I not tell you that if you believed you would see the glory of God?" I do not know how many times Jesus emphasised on 'belief', it only goes to show that we're not the only ones incapable of believing, truly believing. But if we did, we too could see our dead situations come back to life. Having chosen to see through the eye of the spirit, [single eye] we can see things the way we want them to be and not the way they appear. We can declare what we see in our consciousness and bring it to life in the physical realm.

We can create what we call miracles until they cease to be miracles and become our way of life. Jesus did not go around thinking, 'I'm going to perform miracles today'. He simply saw a need and served it. Because He could see both, through the physical eye and the single eye of the spirit where everything was as it ought to be, perfect; He was only correcting a false perception, restoring order where the mind saw disorder. In this context, the healing would not so much be the miracle, the real miracle would be the change in consciousness.

Because health and vitality are the normal or natural state of being, the change in consciousness becomes the real miracle as it removes the block or obstruction, allowing the sick person to see the reality. Once they see it, the body responds and aligns with the truth. At Lazarus' grave, Jesus had asked the people who were with Him to take away the stone that lay against the tomb. It was then that Martha, the sister tried to discourage Him against it. After the little conversation about belief, He insisted they remove the stone.

We can interpret this as removing the blocks that obstruct us from seeing the truth of things or the reality as Jesus saw it. Anything that keeps us from believing in possibility, the doubts and discouraging thoughts that arise when we think of things like healing. The weights we carry in the form of labels, titles, hierarchies, beliefs, egos etc. They are barriers and blocks just like the stone was for Lazarus. We need to remove them so we can free ourselves and resurrect our long dead dreams.

We must silence the Martha in our minds or the Marthas among us, who may be our friends, partners or family members. We need to stop waiting for God to do what He has empowered us to do for ourselves. We are told not to follow miracles. We should not seek miracles, but instead seek the Kingdom of God because there is order in the kingdom, and the miracles we seek are the norm where there is order. Instead of asking God to change this and that, we should ask Him to show us the truth behind it.

We can see it by looking through the eye of the spirit [consciousness] as Jesus did. The true miracle is being able to see through the eye of the spirit, in essence this is to believe. The true miracle is being able to believe. Jesus saw the lame whole even before He asked them to get up and walk. He saw the dead alive and the sick healed in His consciousness before it happened in the physical. He believed.

At Lazurus' grave, when He had thanked the Father, He said something very significant; "I knew that you always hear me, but I said this on account of the people standing around, that they may believe that you sent me." [John 11:38-44] He already knew that His desire to bring the boy back to life was granted even before he asked. Instead of asking God to bring him back, He thanked Him for having already done it.

Now, away from the tomb and back to the well. He told the woman at the well that God the Father is a Spirit, and those who worship Him must worship *in spirit and in truth* [John 4:24]. What did he mean by worship in spirit and in truth? First, we know that the physical is influenced by the spiritual, the seen is birthed from the unseen. To see things the way we want them in the physical, we must see them that way in our consciousness first (in the spirit).

To worship in spirit, therefore, is to worship from within; to not rely on the physical appearance or feelings, but to listen to the spirit within and be open to its guidance. The world of the Spirit is the real world, the world that holds the eternal truth. When you see things in their real form, you then realise you have no need or want [problems] as they are all provided/resolved. You give thanks rather than ask as the things you need in the physical are eternally present in the spiritual realm. In this realm, things are in their true form, perfect and complete, and that does not change.

The physical world on the contrary is a world of appearances. Things can change depending on many things, one of them being our perspective which is altered by our thoughts and emotions. There are no polarities [good or bad] in the world of pure consciousness. This is why Jesus always gave thanks because He saw the fulfilment of all desires in His consciousness, He saw solutions for all needs and answers to all questions. Gratitude is the completion of fulfilment. It is a sign that what you're giving thanks for is complete — done.

We have the mind of Christ, so we can do the same. We can make gratitude our way of life knowing that all our needs are taken care of and all we need to do is start expressing it and living it. We can boldly claim to have the mind of Christ because we are one with Him. Sometimes, when we hear such statements we automatically feel conflicted, almost as though it is blasphemous to make claims like that. This is when we see God as separate from us, when see him as a Holy being who lives in heaven and ourselves as poor sinners at His mercy.

The moment we know without a doubt that we are one with him, it will not sound wrong to make these claims, all of which are Biblical and eternal truths. Jesus did not consider it robbery to be equal with God. When He said to the Jews that they were gods, He asked them a question, 'Is it not written in your law that I said you are gods?' He even added for emphasis, that the scriptures cannot be broken. [John 34-35] He could not understand how they could be so ignorant as to use the law partially.

As we saw in the introduction, the same law they were using to condemn Him for claiming to be God said they too were gods, but they did not know it. Yet they were happy to use the part that served their wicked purpose against Him. They wanted to get rid of Him, they wanted Him dead. If you are going to use the law, you have got to respect the whole law, not just parts of it. This is the point He was trying to make when He delivered the sermon on the Mount. He said,

'If your eye offends you, pluck it out. If your right hand offends you, cut it off.' [Matt.5:29-30] How many people can do that?

About adultery, the sin that the Pharisees wanted to stone a woman to death for, he said whoever looks at a woman lustfully has already committed adultery in his heart, meaning they deserved the same punishment – death. He was indirectly telling them that it was impossible to keep the law. The same law stated that if you broke one of the laws, you were guilty of them all. That's simply impossible. But that was the law, if you're going to observe the law, observe it to the t. It's your choice, you have free will, but can anyone honestly and faithfully keep the law the way Jesus described it?

Similarly, if you are a believer of Christ, you must believe his every word and not just what you understand or what feels comfortable. The same scriptures He said cannot be broken, say that we have the mind of Christ [1 Cor. 2:16] and that as He is, so are we in this world. [1 John 4:17] Quite a few of them say we are one with Christ. It is in him we live, move and have our being. [Acts 17:28] In John 15:4, we are told to abide in him and He in us. For us to live the life He envisioned, we must not be separated from Him, consciously. We must work together.

Jesus knew no one could keep the whole law, especially the way He described it. No one would be willing to cut off their arm or pluck off their eye so as to see no evil. He knew the body was a vessel and not the soul of a man. Even when He was in this world, in a human body and living as one of us, He knew He was not his body, He called it a temple, saying He could rebuild it in three days if it was destroyed. The Jews could not believe He said that. How dare He say he could rebuild in three days, a temple that took four decades to build, almost half a century? Was He out of His mind?

They were enraged. They mocked Him and later used it against Him in court during His trial. They thought He was talking about the building, the synagogue they worshipped in. He spoke from his consciousness and not from his physical reality like everyone else. He knew his life was spiritual, that's why there was often not much separation between the physical and the spiritual in his words. Here, He was speaking metaphorically about His own body and not the physical temple made of stone.

He spoke about physical and spiritual nourishment as though they functioned in the same manner. In the desert when he was being tempted, he got hungry after fasting for forty days and nights. His tempter mocked him, telling him to speak to the stones and command them to turn into bread, He replied:

> 'It is written, Man shall not live by bread alone, but by every word that proceeds out of the mouth of God.' Matthew 4:4

He commanded both the physical and the spiritual worlds and the devil knew that. That's how He could speak to the dead and command them to rise and to the elements, commanding them to calm down like He did the winds and the waves. His power knew no limits. Yet, He acknowledged the father in all His doing, demonstrating to us the need to abide in the Him and to express Him in our activities:

> 'I can of mine own self do nothing: as I hear, I judge and my judgment is just; because I seek not mine own will, but the will of the Father which has sent me.' John 5:30

How do we separate our will from the will of God, or how do we know we're not just doing our own will? When we're guided from within, we are guided by the spirit of God in us. So, we know that our will is His will because He puts it in our hearts and minds. We too can do nothing of our own, but by drawing from within, the power of God our source,

Grace Wairimu

'we can do all things'. As I mentioned earlier, I once found these words conflicting. I had once believed them, but as I grew older and experienced life outside the protective bubble of my parents who were and still are a great man and woman of faith, I began to doubt them.

I had leaned on their faith and prayers for so long that when I started to experience life outside of this bubble I began to question a lot of things because they seemed impractical. The words do not imply that we can do all things by our own strength, but through Christ who strengthens us. [Phil. 4:13] Since understanding that I am one with God, that Christ lives within me, and that his power works in and through me, I have come to see how that is possible. It no longer feels implausible.

This realisation allows me to see myself as a fractal of God. The dictionary describes fractal as a figure, each part of which has the same statistical character as the whole. No matter how small this figure is, it has all the qualities and character of the whole. We are therefore not to belittle ourselves no matter how physically small or insignificant we may appear, we are vessels of the divine. It is not about us or our capability but about what/who is in us.

You are not powerless. All the fullness of God resides in you. You have enough power to influence your world according to your desire. The simple truth is that you are not separate from God. You are an individualised expression of Him. You can speak to your body and command the ailments that afflict it to depart. We do not have to die like mere mortals now that we know we are not mere mortals. God's plan for man is to live a full life, to fulfil his days and to die peacefully in old age. He calls this death sleep, because life cannot die. It is the body/the temple that dies. Man's spirit lives on; it is immortal. The soul returns to its source.

I have heard of people who died peacefully in their sleep. That's the kind of death I'm talking about, not premature death or long painful period of suffering. Like I said earlier in the book, I had the privilege of working in a

238

hospital, where I witnessed things I never could have imagined in a million years. I initially did not want or wish to be there, but I would later realise I was put in that environment for a reason. God wanted me to learn something, a lot of things. I have shared most of it here and will continue to share. My next book, *Grace in Action* will be more practical, sharing insights, especially concerning cancer and dementia.

We were not meant to endure the ravages of disease as we are witnessing today, particularly with the alarming rise in cancer, heart attack, stroke, diabetes, dementia, and the many forms of accidents. It is heart-wrenching to witness the suffering, mental anguish, and grief that is not limited to age, gender, or faith. I feel very strongly about dementia especially, not that I'm indifferent to everything else but with dementia, even the name is questionable.

Many years ago, it was seen as madness. People with dementia were referred to as senile, mad or demented. It's different today but the name still has that connotation. As the disease affects the mind, people living with dementia might struggle to process information, even much of what we have discussed about consciousness and the power of belief. This in my opinion is the worst kind of prison, and it is our responsibility to use the tools given to us to fight for the freedom of people living with dementia, who may not have the capacity to do anything about it.

I have been involved in the care of patients in their last days [palliative care], and it was the most emotionally challenging time I have known. Some of the patients lived their whole lives convinced that there is no God, or having decided not to concern themselves with Him or His existence. In this stage of life, there is not much that one can be offered, but comfort as they wait for that day when they take their last breath. Some ask for prayers, others ask to see a priest, but there are those who remain unresponsive for weeks or months before the eventful day.

There are also those who suffer from severe dementia and lack understanding of what is happening or about to happen. My struggle when I worked in this environment was always whether it was right or even ethical to talk about God at the point of death regardless of the ailment. This stage of life for most people including the family and friends can be very traumatic. There's a feeling of helplessness and frustration, not knowing what the right thing to do is and feeling like they are running out of time to figure it out.

Being unresponsive does not always mean the person is unaware of what is going on around them. Some may see, hear and understand things but cannot respond or react to them. My thoughts in those moments were on what went on in their minds. Could it be possible that people who never believed in God during their active days wonder/wondered about Him in their last moments? Could it be that He talks to people in their death beds and reveals Himself to them? Could it be that He reveals Himself to people who never knew Him at all in their last moments? That I will never know.

I recently read a book by an American author who spent many years working in palliative care. In his book, *Die Wise,* Stephen Jenkinson says that it is everyone's right and responsibility to die well. With that, I agree one hundred per cent. He says that 'there are no atheists in a foxhole'. By this he means there are no atheists in the grave. He says that when the goings get tough, 'some kind of God is going to emerge where your agnosticism used to be'.

Just last night, I was watching a show with my son on TV, a self-declared atheist got through a challenge that saw many of the contestants kicked out of the game. He was ecstatic. He threw his arms up in excitement, looked up and said, 'Thank you God'. That, he did with a lot of joy and genuine gratitude. He then looked at the camera, straightened up and with a serious look on his face, said, 'I'm an atheist, but I'm so glad I made it'.

We witness this kind of double mindedness or double standards if you like, all the time. Somehow, people try to convince themselves that there is no God, but deep down, they know it is not true. They know there is a greater power or intelligence that they may not explain or want to acknowledge as God. Even science will tell you that if you're interested in scientific theories of the order of things. Physicists have spent years trying to explain what they call the Theory Of Everything (TOE) and to this day, all they have is an equation that is yet to be solved — meaning we're yet to know what's behind how our universe works.

Jenkinson, now a consultant to palliative care and hospice organisations asks, '*What is it about living that dying proves?*' In his career spanning decades, he has sat and spent time with hundreds of 'dying people and their families, trying to help them die' as he puts it. What can we learn about death and living from his experience? Palliative care is also referred to as End-of-Life care. It's important to remember though, that life does not end. Life is eternal; it goes on even after we breathe our last breath.

As people come to the end of their physical experience/end of life, they can be in denial, and it's very understandable. I once witnessed a case of a young man who walked into the hospital's Accident and Emergency department complaining of severe stomach pain. He did not expect to be admitted, but doctors wanted to run some tests, so he was admitted. He looked well, strong and healthy, except for the debilitating pain, which came and went. He had been managing it with painkillers for a long time before deciding to go to the hospital.

Long story short, his world was turned upside down when he was informed that he had stomach cancer, which by this time had advanced to stage four. He was placed in palliative care, with only six months to live. It all happened so quickly, it was almost impossible to believe. Though it looked like he had more time than six months, he was gone in four months. Jenkinson's work, according to his book, involved talking to such patients and ensuring they understood what was happening and that they accepted it.

He says death is defeat and urges people to accept it and wrestle it rather than fight it. He encourages people to see death as an angel instead of an executioner. This he says with humility, from seeing people devastated by such news and their lives, and those of their loved ones turned upside down. Most of us have seen how devastating this can be. Jenkinson's advice is to change from fighting for our lives to 'wrestling life for the meaning of our life'.

While he makes a strong case for it, it makes me wonder if it might be a little late to find the meaning of life on a deathbed. Would it be more beneficial if this could be done long before we get to that point in our lives? If we lived as the gods we are—fully owning our place in the Godhead and embodying our true identity, we would stand a far greater chance of changing the course of our lives and, ultimately, our death. This then ties our living to our dying.

Attempting to answer Jenkinson's question, not so much what dying proves, but how it happens — I posit that by changing how we live, we can change how we die. Death, then would not have to be 'defeat', because death in itself is not defeat. It is the way we die that makes it so. When one dies peacefully in their sleep, full of age and having enjoyed a good life, it cannot be defeat. At some point it becomes something to look forward to.

As to what dying proves, I would say it proves that life is transient. This world is not our home and, therefore, cannot be permanent no matter how long or well we live in it. Long life is a blessing and something to aspire to. God promised Job that he would go to his grave in old age. [Job 5:26] He lived to see his children's children to the fourth generation. About Moses, we are told that he was a hundred and twenty years old when he died, 'his eye was not dim, nor his natural force abated'. [Deut. 34:7]

There are many examples of people who died in old age, still strong and compos mentis [being of sound mind] but we tend to expect frailty from the age between seventy and eighty. We expect cognitive decline and even loss of sight or hearing. When we see a 90-year-old who is fully present, mobile and with full mental capacity , we are surprised like it's not normal. It should be the norm. Old age shouldn't mean frailty.

When we expect it or tell ourselves that we do not want to get to that advanced age because we fear being frail, we create that reality for ourselves. We either die young or become frail in old age. God intended for us to live a full life and die in old age. Death, in my imagination, should be a smooth transition, with no pain or fear, preferably like a nice dream while in deep sleep.

While we cannot stop death or change it, we can change how we die by changing how we live. This starts with changing our minds, being transformed by the renewing of our minds. Without repeating myself too much, we can begin right now by changing some of the beliefs we hold. The belief that God is separate from us especially, puts us in a position of weakness. If we can begin to recognise that we are more powerful than the 'devil', that's a good place to start.

Speaking from experience, the thought of the devil trying to sabotage everything we do is paralysing. It makes us feel like we cannot win no matter how much we try. Worse still, when bad things happen and we attribute them to the devil, we give him power and credit he does not deserve, even though it is negative credit. He deserves no credit whatsoever. We must live as though he does not exist because, in the real sense of it, he exists only in our mind as fear. He exists in our imagination, which is meant to be the workshop of our creator.

Our imagination is where creation happens. It is where we create whatever it is that we want to create. When we entertain fear, we create what we do not want because we are creating from fear. We create in reverse. Our power lies in realising that there is nothing to be feared. Everything in life and about life is God's. The Universe and everything in it obey Him, and He and us are one. Jesus expected everything to obey Him; He did not negotiate or beg. He simply spoke just like He had seen his father do. Even demons obeyed Him.

Whenever He saw a need or was called to heal a sick person, He first saw the person already healed in his consciousness as we have already seen. He then spoke according to that and not according to what he saw physically. You probably know the story of the man who lay by the pool of Bethesda waiting for his turn in the pool. When Jesus saw him and asked if he wanted to be healed, the man told him he had no one to help him step into the pool when the water was stirred.

He did not know who he was talking to. If he knew, he would have simply said 'yes, I want to be healed'. But for lack of awareness of who He was, he began to tell Him how difficult it was for him to access the healing in the water when the angel stirred it up. He must have expected Jesus to help him step into the pool. Instead, Jesus told him to get up, pick up his bed and walk. He bypassed the protocol because He could. First, he sent the message that healing was not in the water, and second, he was free — not bound by the law that said he couldn't carry his bed on a Sabbath.

Immediately, the man was healed. [John 5] He got up, picked up his bed and walked away. The Jews questioned him, telling him it was unlawful for him to carry his bed on a Sabbath. Jesus knew it was Sabbath, yet He asked him to carry his bed. He was not disrespectful of the law, but in His consciousness, the law was already fulfilled. He lived from the end/wish-fulfilled. He saw the desired outcome in his consciousness and brought it to life in real-time. He did not see it happening in the future or later, but right in that instant.

When his Father introduced Himself to Moses as I AM, He was describing the essence of eternal presence. He did not say I was, or I will be. But right this instant, I am. When we pray, the answer to the prayer already is. When we say I am healed, for example, we are aligning ourselves with what already is. We are not begging for healing. We know it is already a present reality in consciousness, all we are doing is aligning with it. We are speaking those things that are not as though they are, because though they are physically invisible, they are as they ought to be in the spiritual realm; the unseen world.

In another incident, a twelve-year-old girl had been sick, and her father went to Jesus, who had a multitude of people following him. By the time he got Jesus's full attention, the girl had already died. Jesus heard the news bearer bluntly say to him, "Your daughter is dead, why trouble the Master?" "Do not worry," He comforted the man, "just believe."

Arriving at the girl's house and seeing all the relatives weeping and mourning, Jesus entered the room where the body lay, He took the dead girl's hand and asked her to arise. [Luke 8:54] As if she had been sleeping, she arose. To Him, physical circumstances were not the reality; his consciousness was the reality.

What does this teach us?

First, from the man waiting at the pool to be assisted in when the water was stirred up, we learn that the healing was not in the water. Jumping in the water was just an act of faith, but the healing was in the faith, the belief. Same lesson can be learned when He told the father of the dying girl not to worry that she had already died, but to believe. Believing is having a strong conviction in the good we want to see.

We must hold it in our consciousness that we have the mind of God, the Christ consciousness. Instead of focusing on the problem like the man at the pool who's focus was on the fact that he had no one to lower him into the pool, we should be more like Jesus. We should focus on the state of consciousness where the problem is already solved. Jesus did not identify with the physical surroundings, the stories or the happenings, or even his own physical body.

Inasmuch as He was God, He was having a human experience, just as we all are. He was here to be a man and to live like one. He was even tempted by the devil. His mission was to show us the way to live this life and to transcend its problems and chaos. It is not possible to do that when we identify with every problem. You are not your body, you are not your personal history, you are not even your thoughts or emotions. [1 Cor. 15:50]

Your body is the temple that houses your being, the awareness in which all these experiences arise. That awareness is the consciousness. When you are sick, bypass the sick body and choose to live in your consciousness where there is only wholeness. If you live there consistently and persistently, refusing to entertain any doubt or fear, your body will eventually catch up to your consciousness because as you think in your heart, so are you.

The world around us is not the cause of our experiences, it is the effect. The cause is our consciousness. Our consciousness is made up of the thoughts we think, the words we speak, the emotions we carry and ultimately, the force that drives our actions. Remember, we speak and act according to what is in our hearts — out of the abundance of the heart does the mouth speak. [Luke 6:45] This is why we must guard our hearts and minds.

The heart is where emotions are generated, and the mind is where thoughts are generated. Guard them like your life depends on them because it does.

'And the peace of God, which passes all understanding, shall keep your hearts and minds through Christ Jesus.' **Philippians 4:7**

CHAPTER EIGHTEEN

The Sabbath

Rest & Relaxation

How would you feel if all your needs were met, if all your problems were taken care of? Most of us would feel relief, excitement and joy. You would rest, I imagine. Maybe even go away to some nice place where you can relax and unwind. I imagine this is what the Sabbath was to God after the creation. He rested, looked back at his creation and said, 'It is good'. There is nothing as refreshing as a good rest after hard work.

Rest isn't just about physical relaxation but also mental, emotional and spiritual. If God needed rest, who are we not to need it? God did not rest because He was tired, but because He had satisfactorily finished the work He set out to do. For six straight days He created all that is, and on the seventh He rested. He demonstrated to us the need to rest and the importance of rest. Once we have done what we have set out to do, we should also rest. Scriptures tell us that that we should labour to enter into the rest that is available to God's people. That rest He enjoyed is still available for us.

'There remains, therefore a rest to the people of God. For he that is entered into the rest, he also has ceased from his

own works, as God did from his. Let us labour therefore to enter into that rest, lest any man fall after the same example of unbelief.' Hebrews 4:9-11

The rest spoken of here is the ability to cast our worries and burdens unto God and rest in what Jesus has done. It is to trust in the grace that says, 'Commit your works to the Lord, and he will establish your plans'. [Prov. 16:3] It is to set an intention and to do your part, then take a break from it. Rest. One of the things that keep us from that state of rest is worry. Worry is a state of consciousness that stems from a failure to understand our true nature.

When we worry, we operate from a limited, finite sense of self, and it is very difficult to rest in this state as it rules out trust, thus 'falling into unbelief', the sin that negates God's power. We worry when we identify with our surroundings, our physical circumstances, our physical body or our personal history, having forgotten that we are not these things.

We are spiritual beings with a physical body. That physical body is a house, housing the spirit of God. It's the vehicle that carries us around enabling us to perform tasks and experience the physical world. We must not wear it down in endless pursuit of physical things that won't matter five or ten years into the future. When we pray from this consciousness (worry), we achieve nothing. The prayer that 'avails much' is the one that is prayed from rest.

Scriptures tell us to glorify God in our bodies and spirit, which are His. [1 Cor. 6:20] When we overwork and are constantly worrying about this and that, we're abusing both our bodies and mind, which doesn't glorify God. We cannot be in alignment with our true identity when our bodies and mind are overworked. Worrying about things only affirms their reality in your consciousness and ultimately, your experience. When you rest, on the other hand, you are recognising and affirming that God, the God within, will resolve whatever it is that you are dealing with.

Resting helps to align with the creative power of the universe. Your consciousness contains within it the solution to every problem you could ever face. When you say God will solve it, you are not abdicating responsibility or passively waiting for some external force to intervene, you are declaring your alignment with the infinite intelligence within you. You are acknowledging that the power that created the universe is fully capable of handling whatever situation you are facing once you have done your part.

Instead of focusing on the problem, you are focusing on the state of consciousness where the problem is already solved. You are resting in the knowing that your prayer is answered even before you see the evidence. Just as there are natural laws, there are spiritual laws, and the law of consciousness is one of them. It is what is described in the Bible as 'reaping what you sow'. What you sow in the fertile soil of your consciousness grows to become the experiences you have in the physical world.

If you plant worry and doubt, you reap chaos and confusion. If you pray from worry and doubt, you get nothing. The chaos in your life remain, unless or until you uproot them just as a farmer uproots weed from his garden leaving the desired plants or crop. We must be intentional about this.

According to Jesus' teaching, when we pray we should 'enter into our closet, and when we have shut the door pray to the father which is in secret, and He will reward us openly'. [Matt 6:6] It goes on to say that the father knows what we are in need of. This closet or the secret place of our consciousness is accessed when we shut out the noise and are quiet — when you quiet the voices of worry, doubts, anxiety, fear and judgement and are willing to believe in good, to let go of the past and the fear of the future and ready to receive what is already yours.

In that state of mind, you pray not from fear but from power. You pray from rest, from wholeness. Not from uncertainty or effort but from knowing your request is already granted, and this is what faith is. You're not pleading desperately for God to give you something, you already know He's given you everything and all you do is align with what you need at that moment. Because God already knows what you need, you're not informing Him or trying to convince Him, you are thanking Him and receiving. True prayer is an inner alignment with the good. An affirmation that God already knows and has already done it.

God is good and that good created you to express it. When you know this and affirm it in prayer, your prayer will not sound like this, 'God, if you can, help me/ heal me. I have no way out'. You already know He can, and He does not withhold anything from you. [Psalm 84:11] To affirm these truths your prayer may sound like this, 'Thank you God because I know it is already done. You are my way out and I trust you completely.' You then rest. You do not keep wondering when you will see the results physically. You trust and rest.

Like a farmer, you have planted a seed in consciousness, don't go back and dig it out to see how it's getting on. Rest is an essential part of life, it is the reason we sleep at night. A lot of things happen when we rest. Our bodies and minds repair themselves when we are sleeping/resting. Our subconscious mind also goes to work when the conscious mind is resting. Resting does not mean being idle or lazy. It does not mean doing nothing and simply waiting for a solution to magically appear. When you truly align yourself with the consciousness of the solution, you will be inspired to take the right action.

That is how God answers prayers. You must therefore be in tune with your intuition. Be open to receive inspirations and when you do, act on them without delay, Sometimes these inspirations come in the form of dreams at night, ideas when you are wide awake or synchronicity of events that put you in the right place at the right time or connect you with the right people when you are least expecting. You may also find yourself suddenly interested in something new, which, when pursued may lead to the solution you are seeking.

This is because you are no longer operating from the limited perspective of the problem. You are now operating from the expanded consciousness of the solution. Your actions are no longer driven by fear or worry but by inspiration and inner guidance. Now, the outer world has no power. You have the power that does not come from any achievements or ambition but from within. Connect with your true desire.

Sometimes we pursue things we have no passion for just to give us an edge or maximise our ability to earn a living. You can earn a living doing what makes you come alive on the inside. That's your true desire. There are desires that come from the ego and those that are born from the soul. Unfortunately for most of us, they don't bring home the bacon. We ignore them to pursue those that do because that's how the system works. We live for the bills. But that shouldn't be the case. We can have a balance following our inner guidance, if we ask for it.

What makes you feel alive? What would you do if you didn't have to worry about the bills? If all your cares were provided and taken care of, what would you do even if you weren't paid to do it? What would you do if you didn't fear judgement from others? How would you live if you hadn't learned to fear? That thing that keeps coming to mind and you suppress it out of realism is your true desire. That deep desire is magnetic, it's patient and it remains when time passes and conditions seem to contradict it.

If you embrace it without fear, pride or demands, while remaining at rest, the Christ within will breathe life into it and bring it to pass. This is why you see people in their old age doing things they wanted to do in their youth, and you think they're having a crisis. It's because they waited. They kept pushing it forward for some time in the future when conditions are right. There will always be another bill to be paid, conditions will never be perfect. There has to be a shift in consciousness. You have to seize the moment and there is no better time than now. Don't wait to do things you want to do in life. Just do them.

Remember we have the mind of God. When God said let us make a man in our image and likeness, He had already imagined the man He would create in His consciousness, meaning he had the image in His mind. It started as a thought, an imagination, then a knowing and then He spoke it by saying 'let us make a man…' We have the same faculty that we can use constructively. Instead of imagining things going wrong, we can use it to imagine them going right and life being beautiful and joyful.

When you imagine something that you want to happen, instead of wishing, assume it is already happening and begin to live as though it is, ignoring any contrary suggestion. If it's something you want to do, just take the first step. The next step will be revealed to you when you get to it. With time, it becomes a knowing and once you know, it's a done deal. When you know, you don't hope or believe.

Knowing is beyond physical evidence, it is the faith that moves mountains. When you know, you rest from trying to make things happen, what the scripture calls 'to cease from our 'own' works, as God did from His'. It is to cease from our effort. Having done what we can externally, we trust that the seed we have planted will grow and we will harvest in due course just as a farmer does. We rest.

A farmer does not plant a seed and dig it up every so often to see if it's growing. He fully trusts the laws of nature and waits patiently. He may water it once in a while, but he doesn't keep worrying it might not grow, or how long it'll take. In the realm consciousness, there is no time:

> 'But, beloved, be not ignorant of this one thing, that one day is with the Lord as a thousand years, and a thousand years as one day.' 2 Peter 3:8

Time is an illusion of the physical world. Your prayer is answered the moment you pray. You must believe this to be true when you pray. It is one of the hardest things to do, but it is the secret of prayer. The thing about believing is that saying I believe today and tomorrow you're praying for the same thing is not really believing. If you truly believed you had something, would you keep asking for it? If you lost your keys and later found them, would you keep looking for them? I doubt you would. You'd be grateful you found them and call off the search.

To believe is to have the feeling of having whatever it is that you want with conviction and to rest in that knowing. Where you felt the need for something or lack, you now feel the fulfilment of it. You assume you already have it and behave like you do. You no longer ask for it, but continually give thanks with gladness and joy. It does not happen because you ask persistently but because you maintain the belief, which includes the feeling of its fulfilment. The persistence is not in asking but in trusting it is done and remaining at rest.

This is what it means to live from the end, to embody the consciousness of the solution. Rather than concern yourself with how or when it will happen; you rest in knowing it is done. Think about the vastness of the universe for a moment: billions of galaxies and infinite possibilities, all existing simultaneously, yet you experience only what you accept as possible in your consciousness.

The universe is like an ocean; you are currently only experiencing a tiny drop of that ocean, not because the ocean is withholding some of its water from you, but because you are only drawing that tiny drop. The universe is constantly trying to give you experiences that match your highest vision. You must be open to it to receive these experiences. You must tune your consciousness to the receiver mode. Just as the radio can only receive the frequencies it is tuned to, your consciousness can only experience what it's aligned with.

Most people live their entire lives having never adjusted their frequencies. They stay tuned to the same channel of limited experiences, never realising they have access to the whole spectrum of existence. They end up feeling stuck, stagnant and barely alive when everything they could ever want is available to them. Some experience poverty and settle for it telling themselves that they were born poor, unlucky or in the wrong part of the world, the wrong continent or state or even the wrong family. King Solomon, in his old age, wrote this:

> *'I returned, and saw under the sun, that the race is not to the swift, nor the battle to the strong, neither yet bread to the wise, nor yet riches to men of understanding, nor yet favour to men of skill; but time and chance happen to them all.'*
> Ecclesiastes 9:1

Our experience of life is based not on our status, education or skills, where we're from etc. but what goes on in our minds. We are who we think we are. What we believe we are, we become.

The law of Consciousness
No one needs to be poor when they know how the universe works and when they understand the law of consciousness. The universe only gives you what you are prepared to receive in your consciousness. It becomes a self-fulfilling prophecy if you don't think you can get more out of life or deserve more. That is not because you are incapable or God has forgotten you, but because you have the wrong self-concept and are not open to receiving what is offered to you.

The universe is the bank of God and does not respond to what you want, it responds to what you are. According to the principles that underpin it, you are what you think you are; it does not contradict that. If you think you are unlucky and can't get anything good, you block yourself from receiving good things even though they are well within your reach. Change your mind. Think differently. Transform your life by renewing your mind. Choose now not to remain stuck despite your best effort. People don't remain in the same spot because they're not working hard enough, some poor people work very hard.

Like King Solomon said, favour is not for men of skill or for those who work hard. It is not for the smart either, but time and chance happen to us all. This is your time and chance. This is my time and chance. Our time begins the moment we become aware of the truth. Before that, God overlooks. [Acts 17:30] Your consciousness is not limited to your physical body. It extends to everything you are aware of.

When you feel truly alive, that aliveness permeates your entire world. Everything you touch and everyone you interact with must reflect that state back to you. Just imagine you were doing something you love instead of a stressful job you do just for the money, for example. You'd be happier. You'd radiate joy everywhere you go. Our interactions and experiences are shaped by the states we occupy (our consciousness/state of mind). The universe is not a random collection of events and circumstances but a perfect mirror reflecting back to us our own consciousness.

We must expand our consciousness to embrace more life and appreciate life a little more in our day-to-day existence. We must learn to embrace all experiences, whether we perceive them to be good or bad, knowing they are all happening through us and for us, and not to us. We, therefore, realise that we are not victims but students of life. The sooner we learn, the sooner we transcend the challenging experiences.

We learn, grow and evolve from all experiences, the ones we perceive to be negative often carry the greatest lessons. This is not about positive thinking; it's about occupying expansive states of consciousness rather that limiting ones. Most people live in a state of emotional contraction, suppressing their natural vitality. To dim one's light for any reason is to exist rather than live. We do this for many reasons, sometimes, we do not even realise we are doing it.

We may think we're being humble when we act small,

not realising we're dimming our God-given light, the very light that is meant to light up our path and guide us to unlimited possibilities. We limit ourselves by acting small. We were not created to merely exist but to live life fully. Our natural state is one of expanding aliveness, which we achieve by allowing the power within to express itself through us. This cannot happen when we are acting small.

We tend to think that we need to work harder, do more, and achieve more to feel alive or fulfilled. That should not be the case because feeling alive and fulfilled is our natural state. We do not need to earn it. We just remove the barriers we have placed in our consciousness, which is an infinite ocean of possibilities. Unfortunately, but we are only experiencing a tiny drop of that ocean because we have limited ourselves through assumptions of what is possible and what is not. We assume that some of the things we desire are too big for us, that they're impossible.

Most of us have previously lived in a state of constant preparation, always preparing for something great in the future. We are always getting ready for life while seeing it in a distant future — never today. To our dismay, we realise too late that time waits for no one, not even the king. Everyone runs out of time at some point, and you cannot do all things in a lifetime especially if you start with those that don't come from the heart. We spend half to three quarters of our lives doing what works only to start pursuing what really give us joy in the last half or quarter of our lives.

We wait for the perfect moment, the ideal conditions, or the right circumstances, but the perfect moment is now. Someone famously said that tomorrow never comes. When you get to it, it quickly turns into tomorrow. You never really get to live it. The perfect moment is now. The ideal condition is your current consciousness expanded to embrace more life. Think about a flower, for example. The Bible gives an example of a lily. Lilies do not struggle or strain to bloom or blossom. They do not try to force their petals to open. They simply allow their natural state of blossoming to unfold.

Your consciousness works in the same way. When you stop struggling and striving and start allowing, when you cease trying to be, things change. You become what you are meant to be. Most people do not realise that their current circumstances are their past assumptions made manifest. We often try to change our circumstances while maintaining the same consciousness. We expect different results but continue to operate from the same limited state. It's like trying to harvest a different crop when we have not changed the seed we planted previously.

Every farmer knows that the seed he plants is the crop he harvests. He reaps what he sows, literally. If he desires a different crop he must change the seeds. He must plant a seed that matches his desired crop. The nature of consciousness is to create, just like the nature of the soil is to produce. You are either creating from a state of expanded awareness or that of limited awareness. The choice is always yours. You must live in a state that matches what you want to receive. It you live your life expecting trouble and difficulties, that is exactly what you are going to get in as much as you know it is not what you want.

If you are the kind that prepares for the worst, that contracted state creates more of the very thing you are trying to avoid. Consider how different your life could be if you consciously expected good and moved through each day feeling fully alive, fully present and fully open to receiving. That state is not something to achieve; it is something to allow. Having understood this principle, you must realise that your current state of consciousness is actively creating your future experiences.

Every moment you spend feeling limited, constrained and barely alive is setting the stage for more of the same. Your consciousness is the lens through which your experiences are filtered. Change the lens, and you change everything you see and experience. Most people fail to maintain an expanded state because they are constantly reacting to external circumstances. They allow their state to be determined by what is happening around them rather than allowing their state to determine what happens in their external life.

I once had a dream I thought was childish at the time; it was about a goldfish. The message that came to me while watching a goldfish swim in the water was that 'a goldfish is a goldfish no matter where it is, in deep waters or shallow waters'. It did not make any sense at the time. I was not sure whether the fish was in a fish tank, a pond or an ocean, I just saw it swimming and was captivated by its colours. I now understand it to mean that our surroundings, circumstances or conditions do not change or determine who we are.

No matter what happens in your life, you are still the child of God you were from the beginning, made in the image and likeness of God and an expression of God himself. Life does not happen to you; it happens through you and for you. No matter what you have been through, it did not make you any less of what God created you to be; it was helping you to evolve and reveal what is on the inside. The real you.

Someone described the art of sculpting as removing what is not needed to reveal the treasure that is already in there, waiting to be discovered. I thought it was a brilliant way of looking at life. When a sculptor decides to make a sculpture, whether out of clay, wood, stone, metal etc., he already has an image of the object he wants to create. All he does is remove what is around it to reveal the image he holds in his mind.

It is the same with life. When we remove all the labels we have previously identified ourselves with, we find that spark of light that is God within us. We fun it and watch it grow — we discover our true identity.

CHAPTER NINETEEN

Chaos Precedes Creation

Except a grain of wheat falls into the ground and dies,
it abides alone.

Your assumption of good/success transforms your entire life. Everything must align with your new self-concept. Like every great story of success, there is going to be a period of complete transformation where the old life dies to give way to the new. This is a natural law; it transforms your entire world to match its nature. The process can be painful and chaotic, but the very upheaval that seems to threaten your stability is the reorganisation necessary for success or good to manifest. Nothing can remain in your world that does not align with your new self-concept.

This reorganisation is not random chaos but perfect order taking shape. Everything that does not align with your new state must either transform or be removed from your experience. Even your relationships begin to shift. Some people will be drawn closer, and others will naturally fade away like they never existed. Your opportunities begin to change, some doors close while new ones open. Your way of thinking reorganises itself to match your new state.

Most people resist this reorganisation, trying to hold on to people or things, situations and patterns that no longer serve their new state. You must let the old order dissolve completely. The old life must die to make way for the new. As the scriptures say, you cannot pour new wine into an old wineskin. The skin will burst, spill the wine and ruin the wineskin. [Matthew 9:17, Mark 2:22, Luke 5:37-39] Disorder is often the prelude to a higher order.

Distraction does not always mean that something is going wrong. It may seem that way at first, but then you start to realise that it happened so that something better may emerge. People, circumstances and situations that match your new state are drawn into your experience, while anything that contradicts it is removed. Old habits die, old associations change, and old limitations are transcended. This is not a coincidence or an accident; it is the law of assumption at work.

The very chaos you may be experiencing now may be the evidence that your assumption is taking hold. It is the disturbance of the soil when a shoot is emerging to the surface. If you know anything about how plants grow from seeds, you understand that a seed is planted in the ground or buried under the soil. It dies or decomposes before it germinates into a shoot.

The shoot then breaks through the soil towards the sun. That death that it dies is the chaos we experience before something magnificent breaks forth in our lives; what we call a breakthrough. This is what the scriptures say about it:

> '*I say unto you, unless a grain of wheat falls into the ground and dies, it abides alone; but if it dies, it bringeth forth much fruit.*' John 12:24

By dying, a single seed produces new seeds, multiplied in number. One orange tree, for example, can produce bags of oranges. Same as corn, wheat etc. The divine intelligence in operation in this process is the same intelligence that operates in our lives. It works with a precision and wisdom that far exceeds any human planning or strategy. It knows exactly what needs to be dissolved, what needs to be transformed and what needs to be brought into your experience to manifest your success. It operates beyond the limitations of time and space.

Most people try to plan every detail of their success, they plan how their success should manifest and when. Your conscious planning often limits the infinite ways in which success can come to you. Your task is to maintain the assumption and let this higher intelligence handle the how. You may wonder why 'assumption' and not reality. This is because you do not have to wait for things to change to start living the new life you have envisioned. You assume it and take steps toward it rather than wait.

You know with conviction that it will happen, why wait? Let if find you already living it. Your job is to plant the seed; you do not tell it how or when to grow. The higher intelligence makes the seed grow into whatever tree, fruit or plant it is intended to be. It knows your deepest desires better than you do and is able to bring it to pass. It knows what form of success will bring you the greatest fulfilment. For some, it is financial, for others, it's family or relationships, for others yet, it is perfect health, perfect expression etc.

The intelligence that keeps your heart beating, maintains the rhythm of your breathing, and orchestrates the movements of the planets is the same intelligence that works through your assumptions to bring about your success. To cooperate with this divine intelligence, you must develop an unshakable faith in its operations and maintain the consciousness of success. Once you have those boxes checked rest and let Him handle the details of its manifestation.

Every moment of doubt is like taking the seed out of the ground to check if it is growing. It ruins the seed and the whole process of its growth. You must plant your seed/assumption in your consciousness/soil and let it grow undisturbed. Do not forget that great things take time. The most profound transformations often require a gestation period. A human baby for example, takes nine months from conception to birth.

A mighty oak tree takes years, even decades, to reach its full glory and majesty. It does not spring forth from an acorn overnight or in a week or two, yet within that tiny acorn lies the complete blueprint of the oak tree. It contains within it the pattern of perfection waiting to unfold in divine timing and order. It does not matter where you are in your life, how old you are or how young. It is never too late or too early to plant a different kind of seed, one that aligns with the harvest you desire. You have in you the complete blueprint of your life purpose. Your responsibility is to awaken to it.

When we plant a seed in consciousness, we must be patient with it. Imagine standing before a locked door with a bunch of keys in your hands and you know for sure one of those keys will unlock the door. You, however, do not know which one. You patiently try them one by one, knowing that one of them will unlock the door even if it is the last key in the ring. You are, therefore prepared to try them all no matter how many they are, or how long it takes.

This is the essence of persistence and unwavering faith. It is the knowledge that your assumption must manifest, coupled with patience to allow it to unfold in divine timing.

The concept of time
In the natural world, time is linear. We perceive it as occurring in a sequence, but in the realm of imagination, in the world of consciousness, time is fluid. Past, present and future exist simultaneously. When you assume the feeling of wish fulfilled, when you live from the end, you are transcending time. You are bringing the future into the present moment by living as if your desire has already been realised.

Your external world is always catching up to your internal assumptions. It is always conforming to the contents of your consciousness. Whether it takes a minute to reflect on the outside or a year, one way or another, it will catch up. So, why not start living that life right now as you wait for it to catch up? When you persistently live your assumed state, you are creating a new pattern in consciousness. Your external world is bound to reconstruct itself to match this new pattern.

This reconstruction takes time in the natural world, but in the world of consciousness, it is instantaneous. The moment you assume the feeling of wish fulfilled; it is done. Never give up on the reality of your assumption [you assume what you have imagined]. In the scriptures, prophet Elijah prayed for rain during a severe drought. He then sent his servant to go look for signs of rain. The servant returned to report no signs of rain. Elijah persisted. He did not give up the first time, second time or even the third time that the servant came back with the same news: no signs of rain.

He sent him seven times, and seven times the servant went and looked. It was the seventh time that he saw a tiny cloud on the horizon. From this tiny seed of manifestation, a mighty rainstorm was born. The prophet never gave up, even when no signs were reported. He persisted in his assumption and belief that the rain would come, even when there was no external evidence to support the belief. [1King 18:44]

His faith brought an end to a severe drought. We are all prophets and creators. Our assumptions are prophesies that must be fulfilled. Our every imagined act or experience is a seed planted in the soil of our mind that must bear fruits. The question is not whether your assumption will manifest but whether you will persist long enough to see its fruition as Elijah did.

Many believe that to never give up is to struggle or to fight against adversity, but true persistence is not a battle against external circumstances. It is a steadfast adherence to your internal assumptions. It takes time for your old beliefs and patterns of thinking to fall away, making your assumption your dominant state. It takes time for your external world to reconstruct itself to match your internal reality, but this reconstruction is inevitable. Just as an acorn must become an Oaktree, your assumption must become a reality. The only variable is time.

Time is a construct of consciousness. When you are fully immersed in your wish fulfilled, when you are living from the end, time ceases to exist. In that state of assumption, your desire is not something to be achieved in the future; it is a present fact. This is a state in your consciousness where miracles are born. A state that can compress time and bring about manifestation with speed that defies logic.

To reach this state requires that you believe in the power of your imagination and that you never give up on your assumption. In so doing, you engage the infinite power of your subconscious mind, setting in motion forces beyond your conscious comprehension. You will then find that time mirrors your consciousness. When you're having a great time, for example, time appears to fly, but when you're bored and want time to move fast, it appears to stand still.

The gap between your imagined world and the physical reality narrows with increasing speed and efficiency. As you witness this acceleration, as you marvel at the synchronicities and coincidences that begin to fill your life, you must never lose sight of the fundamental truths. In your imagination, the realm of consciousness, your desire is already fulfilled. Your prayer is already answered. It is already a present fact and not something waiting to happen in the future.

Your persistence and refusal to give up is not about making something happen in the future. It's about aligning yourself with the present reality that already exists in the realm of potential, then bringing that potential into manifestation through the assumption. This is why great things take time and yet, also timeless. In the natural world, there is a gap between the planting of the seed and the harvesting of the fruit. In the consciousness, the seed and the fruit exist simultaneously.

Your job is to bridge these two worlds by being steadfast in your faith in the assumption you hold in consciousness. This is the alchemical process by which thought is transformed into thing, by which imagination becomes reality. The catalyst that drives this transformation is your persistence. Your refusal to give up no matter what your senses may tell you, no matter what your physical eyes see. Since time does not exist in your imagination, you can revise activities that already happened by imagining them happening differently.

You can make peace with past experiences that did not go too well by seeing them in a better light than they occurred. This helps to check the box as resolved. The exercise can be used to revise activities of the day before going to bed. The Bible tells us not to go to bed angry. Revising anything negative that might have happened in the day and seeing them play out as you would have liked them to play out prevents unwanted seeds from taking root in your subconscious mind. By so doing, you rewrite your past in your consciousness altering the trajectory of your future.

Your imagination can go back to the past and to the future as it is not bound by time, nor is it restricted. This practice reinforces your persistence and strengthens your ability to create your desired reality consciously without repeating unwanted experiences. Through the act of revision, you declare to your subconscious mind that you refuse to accept any experience that does not align with your desired outcome. By so doing, you are training your mind to automatically reject any experience that contradicts your assumption of wish fulfilled.

This is self-love. Self-love is when you know what you want and love yourself enough to want to see it fulfilled. Honouring your desires is a vital part of self-love. All love begins within; you cannot truly love another until you have learned to love yourself fully and completely. Part of this is knowing that you are worthy of all the good things that life has to offer.

As a vessel and a channel through which divine love flows, self-doubt, second-guessing or self-criticism can block the flow rendering the vessel useless. It is important to keep the channel clear and open, ensuring that the love flowing through you radiates to all around you, which is the true power of love. To love others effectively, we must love ourselves, then we can love them as we love ourselves.

Self-love is the most selfless act you can perform, for in loving yourself, you raise your vibration and consciousness, and in so doing light up and lift the world around you. The belief that it is selfish to want good things for ourselves and that it is more virtuous to put others' needs before our own is not in alignment with loving your neighbour as you love yourself. If you did not love yourself, how would you love your neighbour?

When you love yourself you learn to honour your desires. Your desires are not random; they are divine inspirations. They are God speaking through you and guiding you towards the highest expression of self. When you ignore them and push them aside in the name of humility and selflessness, you are denying the divine expression that seeks to manifest through you. The Bible tells us not to gratify the desires of the flesh, but when we are guided from within, our desires are not of the flesh as they are aligned with the spirit within. They are of the spirit, the Christ within us.

When you honour your desires, you are appreciating and acknowledging the gift of the divine within you. The natural part of us that is more inclined to play small, to doubt our capabilities and to look outside of ourselves for approval and validation cannot exist in the consciousness where miracles happen. It is devoid of self-love. True self-love requires that we embrace our identity, seeking not the approval of others. We are not being humble when we act small or compare ourselves to others; we are denying the very essence of our being.

Embrace your power, love it and honour it. The path you are on is yours alone. The divine expresses itself through you in a unique way that is perfect for you. When you compare yourself to others, you are denying the perfection of your own divine expression and the wisdom of the divine plan unfolding in your life.

CHAPTER TWENTY

Choose Freedom

Be not entangled again with the yoke of bondage.

Freedom is the greatest and noblest thing that anyone could have. Of what benefit would it be if you had all the wealth in the world and no freedom to enjoy it? Imagine all the wealthy people behind bars with no freedom to enjoy their wealth, or those who spent their whole lives acquiring wealth only to spend it all trying to regain the health they lost when they should be resting and enjoying it. True freedom does not come from financial security or material abundance inasmuch as all these are good and noble.

Paul wrote about the yoke of bondage, which is slavery or the absence of freedom. 'It is for this reason that Christ came,' he wrote. *'For freedom did Christ set us free,'* he says in Galatians 5:1 [NIV] then goes on to say that we must not be entangled again in the yoke of bondage. Once set free, you do not want to go back to slavery. It is a profound statement when you think about all the do's and don'ts attached to His mission. Christ's mission to bring freedom to mankind has been, for many, a prison, keeping them from expressing themselves fully lest they're misunderstood or appear worldly.

The fear of judgement keeps many from authentically

expressing what God has put in them. They just go with the flow and do what they are expected to do. They end up following what Jesus called traditions of men. It becomes more about pleasing others than living life to the fullest, which is the real reason Christ came according to His words in John 10:10. Paul, being aware of this urges us in a letter to the churches in Galatia to 'Stand fast and be not entangled again in a yoke of bondage.' [Gal. 5:1]

He was telling the people that most of the things they did were no longer necessary. There were certain things that were practised as law before the coming of Christ, but now that Christ had come and brought freedom, they needed not remain bound by those laws. Certain beliefs and practices were no longer needful. They could continue practising them if they wished to, but as a choice. If an individual chose to practise them, they needed not drag others into it or judge them for not doing the same.

This was not just a problem back then, it is a problem even today. Traditions are hard to break free from even when they no longer reflect present realities or personal convictions. They are inherited patterns of thought, behaviour, and beliefs passed down from generation to generation. In some communities, tradition runs so deep it feels sacred. According to Paul, practicing some traditions and demands of the law means Christ is of no effect to us and profits us nothing. Some of those practices have nothing to do with faith, and by engaging in them we fall from grace. [Gal. 5:1-4]

Today, there are things we do just because they have always been done. They may offer comfort, structure, and a sense of belonging – but they can also become limiting. In some cases, we may be aware that they no longer serve the truth we're now aware of, or the growth we seek, yet we cannot break free from them because of judgement from others. We feel that letting go of them is betrayal to everything we have held on to for decades or generations.

That reminds me of a news article I read this morning.

It was after the announcement of the passing of Pope Francis, who brought some radical changes to the Catholic Church and tried to unite people of different faiths and backgrounds among other things. His inclusive and compassionate stance enraged some traditionalists who felt he was moving away from the teachings of the church. People can be uncomfortable with change, not necessarily because it's bad or wrong, but because they are more comfortable with how things have always been.

Jesus was not a fan of traditions. When the Pharisees asked Him why His disciples never observed the traditions of the elders, He called them hypocrites who worshipped God in vain while they taught doctrines of men. [Mark 7:7] He accused them of rejecting the laws of God in order to establish their tradition. They had certain ways of doing things, foods that were prohibited and many other rules and practices that kept them in bondage.

They had no freedom even to eat what they desired or do the things they genuinely wanted to do. About what they ate and drunk, Jesus told them that nothing that went into their mouth could defile them but that which came out of their mouth. By that He meant they were free to eat or drink anything they wanted. What they needed to watch was what went into the heart because, 'out of the abundance of the heart the mouth speaks'. [Matt. 12:34]

Your words are influenced by your thoughts, which arise from feelings. If something hurts you, it creates negative emotions which give birth to negative thoughts and ultimately negative words or actions. These directly impact your life and sometimes even the lives of others negatively. What they needed to watch was their thoughts and feelings as opposed to what they ate or drank.

Today, we are obsessed with healthy eating. We measure our food like medicine and while this is all good, the real medicine is in our words and emotions. Some of the things we concern ourselves so much with are distractors. They obstruct us from seeing what's important. What's important is our own evolution, we are here to evolve and be more like Christ—to transcend the limitations of this life, but as long as we keep looking at each other to see who is doing or not doing what, we get distracted.

Like Paul, we must forget what no longer serves us and fix our eyes on what is important: the prize.

'Forgetting those things which are behind, and reaching forth unto those things which are before, I press toward the mark for the prize of the high calling of God in Christ Jesus.' Philippians 3:13-14

We must free ourselves of all the things that hold us back from reaching our high calling. We must choose freedom. With freedom comes authentic expression, limitless abundance, unconditional love, and radiant well-being. When we immerse ourselves fully in this vibration without mental reservations or doubt, we realise that all materialised reflections of lack, struggle or unease dissolve as our new frequency floods the reality we experience.

We owe it to ourselves to change the narrative of struggle and straining outwards and commit to living from the empowered vibration of abundance, which can only come from within. We do not have to strive, chase or keep pushing towards our ideal experiences; they already exist within us. We can transcend any circumstance by the power given to us and the freedom we already enjoy as children of God.

We are rightful heirs of the Kingdom, why should we live entangled in a yoke of bondage, enslaved to poverty, disease, anxiety, hatred, anger, resentment, fear, guilt, shame, unforgiveness, division and judgement? There is no scarcity or limit in the source of all good. The only thing that can prevent its manifestation is obstruction of your channel which is your consciousness. If that channel is filled with these things, you cannot receive the good you're entitled to – your rightful inheritance.

This is not about being perfect or flawless but embracing

all aspects of ourselves including our perceived flaws and weaknesses; recognising that we are made righteous, not by our effort, goodness or faithfulness but by the grace of God. As you embrace your new consciousness of grace, you will see that nothing is impossible or unattainable.

You will also see that everything in your life, every person, every circumstance and experience is a gift, a perfectly orchestrated opportunity for you to know yourself more fully, to express your divine nature wholly, and to live a more authentic life. In this state of consciousness, even the difficulties you encounter will be recognised as invitations to grow and evolve. This new way of experiencing life is the realization of your divine nature, the embodiment of your creative power. It is the fulfilment of your purpose as a unique expression of the Infinite.

This state of consciousness is not some distant goal to be achieved in the future. It is your true nature, your natural state of being. It is the amazing grace that helps you transcend the limitations of this life, enabling you to live a full life as your creator intended. Realise you have all the power you need to shape your life, to create your reality and to fill your deepest desire.

As you now have a new understanding of your true nature, a new appreciation of your creative power, let your life be an expression of truth. Remember, there are many philosophies, religions and beliefs, but the truth is just one.

You are one with this truth, one with the source of all creation, one with the infinite possibility that exists within consciousness — You are one with the power that raised Jesus from the dead because that power is in you. You are one with Christ. Step boldly into your divine inheritance:

> *'Let us therefore come boldly unto the throne of grace, that we may obtain mercy, and find grace to help in time of need.'* Hebrews 4:16

Instead of waiting for someone to come and save you, realise that God already did. He is waiting on you to wield the power He has given you to transcend whatever it is you want to be saved from. Is it an illness, is it poverty, is it a low image of yourself? He paid the price and wants you to know He created you in His own image. To have a low image of yourself is an insult to Him. You are His very own expression. Claim your rightful place as a conscious creator and a living expression of the infinite.

Discover your inseparable oneness with the divine intelligence, the living God, the beginning and the end, the truth and the way. Let your life be a testament to the power of God that resides within you. Believe God's word when it says you can do all things, and nothing shall be impossible because the one who lives within you is greater than anything outside of you. He is the Great I AM. He is your true fortune and your perfect provision. He is your source, your healer and the lifter of your head. [Psalm 3:3]

Remember, true greatness lies not in external achievements but in the realisation of your divine nature. The greatest thing you can achieve in this life is the realisation that you are God made manifest, that the power of creation lies within you and that your imagination is not merely a faculty for daydreaming but the workshop in which you create your reality. This realisation and awakening to your true nature are the greatest of all manifestations.

EPILOGUE

In September 2024, I went on my first-ever retreat, driven by curiosity and a deep desire to find answers to two questions that had surfaced while writing this book. The foremost question was the bold claim that we are gods. It was not that I doubted it, but I needed clarity. The second question emerged naturally during my exploration of the first. When I learned about a teacher plant said to hold answers to life's most complex questions, I felt compelled to explore—though cautiously sceptical.

The teacher did not speak to me audibly, but through visual impressions and telepathic perception. I have given a detailed account of the experience in chapter five, where I saw the sun emerge from my right as illustrated on the book cover. It slowly moved to the centre, getting brighter and brighter as it moved and stopped directly facing me. It had a face of a human and as I wondered if it was the face of God, it gently cracked a smile, which grew wider and brighter as if to confirm my thoughts.

The rays grew brighter, softening into a pure white light as they reached me, wrapping me in a warmth and love I had not experienced before. From the opposite side emerged trees and mountains, dancing as they also moved to the centre. The scene was spectacular. To say it took my breath away is an understatement. As I wondered if that too was God and what message He was trying to communicate, I got the answer that He animates everything He created and that they are all intertwined in unconditional love.

Around the time I completed the book about eight months from this experience, I came across some scriptures that made me stop and think, 'Isn't that what I saw, a face shining like the sun?' Not exactly. I saw a bright, shining sun with a human face. I saw in reverse — but I could draw some similarities which prompted me to investigate further.

The scriptures say, 'There he was transfigured before them. His face shone like the sun, and his clothes became as white as the light'. [Matt. 17:2] It was the face of Jesus as His disciples, Peter, James and John saw it on the mountain where they had gone to pray, not long before his crucifixion. In the lines that followed was the answer to my second question that had been elusive during the experience.

I had come across the concept of reincarnation during my research, and I had dismissed it even as I quietly wondered if there was any truth in it. *If it was real, why was it not in the Bible?* I had wondered, assuming it was not real or true as it was neither referenced in the Bible, nor mentioned in any Christian circles I was familiar with. I however, intended to ask but the thought never crossed my mind throughout the experience with the teacher plant. It completely eluded me.

Reincarnation is a concept unfamiliar to many, especially within Christianity. During the transfiguration, as Peter, James and John witnessed this glorious transformation where Jesus' face shone like the sun and his clothes white as the light, they also saw Moses and Elijah, both of whom had lived many years before the birth of Jesus; centuries to be precise. The disciples saw them talking with Jesus. Overwhelmed by what they were witnessing, they suggested building shelters for them.

A bright cloud appeared, covering them, and from it came a voice that terrified them, causing them to fall to the ground. As they lay there, Jesus touched them and asked them to get up. When they looked up, He was alone—Moses and Elijah had vanished. Had they imagined them or were they hallucinating? They all saw them; they couldn't all have imagined them or seen something that wasn't there. Jesus instructed them not to tell anyone until He had been raised from the dead.

They then asked Him why the teachers of the law had said that Elijah would come first (before his crucifixion). "To be sure," He replied, "Elijah comes and will restore all things. But I tell you, Elijah has already come, and they did not recognize him." Elijah had walked the earth about 800 years before the birth of Jesus, around 874–853 BC. He was one of the prophets of the Old Testament, and unlike the other prophets, he did not die. He was taken up to heaven in a whirlwind according to the scriptures in 2 Kings 2:11.

When the disciples heard his answer, 'they understood that He was talking about John the Baptist'. [Matt. 17:10-11] John the Baptist lived before and during the early years of Jesus' ministry, he baptised Him. Does that mean Elijah came back over 800 years later as John the Baptist? Could this mean reincarnation is real? If it is, this is the closest the Bible gets to addressing it. It is reinforced by Matthew who describes him [John the Baptist] as the greatest 'among them that are born of women'.

He continues to say, 'And if you will receive it, this is Elias, which was to come. He that has ears to hear, let him hear.' [Matt. 11:11-15] That last sentence is almost cryptic, *'He that has ears to hear, let him hear'.* He is referring to the inner ears, the ones that allow you to hear what the physical ears don't — the spirit. The ability to understand something that defies logic. There are some things you cannot hear with your physical ears or see with physical eyes. An angel, speaking to John the Baptist's father before his birth said he would have the spirit and power of Elias. [Luke 1:17] Elias is Elijah, who, like Enoch did not die.

Concerning the dancing trees and mountains as mentioned earlier, I recently stumbled on some words I couldn't recall having seen before: 'For you shall go out with joy and be led forth with peace: *the mountains and the hills shall break forth before you into singing, and all the trees of the field shall clap their hands.*' [Isaiah 55:12] I have no doubt that the creator of the universe animates his creation. He is the engine that keeps everything going, the bright light in us.

Today my prayer His word would come alive in our live and that we would see Him in everything. Like Paul who had to temporarily lose his physical sight in order to see clearly, we would see beyond what our natural eyes and ears reveal. There is more to this life than we can see. My second book, *Grace in Action,* goes beyond theoretical understanding of these truths to their practical application in everyday life.

We are powerful beings; whatever we bind here on earth is bound in heaven, and whatever we loose is loosed in heaven. Think about that for a moment — 'whatever' we loose, 'whatever' we bind. It means we decide, we act, and heaven passes it as 'done'. Whatever we declare here on earth is endorsed in heaven. Declare something today. [Job 22:28] That's how powerful we are. Embrace it and walk in this power. It's your birthright.

Dare to be a Joshua and command that mountain standing in your way to move. Joshua commanded the sun and the moon to stand still. In other words, he stopped the time until the battle was won. You have that same power. You too can practically apply these eternal truths to win your battles and rise above every limitation. You were created for this — to transcend limitations and walk in freedom.

The word of God is eternal, and it says you're immortal. It says you are gods, most valuable children of the Most High. Your soul has no beginning or end, let it become your centre and live from this centre; live from inside out, allowing the light in you to shape your outward life. This is the divine plan of our creator — the blueprint for a life without limits.

BIBLIOGRAPHY

Beckwith, M. B. (2016) *Life Visioning*. Sounds True Inc.

Beckwith, M. B. (2009) *Spiritual Liberation*. Beyond Words.

Clark, G. (1929) *The Man Who Tapped the Secrets of the Universe*. Martino Publishing.

Dispenza, J. (2017) *Becoming Supernatural*. Hay House.

Dispenza, J. (2012) *Breaking the Habit of Being Yourself*. Hay House.

Dispenza, J. (2007) *Evolve Your Brain*. Health Communications Inc.

Dispenza, J. (2014) *You Are the Placebo*. Hay House.

Dyer, W. (2012) *Wishes Fulfilled*. Hay House.

Fox, E. (1934) *The Sermon on the Mount*. Harper Collins Publishers.

Goddard, N. (1952) *At Your Command*. Penguin Random House.

Goddard, N. (1952) *The Power of Awareness*. Dover Publications.

Goddard, N. *The Power of I AM*. [Audiobook]. Paths of Illumination.

Goddard, N. *When You Give God Your Best*. [Audiobook] Paths of Illumination.

Goldsmith, J. S. (1998) *Beyond Words and Thoughts*. Acropolis Books.

Goldsmith, J. S. (2003) *The Infinite Way*. DeVorss & Company.

Holmes, E. (1994) *Words That Heal Today*. Health Communications, Inc.

Jenkinson, S. (2015) *Die Wise: A Manifesto for Sanity and Soul*. Berkeley, California: North Atlantic Books.

Larson, C. D. (2024) *Steps in Human Progress.* [audiobook] Paths of Illumination.

Murphy, J. (2016) *Love Is Freedom.* [audiobook] Ascent Audio.

Murphy, J. (2016) *I AM That I AM.* [audiobook] Ascent Audio.

Murphy, J. (2016) *The Magic of Faith.* [audiobook] Lgt Digital.

Murphy, J. (2019) *The Power of Your Subconscious Mind.* Revised edition. New York: Simon & Schuster.

Osteen, J. (2015) *The power of I am: Two words that will change your life today.* New York: Faith Words.

Long, J. and Perry, P. (2010) *Evidence of the afterlife: The science of near-death experiences.* New York: HarperCollins Publishers.

Prince, J. (2007) *Destined to reign: The secret to effortless success, wholeness and victorious living.* Tulsa, OK: Harrison House Publishers.

Russell, W. (1948) *The Message of the Divine Iliad, Vol. 1.* The University of Science & Philosophy.

Russell, W. (1973) *The Secret of Light.* Parker Publishing Company.

Russell, W. (1929) *The Universal One.* Parker Publishing Company.

St. John of the Cross (2003) *Dark Night of the Soul.* Dover Publications, INC.

Tolle, E. (1997) *The Power of Now.* Hodder & Stoughton.

Other titles by BLKDOG Publishing for your consideration:

Britannia: The Wall
By Richard Denham & M. J. Trow

THE END OF ROMAN BRITAIN BEGINS.

The story opens in 367 AD. Four soldiers - Justinus, Paternus, Leocadius and Vitalis - are out hunting for food supplies at an outpost of Hadrian's Wall, when the Wall comes under attack.

The four find their fort destroyed, their comrades killed, and Paternus is unable to find his wife and son. As they run south to Eboracum, they realize that this is no ordinary border raid. Ranged against the Romans at the edge of the world are four different peoples, and they have banded together under a mysterious leader who wears a silver mask and uses the name Valentinus - man of Valentia, the turbulent area north of the Wall.

Faced with questions they are hard-pressed to answer, Leocadius blurts out a story that makes the men Heroes of the Wall. Their lives change not only when Valentinus begins his lethal sweep across Britannia but as soon as Leo's lie is out in the world, growing and changing as it goes.

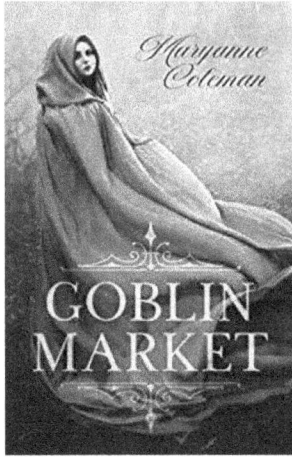

Goblin Market
By Maryanne Coleman

Have you ever wondered what happened to the faeries you used to believe in? They lived at the bottom of the garden and left rings in the grass and sparkling glamour in the air to remind you where they were. But that was then – now you might find them in places you might not think to look. They might be stacking shelves, delivering milk or weighing babies at the clinic. Open your eyes and keep your wits about you and you might see them.

But no one is looking any more and that is hard for a Faerie Queen to bear and Titania has had enough. When Titania stamps her foot, everyone in Faerieland jumps; publicity is what they need. Television, magazines. But that sort of thing is much more the remit of the bad boys of the Unseelie Court, the ones who weave a new kind of magic; the World Wide Web. Here is Puck re-learning how to fly; Leanne the agent who really is a vampire; Oberon's Boys playing cards behind the wainscoting; Black Annis, the bag-lady from Hainault, all gathered in a Restoration comedy that is strictly twenty-first century.

Fade
By Bethan White

There is nothing extraordinary about Chris Rowan. Each day he wakes to the same faces, has the same breakfast, the same commute, the same sort of homes he tries to rent out to unsuspecting tenants.

There is nothing extraordinary about Chris Rowan. That is apart from the black dog that haunts his nightmares and an unexpected encounter with a long forgotten demon from his past. A nudge that will send Chris on his own downward spiral, from which there may be no escape.

There is nothing extraordinary about Chris Rowan...

www.blkdogpublishing.com